Highway of Missionaries:

AN ILLUSTRATED HISTORY OF

THE DIOCESE OF HARRISBURG

AUTHORSHIP

Editor
Very Reverend William J. King, J.C.D.
Secretary for Canonical Services

Author
Linda V. Itzoe, Ph.D.
Diocesan Archivist

with contributions by
Reverend Monsignor Thomas J. Kujovsky, Director of History and Archives
Rosalia Scalia
Kathleen Signor, Consultor for the Pontifical Commission for
the Cultural Heritage of the Church

ACKNOWLEDGEMENTS

The author thanks Joseph Aponick, Betsy Baker, Charles Blahusch, Betty J.L. Curtis, Annette Eurieck, Very Rev. T. Ronald Haney, Sue Hartman, Chris Heisey, Connie Hess, Roy Horner, Mary Klinger, Jodi Lasecki, Rev. Edward R. Lavelle, Father Clarence Olszewski, Jennifer Reed, Christine Schwartz, Mary Shriver, Rev. Msgr. Vincent J. Smith, Joanne Weber, Barbara Zogby, Regina Zogby, and parish priests, historians, and administrative personnel throughout the diocese—all who have given so generously of their talent and time to contribute to the preparation of this illustrated history of the Diocese of Harrisburg.

PUBLISHER
Éditions du Signe
B.P. 94
67038 Strasbourg - France
Tel: 011 333 88 78 91 91
Fax: 011 333 88 78 91 99
Email: info@editionsdusigne.fr

PUBLISHING DIRECTOR
Christian Riehl

DIRECTOR OF PUBLICATION
Joëlle Bernhard

PUBLISHING ASSISTANT
Audrey Gilger

DESIGN AND LAYOUT
Juliette Roussel

PHOTOGRAPHY
Frantisek Zvardon
Chris Heisey

COPYRIGHT TEXT
© The Diocese of Harrisburg, 2006

PHOTOENGRAVING
Atelier du Signe - 105291

COPYRIGHT DESIGN AND LAYOUT
© Éditions du Signe, 2006
All Rights reserved
Reproduction forbidden

ISBN-10:   2-7468-1548-6
ISBN-13: 978-2-7468-1548-3

Printed in China

ON THE FRONT COVER:
Five historic churches of the Diocese of Harrisburg are Saint Joseph, Milton, 1805 (top center), Assumption of the Blessed Mother, Lancaster, 1742 (lower right), Conewago chapel, now the Basilica of the Sacred Heart, Hanover, 1740, (lower left), Sacred Heart, Lewistown, 1828 (upper left), and Saint Patrick, later the cathedral, Harrisburg, 1827 (center). The Susquehanna River flows through the center of the Diocese.

TABLE OF CONTENTS

DIOCESE OF HARRISBURG — Office of the Bishop

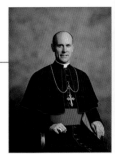

4800 Union Deposit Road — Box 2153 • Harrisburg, Pennsylvania 17105-2153
(717) 657-4804

February 2006

My Dear Friends in Christ,

The publication of this history of our diocese is an occasion for grateful reflection on the manifold blessings of the Lord in the lives of our ancestors in the faith and in the growth of the Church in this portion of the Lord's vineyard which is the diocese of Harrisburg.

To read this book is not only to study with historical interest the events of our past, but also to discover in our rich history the Spirit of God at work. The beginnings of the faith in our area date back to the days of Jesuit missionaries in the 17th and 18th centuries. There were already 19 parishes and 34 missions and Mass stations in the area encompassing our diocese when it was established by Blessed Pope Pius IX on March 3, 1868. From that time on, as this book illustrates, the Church has grown and flourished in the diocese of Harrisburg.

Our history is the story of men and women of faith: clergy, religious, and laity who built parishes and missions, schools and orphanages, hospitals, homes and institutions, all for the glory of God and the service of the Church's mission. Animated by the gifts of the Holy Spirit, these men and women, committed to the task of building up the Body of Christ and dedicated to works of mercy, have left us a beautiful heritage.

Knowing and appreciating our history helps and inspires us today to continue the noble mission entrusted to us by the Lord. We share the same mission as those who have gone before us: the proclamation in word and deed of the Gospel of Jesus Christ. This is accomplished through evangelization and catechesis, the celebration of the saving mysteries of Christ in the sacraments, and living as a vibrant community of faith, hope, and charity.

Inspired by this diocesan history and urged on by the love of Christ, may we proclaim, celebrate, and live with renewed vigor the faith we have received. May the Blessed Virgin Mary, Mother of God and Mother of the Church, and Saint Patrick, our patron, intercede for us!

Sincerely yours in Christ,

+ Kevin C. Rhoades

Most Reverend Kevin C. Rhoades
Bishop of Harrisburg

INTRODUCTION

On March 3, 1868, Pope Pius IX, accepting the recommendation of the Second Plenary Council of the bishops of the United States of America, issued a decree establishing the Diocese of Harrisburg. The decree, translated from the Latin, reads:

"Wherefore, in keeping with the counsel of the afore-mentioned Cardinals [Sacred Congregation for the Propagation of the Faith], and exercising Our Full Apostolic Authority, We hereby establish and constitute in the City of Harrisburg a new Episcopal See, under the care of its own Bishop, to be known henceforth as the 'Diocese of Harrisburg.' We wish this diocese to include the civil counties of Clinton, Centre, Mifflin, Franklin, Cumberland, Adams, York, Dauphin, Cumberland, Northumberland, Columbia, Lebanon, Lancaster, Montour, Union, Snyder, Juniata, Perry and Fulton."

Named to lead this newly established diocese was Bishop Jeremiah F. Shanahan, a thirty-four year old priest and seminary rector from the Archdiocese of Philadelphia. By 1868 when this new diocese was established, Catholicism already had a long history in the New World. Through the years, Catholics residing in what is now the Diocese of Harrisburg have been successively under the jurisdiction of bishops of four dioceses.

Originally, all the American colonies were officially part of the Diocese of London, headed by the Vicar-Apostolic of London. In 1790 the Diocese of Baltimore was established as the first American diocese, encompassing all of the thirteen states of the new nation. Eighteen years later, in 1808, the Diocese of Baltimore was divided into several new dioceses, including the Diocese of Philadelphia, which encompassed the territory that in 1868 became the Diocese of Harrisburg.

Chapter 1

THE COLONIAL YEARS

1673-1790

The history of the Church in what is now the Diocese of Harrisburg began in the 1600s. In these early years the rivers of colonial America formed the "highway of missionaries." Priests from the French settlement of Quebec traveled south on the Susquehanna River to minister to the American Indians and the early settlers. Father Jean Pierron, traveling from Quebec in 1673, was the first priest who can be traced to the area that is now the Diocese of Harrisburg.

In 1682 Charles II of England gave William Penn a charter for land in the New World, land that Penn named "Penn's Woods," and hence, "Pennsylvania." However, from the beginning Penn quarreled with Lord Baltimore about the border separating the provinces of Pennsylvania and Maryland. It was a dispute that would continue for three quarters of a century until the Mason-Dixon line was established.

Penn, a Quaker, promised religious freedom to Quakers as well as to other faiths that settled in his province. A handful of the early settlers to this new province were Catholic.

In 1704 Jesuit priests established a base in Bohemia Manor, Maryland, which became known as "Old Bohemia." The earliest parishes in the Diocese of Harrisburg are closely linked to the Jesuit missionary priests who traveled from Bohemia Manor to Pennsylvania during the early eighteenth century to minister to the few Catholics settled there.

By 1720 a Jesuit mission headquarters for all of Pennsylvania was located in Philadelphia and was led by Father Joseph Greaton, a Jesuit missionary who had come from Bohemia Manor to be in charge of the entire Pennsylvania mission field. He was the first priest to travel to Conewago in what is today Adams County. He celebrated Mass there as early as 1721 and in 1730 founded the "Conewago Mission," which is today the Basilica of the Sacred Heart of Jesus, close to Hanover, the oldest parish in the Harrisburg diocese.

WILLIAM PENN'S "HOLY EXPERIMENT"

William Penn (1644-1718) was the founder, proprietor, and governor of the colony of Pennsylvania. He gave his colony this name, meaning literally "Penn's woods," in honor of his father at the suggestion of King Charles II. On March 4, 1681, the king signed the charter granting Penn 45,000 acres in the New World, thus enabling Penn, a Quaker and staunch believer in individual freedom and, most especially, religious toleration, to establish what he called his "Holy Experiment." Unlike other charter recipients who simply assumed possession of the land given them by English authority, Penn negotiated with the various Indian tribes of the region to purchase their land, the very acreage that Charles II had granted to him. His biographers report that his refusal to carry a weapon, his prowess as a sprinter able to outrun Indian braves, and his readiness to learn to converse with the Indians in their own language all helped him gain the respect and trust of the Indians. The laws he developed to govern his colony expressed ideals anticipating the Declaration of Independence. Catholic immigrants, who were persecuted in most areas of the New World, felt welcome in Penn's colony, though English law barred them from holding public office. The Catholic presence in colonial Pennsylvania is reflected in the census in 1756, which reported a population of about 200,000 residents in the colony, of whom 1,365 were Catholic.

FATHER FERDINAND FARMER

Father Ferdinand Farmer (1720-1786) known as "the priest on horseback," ministered to the faithful in Lancaster and surrounding areas in the 1750s, when Lancaster was part of the "western frontier."

Father Ferdinand Farmer (born Andreas Steinmeyer) is remembered as "the priest on horseback." Born in Germany on October 13, 1720, he entered the Jesuit novitiate in 1743. Upon ordination he joined the English Province of the Jesuit Order, and in 1752 arrived in the colonies to begin his work as a missionary. To blend in with the English settlers in the New World, he "translated" his name from Andreas Steinmeyer to Ferdinand Farmer ("meyer" is German for "farmer").

He was assigned to Saint Mary's, Lancaster, and the surrounding area, which encompassed what are now Lancaster, Berks, Dauphin, Chester, and Cumberland counties. In his first months he established the "Donegal Mission" (now Saint Peter), Elizabethtown. During the six years in this assignment, he traveled on horseback to minister to the scattered 394 souls in his care. In 1758 he was transferred to Philadelphia and later New York City. After the Revolutionary War he built Saint Peter on Barclay Street, where years later (now Saint) Elizabeth Ann Seton would be received into the church.

His lifelong correspondence with members of learned societies in Europe earned him recognition as an intellectual as well as a missionary priest. The high esteem accorded him is reflected in his being granted membership in the Philadelphia Philosophical Society and his election as a trustee of the University of Pennsylvania, both recognitions rarely bestowed on Catholics in these early days of the nation.

The registers he maintained throughout his life recorded his performing 3,317 baptisms and officiating at 568 marriages. He died in August 1786 at the age of sixty-five.

Jesuit priests, especially from Germany, England, and Ireland, accepted missionary assignments to join Father Greaton in the Pennsylvania province. These included Father Henry Neale, Father William Wappeler, Father Mathias Manners, Father Ferdinand Farmer (born Andreas Steinmeyer), Father Robert Molyneux, and Father Theodore Schneider.

Additional parish communities were established by these pioneer Jesuit missionaries. These included Saint Mary's, originally named the Mission of Saint John Nepomucene, now called "Historic Saint Mary's," Lancaster (1741), Saint Peter, originally called the "Donegal Mission of the Assumption of the Blessed Virgin Mary," Elizabethtown (1752), and Saint Patrick, York (1776). In addition, although no chapels were built in Northumberland, Lewisburg, and Chillisquaque prior to the Revolutionary War, these northern areas were served by the missionary priests from Conewago and Lancaster.

The colonists, struggling to survive in this new land, lacked the means to support the priests who ministered to them. Sir John James, an English convert to Catholicism aware of this financial

The first Saint Mary's, Lancaster, the second parish established in the diocese.

The title page of the book recording marriages and baptisms: the only tangible remainder of the chapel built on the farm of Henry Eckenroth outside of Elizabethtown, where the faithful worshiped in the second half of the 1700s.

hardship, established an endowment specifically for the support of missionaries in Pennsylvania. This James Fund was dispersed through Saint Mary's in Lancaster.

Under English law, public celebration of the Mass was officially prohibited in the colonies. Sadly, because of suspicion and prejudice, Catholic places of worship faced the constant threat of arson. As a result, the early colonists quietly opened their homes for area Catholics to attend Mass there. These "Mass Houses," as they were called, included the Robert Owings Mass House in Conewago and the homes of Thomas Doyle in Lancaster and Henry Eckenroth in Elizabethtown. The construction of modest chapels followed in these three mission locations.

The missionary priests served untiringly, traveling by horseback to minister to the Catholics scattered through the region. They often disguised themselves as physicians, teachers, Quakers, and itinerant tinsmiths to avoid attracting attention to their presence.

As English subjects, the colonists were bound by the law requiring the "Test Oath." This oath was particularly hostile to Catholics, for it contradicted Catholic teaching regarding the Eucharist and veneration due the Blessed Virgin Mary.

Nevertheless, Catholics, attracted to the promises offered by Penn's "Holy Experiment," continued to settle in the Pennsylvania province. A census ordered by the governor of Pennsylvania in 1757 recorded 394 Catholics, primarily of German and Irish ancestry, in the counties of Lancaster, Berks, Dauphin, Chester and Cumberland.

The Owings Mass House, Conewago, was used for Catholic worship in the 1720s

DIGGES' CHOICE

In 1727 John Digges was granted a 10,000-acre warrant by Charles Calvert, 4th Lord of Baltimore, for a plot of unsettled land of his choosing in the Maryland Province. His land became known as "Digges' Choice" and, later, the Conewago Settlement. As chance would have it, Digges claimed his acreage in a section of Maryland that was also claimed by Pennsylvania. The root of the problem was that the descriptions of boundary lines given to the first Lord Baltimore by Charles I in 1632 and to William Penn by Charles II in 1682 did not match, and as a result, a strip of land in the northern portion of the fortieth parallel, was claimed by both. The Conewago Mission, settled by Jesuit missionaries in the 1720s, was located within the disputed area and was adjacent to "Digges' Choice." As might be expected, tempers flared when two parties, each with official documents of ownership issued by their respective Provinces, Pennsylvania or Maryland, both laid claim to the same acreage.

Sadly, in February 1752, John Digges' son Dudley was accidentally shot and killed in a dispute that turned violent when he confronted Martin Kitzmiller, who had obtained the same land under a Pennsylvania land warrant. Dudley Digges was the first person buried in what was to become the cemetery for the Conewago Mission.

The whole matter was too complex for the colonial authorities to resolve; survey after survey was rejected for one reason or another. Finally in November 1763 Charles Mason and Jeremiah Dixon, surveyors from England, arrived to settle the matter. Their task was not easy. It was four years later, October 9, 1767, that the Mason-Dixon line was finally established to set the dividing line between Maryland and Pennsylvania.

Artifacts discovered during excavation of Owings Mass House, Conewago

Anti-Catholic sentiment continued during the French and Indian War (1756-1763), when colonial Catholics were suspected of sympathizing with the predominantly Catholic French in the dispute. In 1760 Saint Mary's original church in Lancaster was destroyed by arson. The sacramental records also were lost in the fire. In 1762 a letter written by a Protestant clergyman to his superiors in London captured the suspicions faced by the Catholic populace: "Popery has gained considerable ground in Pennsylvania of late years. ...Their behavior in outward appearance is quiet and inoffensive, but they have been often suspected during this war of communicating intelligence to the enemies of our Religion and County."

By the end of the 1760s the general population had begun to be more tolerant of their Catholic neighbors. In 1768 Conewago became the headquarters of the Jesuits' Saint Francis Regis mission circuit, including all of Pennsylvania west of the Susquehanna River, all of western Maryland, and the Shanandoah Valley of Virginia. Placed in charge was Father James Augustine Pellentz, who had ministered in the Lancaster mission and its surrounding mission posts for a decade. He would continue to serve at Conewago until his death in 1800. Under his leadership the Conewago chapel

A profile sketch of the type popular in colonial days: Father James Pellentz, SJ, (1727-1800), who ministered to Pennsylvania Catholics for forty years, the latter thirty at the Conewago Mission.

was enlarged and the Catholic population continued to grow. The sacramental records maintained there are the oldest source of Catholic genealogy in the diocese. When the Jesuit Order was supressed from 1773 to 1814, Father Pellentz, like his fellow missionaries, continued his ministry among the colonists.

As the American Revolution approached, Catholics continued to gain acceptance. When the war began, they made up only about one percent of the population of the thirteen colonies, but their contributions were significant. Their acceptance was reflected in the key roles played by statesmen such as Thomas Fitz-Simons, who, elected as a Provincial Deputy, was the first Catholic to be named to a public office in Pennsylvania, and Charles Carroll, who, in addition to being the cousin of the soon-to-be named first bishop in the United States, was one of the signers of the Declaration of Independence.

The opening of Catholic parishes continued during the years of the war with the establishing of Saint Patrick, York, in 1775 and Saint Patrick, Carlisle in 1779. In 1787, a new stone church was built at Conewago, and the name was changed to the Sacred Heart of Jesus, making it the first church in North America named for the Sacred Heart of Jesus. A charming tradition connected

SIR JOHN JAMES FUND

In the 1700s Sir John James, a wealthy British convert to Catholicism, established a fund to support German Jesuit missions in Pennsylvania. Officials funneled the monies through Saint Mary's in Lancaster in order to sidestep the growing demands of trustees of Philadelphia's "Old Saint Mary's" for control of church matters. Many colonial mission stations in the Province benefited from this funding.

with the building of the chapel is that all neighbors, Catholics and Protestants together, used their wagons to haul the stone. They walked beside their teams with hats off because the stone was to be used "for a house of God."

In 1789 the first diocese in the new nation, the Diocese of Baltimore, was established. John Carroll was chosen bishop of the new See and the following year was consecrated as the first Bishop of Baltimore.

EXCERPTS FROM THE TEST OATH AND ARTICLE VI OF THE CONSTITUTION

A portion of the Test Oath required of colonists until the adoption of the Articles of the Constitution:

"I, [name] do solemnly and sincerely in the presence of God, profess, testify and declare that I do believe that in the sacrament of the Lord's Supper, there is not any transubstantiation of the elements of bread and wine into the body and blood of Christ, ... and that the invocation of the Virgin Mary or any other saint, and the sacrifice of the Mass, as they are used in the Church of Rome, are superstitious and idolatrous."

Excerpt from Article VI of the U.S. Constitution:

"...no religious test shall ever be required as a qualification to any office or public trust under the United States."

1673	Father Jean Pierron, a French missionary from Quebec, visits the area that is now the Diocese of Harrisburg
1676	Blessed Innocent XI becomes pope, succeeding Pope Clement X
1682	William Penn receives charter for Pennsylvania province
1685	James II crowned king of England
1688	"Glorious Revolution" in England results in unseating of James II, primarily because of his Catholic sympathies
1689	Alexander VIII becomes pope; William and Mary begin rule of England
1691	Innocent XII becomes pope
1693	Test Oath required throughout British Empire
1700	Clement XI becomes pope
1704	Jesuits establish mission at Bohemia Manor in Maryland province
1707	Anne crowned queen of England
1714	George I crowned king of England
1720	Father Joseph Greaton establishes mission in Philadelphia to serve all of Pennsylvania province
1721	Mass celebrated in Conewago area by Father Greaton; Innocent XIII becomes pope
1724	Benedict XIII becomes pope
1727	King George II crowned king of England
1730	"Conewago Mission" established; Clement XII becomes pope
1740	Benedict XIV becomes pope
1741	Conewago Chapel, originally named "Saint Mary of the Assumption," built; Saint Mary, Lancaster, founded
1742	Original chapel of Saint Mary, Lancaster, built
1752	Saint Peter, Elizabethtown, founded
1757	Pennsylvania census reports 394 Catholics in area; French and Indian war begins
1758	Clement XIII becomes pope
1760	Saint Mary, Lancaster, destroyed by arson; King George III crowned king of England
1768	Conewago becomes headquarters for Saint Francis Regis mission circuit
1769	Clement XIV becomes pope
1773	Jesuit Order suppressed
1775	Saint Patrick, York, founded; Test Oath revoked in colonies; Pius VI becomes pope
1776	American Revolution begins
1779	Saint Patrick, Carlisle, founded
1787	Stone church constructed at Conewago, name changed to Sacred Heart of Jesus
1788	Bishop John Carroll elected Bishop of Baltimore with jurisdiction over all Catholic churches in the United States
1789	Earliest record of Catholic colony in Lebanon; George Washington elected President of the United States on April 30; Diocese of Baltimore established by Pope Pius VI on November 6

PART 1
DIOCESE OF BALTIMORE: 1790 - 1808

As the American Revolution came to a close, the Catholic Church in America entered a new phase. Though prejudice against the faith still lingered, finally, with the birth of the new nation, Catholics were legally free from the strictures of religious oppression.

Just as the nation was now independent, so the Catholic Church in America was now ready to have its own diocese and bishop. In 1784 Father John Carroll, having received the title Superior of American Missions, took charge of all Catholics in the new nation. Five years later, on November 6, 1789,

BISHOP JOHN CARROLL, FIRST BISHOP OF BALTIMORE

Bishop John Carroll First Bishop of Baltimore

John Carroll (1735-1815), born in Maryland, attended the Jesuits' grammar school in Bohemia and later continued his education in Flanders. He returned to Maryland after being ordained. However, because of laws in Maryland forbidding public Masses, he celebrated Mass in a chapel on his family's estate.

Father Carroll became involved in the struggles of the emerging American nation. He was a cousin to Charles Carroll, a signer of the Declaration of Independence. In the 1770s he traveled with his cousin, Benjamin Franklin, and others to Canada to seek Canadian neutrality during the Revolutionary War. Historians agree that it was mainly through his efforts that the provision for the protection of religious liberty was included in Article Six of the Constitution.

In 1784 Father Carroll was named by Pope Pius VI as Superior of the Missions in the new nation, and in 1789 he was appointed bishop of the newly established See of Baltimore, which encompassed all of the United States.

He was consecrated at Lulworth Castle, England, in 1790. The next year he convened the First Synod of Baltimore, which produced guidelines for the clergy and laity of the new See. At his invitation the Fathers of the Company of Saint Sulpice came to Baltimore, where they founded Saint Mary's College and Seminary. Likewise, Bishop Carroll established the academy that would become Georgetown University.

In 1808 with the establishment of four suffragan sees, including the Diocese of Philadelphia, Baltimore was raised to the dignity of an Archdiocese. Archbishop Carroll died in the fall of 1815, just weeks after ill health prevented him from accepting the honor of laying the cornerstone of the Washington Monument in Baltimore.

Pope Pius VI issued a Papal Bull erecting the first diocese in the United States, the Diocese of Baltimore, comprising all of the United States; the next year Father Carroll was consecrated as its bishop.

Bishop Carroll's leadership was immediately evident. In 1791 he named Father James Pellentz Vicar General of the new diocese and in November of the same year convened the First Synod of Baltimore.

Conewago Missal, printed in 1769, was used by the clergy stationed at Conewago from 1770 until the mid 1880s. It was used by Bishop Carroll, Father "Prince" Gallitzin, and Father James Pellentz, among others.

FATHER LOUIS DE BARTH (1764-1844)

Father Louis de Barth came to America in 1791. He was born in Munster on November 1, 1764, the second son of Count de Barth and Maria Louisa de Rohmer. He entered the seminary at Strasbourg, France, where he was ordained in 1790. Tensions caused by the French Revolution forced him to flee to America. He served first at Bohemia, Maryland, and subsequently at parishes throughout the area, including Saint Mary's (Lancaster) and its mission Saint Peter (Elizabethtown), Saint Patrick (Carlisle), and Saint Patrick (York).

He became the administrator at Conewago and later was named Vicar General of the newly formed Diocese of Philadelphia. Upon the death of Bishop Egan in 1814, Father de Barth declined the invitation to become bishop. Instead, he served as administrator of the diocese until the Most Reverend Henry Conwell was appointed bishop in 1820. Father de Barth then returned to Conewago, where he ministered until 1828. Then, undoubtedly feeling frustrated by the persistent difficulties with trustees in the Diocese of Philadelphia, he left the diocese to become pastor of what is now Saint Alphonsus Church, Baltimore. He spent his final years in retirement at Georgetown College, now University. He is buried at Trinity Church in Georgetown.

Also in these first years of his episcopacy Bishop Carroll declared the Blessed Virgin Mary the patron saint of the diocese and founded both Saint Mary's Seminary, under the leadership of the Sulpicians, and Georgetown College (now University).

One of the difficulties continuing from the colonial period was the limited number of priests, only thirty-five when the diocese was formed. A letter to Bishop Carroll from Father William Elling, who was stationed at Saint Mary's in Lancaster in the 1790s, captures a glimpse at how vast an area was under the care of one priest. He records the monthly Mass schedule of the mission: first Sunday, Lancaster; second, Donegal (Elizabethtown); third, Harrisburg; fourth, Lebanon; and in months with five Sundays, fifth, Chester County. Sadly, even though the Lancaster mission had by then been in existence for half a century, its faithful were still able to attend Mass only one Sunday a month.

In the 1790s refugees fleeing the French Revolution came to the United States in search of a new life free from oppression. Among the refugees were Catholic missionaries, in particular, Father Louis de Barth de Walbach, whose brother John had fought under George Washington in the Revolutionary War. Father de Barth served

Excerpt of a 1790s letter from Father William Elling to Bishop Carroll stating the monthly Mass schedule for Lancaster and its missions: "... I Lancaster, II Donegal [Elizabethtown], III Harrisburg, IV Lebanon, V [if the month had five Sundays] Chester county ..."

missions throughout southcentral Pennsylvania, urging them to build churches, for now Catholics were free to worship in public. Churches constructed under his leadership included Saint Peter's in Elizabethtown in 1799 and Saint Patrick's in Carlisle in 1806. Church records from throughout the diocese reflect his active ministry.

Another especially active priest at this time was Father Demetrius Augustine Gallitzin, who became known as the "Apostle of the Alleghenies." He served at the Conewago Mission in the 1790s before moving west to found parishes and towns, including Loretto. There he ministered for over forty years, during

Baptismal entry by Father Louis de Barth in the 1795 Record Book of Saint Peter, Elizabethtown

which he drew 10,000 souls to the faith.

During the early years of the new century, the numbers of Catholics continued to grow in the area that is now the Diocese of Harrisburg. Three new parishes were established: Corpus Christi in Chambersburg, Our Lady of Refuge in Doylesburg, and Saint Joseph, in Milton. In addition, Catholic communities took root in Buchanan Valley, Danville, Sunbury, and Lewisburg.

FATHER DEMETRIUS AUGUSTINE GALLITZIN (1770-1840)

Father Demetrius Augustine Gallitzin (1770-1840) was born at the Hague in the Netherlands on December 22, 1770. His father was Prince Dimitri Alexeievich Gallitzin, envoy of Catherine the Great of Russia at the Hague, and his mother was Countess Adelheid Amalie von Schmettau, whose father served under Frederick the Great of Prussia. In October 1792 young Prince Gallitzin arrived in Baltimore as part of his plan to complete his education through travel. However, almost immediately upon arrival, he answered a call to the priesthood. He studied at Saint Mary's Seminary in Baltimore and on March 18, 1795, was ordained by Bishop John Carroll, Bishop of Baltimore. Father Gallitzin was the first priest to receive all his sacred orders in the United States. Known also as Augustine Schmet (a contraction of his mother's name) or Smith, Father Gallitzin served initially at the Conewago Mission near Hanover and then established a mission at Loretto and, in

Father Demetrius Gallitzin, the "Apostle of the Alleghenies"

the course of time, in many other burgeoning towns in western Pennsylvania, which was then the American frontier. In the forty-one years of his ministry there, he became known as the "Apostle of the Alleghenies."

Throughout his life Father Gallitzin was an advocate for the oppressed and the downtrodden. He used his family wealth to purchase land in western Pennsylvania that he in turn sold to Catholic immigrants at minimal cost. In his church his parishioners sat without distinction of rank or status instead of in the traditional arrangement of families occupying pews for which they had paid pew rent. He was recognized as the first Catholic apologist in the young nation, writing widely circulated defenses of the Catholic faith. By his death on May 6, 1840, the number of Catholics in this western area of the state had increased from about a dozen to approximately 10,000. He is buried at Loretto, and his Coat of Arms is displayed in the church, now a minor basilica.

THE

NEW TESTAMENT

OF

OUR LORD AND SAVIOUR

JESUS CHRIST,

TRANSLATED FROM THE

LATIN VULGAT:

DILIGENTLY COMPARED WITH THE ORIGINAL GREEK:

AND FIRST PUBLISHED BY

THE ENGLISH COLLEGE AT RHEMES, A. D. 1582.

WITH

ANNOTATIONS, REFERENCES, AND AN HISTORICAL AND CHRONOLOGICAL INDEX.

FIRST AMERICAN, FROM THE FIFTH DUBLIN EDITION.
NEWLY REVISED AND CORRECTED ACCORDING TO THE CLEMENTIN EDITION OF THE SCRIPTURES.

PHILADEPHIA:

PUBLISHED BY MATHEW CAREY.
No. 118, Market-Street.

1805.

Title page of the first edition of the Catholic Bible in English, printed in the United States in 1805

In 1805 the first edition of the Catholic Bible in English printed on American soil was published in Philadelphia. Bishop Carroll helped oversee the project, reviewing the proofs as the production proceeded.

As the new diocese continued to establish its identity, one of its major internal problems was to have its authority recognized. During the colonial years, with the central authority of the church far away in Europe, the mission churches were by necessity largely self-reliant. With the establishment of the diocese on American soil, some of the churches were slow to accept the authority of the new now-local diocese. What resulted was a tug-of-war between the diocese and the trustees of some individual churches. It was a struggle that would continue well into the nineteenth century.

Despite these tensions, the Church continued to grow in the new nation. In 1808 four new dioceses were erected out of the Diocese of Baltimore, and Baltimore became an archdiocese.

One of the new dioceses was the Diocese of Philadelphia, which encompassed all of Pennsylvania and Delaware and part of New Jersey.

TRUSTEEISM

During the colonial period and into the early years of the American nation, lay trusteeism caused tensions to develop between the clergy and the laity. Under American civil law, trustees elected by their congregations were a legal body empowered to manage the day-to-day affairs, property, and finances of their congregation.

This law was built upon the Protestant model of church administration in which a lay body oversees all aspects of church administration. The new states felt that the Catholic hierarchy would too closely resemble the monarchy which had only recently been overthrown. Some of the Catholic trustees demanded the same scope of authority as their Protestant neighbors and thus claimed the right even to select and dismiss priests.

Further, these early parishioners, most of whom were either immigrants or first-generation Americans, still felt connected to the episcopal authority of their homeland rather than to the church authority in this new country. Also, since many of the missionaries did not speak the language of the predominantly English- and German-speaking congregations they came to serve, communication was sometimes strained. In many of the missions, the priest was able to come just once a month, so the laity held prayer services and instructed their children in the faith.

In sum, while serving many practical functions, the system of trusteeism introduced problems that caused it to be a troublesome element in the early years of the American nation. It was in conflict with a truly Catholic ecclesiology or understanding of the Church, and unscrupulous trustees occasionally used church finances as a way to protest spiritual and doctrinal issues.

In 1808 Reverend Michael Egan, who had served the mission churches in southcentral Pennsylvania, was named the first Bishop of Philadelphia. What is today the Diocese of Harrisburg would have to wait another sixty years to come into being. In the interim, five successive bishops would lead the Diocese of Philadelphia.

During Bishop Egan's episcopacy, the church continued to grow in what is now the Diocese of Harrisburg. Immaculate Heart of Mary, Abbotstown, and Assumption of the Blessed Virgin Mary, Lebanon, were founded, and a chapel was built at Sylvan Heights in Harrisburg.

Bishop Egan struggled with the two burdens of ill health and the tensions caused by trustees in scattered churches in the Philadelphia diocese. Upon the death of Bishop Egan in 1814, Father de Barth declined the offer to be named bishop but served as administrator of the diocese until a new bishop was named. In 1820 the Most Reverend Henry Conwell from Armagh, Ireland, accepted the call to become the second Bishop of Philadelphia.

Bishop Conwell, seventy-three years old and a stranger in the young nation, faced a difficult task. His problems with trustees who were determined to have a voice in ecclesiastical matters intensified to the point that the Bishop could not use the pro-cathedral church of Saint Mary's in Philadelphia. Because the trustees wanted another priest as their bishop, they refused to pay the salary of the new bishop or allow him to move into the rectory. To bypass the trustees, Bishop Conwell channeled diocesan funding through Saint Mary's in Lancaster. During the colonial days, Saint Mary's had served as the distribution point for monies from the Sir John James Fund, which had helped finance the work of German missionaries in the Pennsylvania province.

Despite all the wrangling, parishes that would soon be part of the Diocese

Bishop Michael Egan
First Bishop of Philadelphia

of Harrisburg took root in Abbotstown, Lebanon, Millerstown, Harrisburg, Columbia, and Lewistown.

In 1830 the Most Reverend Francis Patrick Kenrick was named coadjutor of the diocese, with full power of administration, although Bishop Conwell retained the title of bishop. Bishop Kenrick dealt decisively and effectively with the trustee problem, which had by then dragged on for over thirty years. Upon the death of Bishop Conwell in 1842, Bishop Kenrick became bishop in name as well as in authority.

BISHOP MICHAEL EGAN (1761-1814)

The Most Reverend Michael Egan, O.S.F., a native of Ireland, entered the Franciscan Order and, upon ordination, served first in Rome as Prior of the Convent of Saint Isadore and then as a missionary in his home country. In 1802 he joined Father Louis de Barth to minister to the Catholics of Saint Mary's, Lancaster, and the surrounding missions. An early account of his ministry at Saint Mary's notes that, in addition to being an eloquent speaker able to preach in English and German, he sometimes joined the choir as a member of the bass section. With the erection of the Diocese of Philadelphia in 1808, he was, upon the recommendation of Bishop Carroll, named by Pope Pius VII to be the first bishop of Philadelphia, although he was not consecrated until two years later in 1810. Ill health and the difficulties he faced in his new role, most especially the opposition of lay trustees who challenged his episcopal authority, contributed to his death just four years later in 1814.

Saint John Neumann, born in Bohemia on March 28, 1811, began his seminary studies in Europe but emigrated to the United States in 1835 to serve as a missionary. The following year he was ordained and six years later, in 1842, joined the Redemptorist Order in Baltimore. He was the first Redemptorist to make his religious profession in the United States.

From the beginning of his ministry in the United States he was known widely for the qualities noted by Pope Pius XII in 1958: "his holy life, his childlike gentleness, his hard labor, and his tremendous foresight."

He was consecrated as fourth bishop of Philadelphia on Passion Sunday, March 28, 1852, his forty-first birthday.

His accomplishments during his episcopacy were numerous. In particular, he authored the Baltimore Catechism, established the parochial school apostolate in his diocese, instituted the diocesan schedule for the Forty Hours Eucharistic Devotion, founded the Sisters of the Third Order of Saint Francis of Glen Riddle and encouraged other Orders of sisters within the diocese, fostered the founding of hospitals and orphanages, fostered an increase in the number of vocations of men and women, and labored untiringly to minister to the souls within his See.

At least biannually he visited every parish and mission within his See. It is reported that on one occasion he accepted a ride on a humble piece of farm machinery en route to Elizabethtown and in one day trudged twenty-five miles in the Allegheny Mountains to reach a mission site with just one person to be confirmed. In his visits he encouraged the construction of churches and the opening of schools. Sacramental registers in many of our parishes attest to his zealous ministry, and the descendants of those baptized or confirmed by a saint still fill our churches today.

Bishop Neumann collapsed and died on the sidewalk at the corner of Vine and Thirteenth

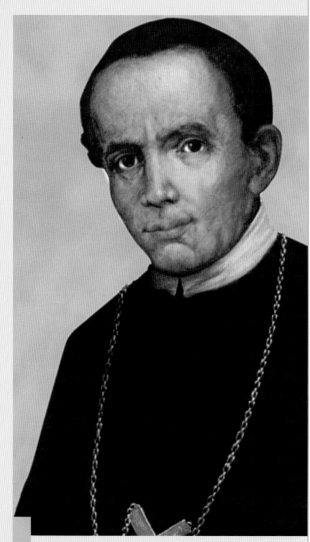

Saint John Nepomucene Neumann,
fourth Bishop of Philadelphia

Streets in Philadelphia on January 5, 1860, the day before the Feast of the Epiphany. He was only forty-nine. The national shrine in his honor is at Saint Peter the Apostle Church, Philadelphia, where his earthly remains lie in a glass-covered tomb under the Mass Altar in the Lower Church.

Bishop John Nepomucene Neumann was declared "Venerable" by Pope Benedict XV in 1921, "Blessed" by Pope Paul VI in 1963, and "Saint" in 1977, also by Pope Paul VI.

S aint Elizabeth Ann Seton, the first American-born saint and "foundress of modern-day Catholic Education" was born in New York City of a wealthy and devout Episcopalian family, the daughter of a professor of anatomy at Columbia University. She was the stepsister of Archbishop James Roosevelt Bayley of Baltimore. In 1794 Elizabeth Ann Bayley married William Magee Seton, a wealthy merchant with whom she had five children. After the death of her husband, during a trip to Italy, she converted to Catholicism in 1805. In 1809 with four companions she founded a religious community near Emmitsburg, Maryland. Thus began the first American religious society, the Sisters of Charity of Saint Joseph.

By the time of her death the new order had spread through the United States. The Sisters of Charity opened an asylum for girls in Harrisburg in 1828. The Sisters also staffed Saint Catherine Laboure School in Harrisburg from 1949 until 1975, the year of Saint Elizabeth Ann Seton's canonization.

Saint Elizabeth Ann Seton

During his tenure the seminary that would become Saint Charles Borromeo was established and a number of new parishes were formed, both within Philadelphia and across the diocese.

Growth occurred also within the area that is now the Diocese of Harrisburg with the founding of churches at Shamokin, New Freedom, Quarryville, Bloomsburg, Danville, Trevorton, Dallastown, Waynesboro, and New Oxford.

In the late 1840s the potato famine in Ireland brought many Irish newcomers to Pennsylvania, swelling the already large number of Irish Catholics within the state. Many labored with picks and shovels to build the canal system, the "water highway" that opened up travel throughout the Commonwealth.

In 1852 Bishop Kenrick became Archbishop of Baltimore, and the Most Reverend (now Saint) John Nepomucene Neumann was named the fourth bishop of Philadelphia. The strides made by the Catholic Church during his episcopacy were both numerous and monumental. Only a few of them can be noted here.

Born in Bohemia, Bishop Neumann was the first non-Irish bishop of Philadelphia. The bias that

1942 edition of The Baltimore Catechism, *developed by now-Saint John Nepomucene Neumann: the Catechism was a product of the First Plenary Council of Baltimore, 1852.*

he suffered because of his "German accent" made him all the more sensitive to the trials of the various nationalities that immigrated to the new nation. He championed the building of parish churches throughout the diocese, over sixty-five in the eight years of his episcopacy, a number of which were founded for specific ethnic groups.

In the area that is now the diocese of Harrisburg, Saint Joseph in Lancaster, Immaculate Conception in York, Saint Lawrence in Harrisburg, Saint Hubert in Danville, and Holy Trinity in Columbia were established as German parishes. In addition, churches were founded in Lykens, Gettysburg, Middletown, and Bonneauville.

Bishop Neumann was the principal author of the Baltimore Catechism, which was a product of the First Plenary Council of Baltimore in 1852. In

THE COUNCILS OF BALTIMORE

Seven provincial and three plenary councils of Baltimore were convened between 1829 and 1884. At these gatherings the hierarchy of the U.S. Catholic Church addressed various pastoral challenges facing the young Catholic community in America. A plenary council is composed of bishops from more than one ecclesiastical region. Laws promulgated in its sessions bind the dioceses represented in the plenary council, whereas provincial councils legislation affects only the territory of that ecclesiastical province. From 1808 until 1846, Baltimore functioned as the only ecclesiastical province in the United States. Therefore the first seven provincial councils of Baltimore were practically, though not formally, plenary councils of the United States.

The decrees of the early councils reflected the concerns of the U.S. Church in regard to the sacramental life of the Church, trusteeism, priestly conduct, the need for Catholic publications, a uniform catechism, and the establishment of Catholic schools. The plenary councils called for unity among Catholics after the Civil War, a need to respond to the emancipation of blacks, a Catholic university, aid to blacks and Native Americans, and better seminary and clergy education.

The Councils of Baltimore created a strong diocesan organization, brought uniformity to church discipline and worship, and strengthened ties to Rome.

1853, on the Feast of Corpus Christi, he inaugurated the annual observance of the Forty Hours Devotion in the parishes of the diocese. He himself developed the diocese-wide schedule for the devotion. He introduced the Saint Vincent de Paul Society into the diocese. Likewise, he was ever sensitive to the care of orphans and the infirm. He founded the Congregation of the Philadelphia Sisters of the Third Order of Saint Francis and

Saint Francis Xavier church, Gettysburg, and other local churches served as temporary hospitals for casualties from the Battle of Gettysburg. Sisters of Charity from Saint Joseph College at Emmitsburg, Maryland, came to minister to the wounded and dying soldiers.

The sanctuary of the church served as the operating room for amputation cases. The injured lay on the pews, under the pews, and in the aisles. An entry from the annals of the Sisters of Charity describes the wretchedness: "The Catholic Church was filled with wounded, mutilated men …There was scarcely room to pass among them in the sanctuary and in the gallery. Their own blood, the water used for bathing their wounds, and all kinds of filth and stench added to their misery, for already gangrenous wounds had begun to infect the air."

The church continued to serve as a hospital for several weeks in the aftermath of the battle. During these weeks Mass was celebrated in the home of a parishioner. A stained-glass window in the church pays tribute to the Sisters of Charity for their ministry to the battle casualties, both Union and Confederate.

Stained-glass window in Saint Francis Xavier Church, Gettysburg, depicting the care of the injured during the Battle of Gettysburg. Saint Francis Xavier church was used as a hospital during this period of the Civil War.

The April 15, 1865, edition of The New York Herald *reports the assassination of President Abraham Lincoln.*

welcomed other orders into the diocese, in particular the Sisters, Servants of the Immaculate Heart, and the Good Shepherd Sisters.

It was during Bishop Neumann's episcopacy that the dogma of the Immaculate Conception was proclaimed by Pope Pius IX. However, long before this proclamation, Bishop Neumann was a strong advocate for celebrating this December 8 Feast as a holy day.

This fourth bishop of Philadelphia was a tireless visitor to every corner of his see, then the largest diocese within the United States. His visitation records show that he made at least biannual visits to every parish and mission within the diocese. As early as 1855 he began to call attention to the need to establish a suffragan diocese within the western portion of his see, though it was not until after his death that the Diocese of Harrisburg was established.

He likewise had a keen interest in education. He fostered formal learning at all levels for boys and girls alike across his diocese. Today he is known as the founder of the parochial school apostolate. As bishop he saw schools open in McSherrystown, York, and Lebanon in what is now the Diocese of Harrisburg.

Major seminaries were already in place in the new nation, but Bishop Neumann saw the need also for minor seminaries to help foster vocations. One result was the opening of a preparatory seminary at Glen Riddle in 1859. The rector was the newly ordained Father Jeremiah F. Shanahan, who a decade later would become the first bishop of Harrisburg.

Bishop Neumann's episcopacy was not without problems. Even with the erecting of a diocese for New Jersey in 1852, the Philadelphia see still covered 26,000 square miles. Determined to minister to all his flock, Bishop Neumann was away from Philadelphia for weeks at a time, and much administrative work was given scant attention. In 1857 Father James Fredric Wood was appointed as coadjutor-bishop of Philadelphia with the right of succession. For the next three years he attended to the day-to-day affairs in Philadelphia while Bishop Neumann traveled with missionary zeal to the Catholic communities within his see.

With the death of Bishop Neumann in 1860, the Most Reverend James Frederic Wood became the fifth bishop of Philadelphia. The War Between the States, the assassination of President Abraham Lincoln, and the bitter years of Reconstruction all occurred during his episcopacy. During the War, sisters from a number of orders served as nurses in hospitals and on the battlefields, and Saint Francis Xavier Church in Gettysburg was used as a hospital to treat the casualties of the Battle of Gettysburg.

Against this national backdrop, Bishop Wood oversaw the completion in 1864 of the Cathedral of SS. Peter and Paul. It was designed by Napoleon LeBrun, the architect also of the U.S. Capitol in Washington, D.C. He also spearheaded the building of Saint Charles Borromeo Seminary in Overbrook, on the outskirts of Philadelphia. Early on, he was ridiculed for his plan, dubbed "Wood's Folly," to relocate the Philadelphia seminary outside the city limits.

Despite the turmoil within the nation, Catholic churches were founded in Columbia, Sunbury, Hanover, and Mount Carmel, and schools opened in New Oxford, Columbia, and Littlestown.

Finally, a key event during his years as bishop was the erection of the Diocese of Harrisburg, along with the dioceses of Wilmington and Scranton, in 1868. Thirty-four-year-old Father Jeremiah F. Shanahan, rector of the seminary at Glen Riddle, was named the first Bishop of Harrisburg.

1790 Bishop John Carroll consecrated at Lulworth, Dorchester, England, on August 15

1792 Arrival of priests from France escaping the French Revolution, including Father Louis de Barth de Walbach; Corpus Christi, Chambersburg, founded

1794 Lancaster Pike connecting Philadelphia with Lancaster completed

1800 Pius VII becomes pope

1802 Our Lady of Refuge, Doylesburg, founded

1805 Saint Joseph, Milton, founded

1808 Diocese of Philadelphia established by Pope Pius VII, comprises Pennsylvania, Delaware, and western and southern parts of New Jersey

1809 Immaculate Heart of Mary, Abbottstown, founded

1810 The Reverend Michael Egan installed as the first bishop of Philadelphia; Assumption of the Blessed Virgin Mary, Lebanon, founded

1812 Harrisburg becomes capital of Pennsylvania

1813 Chapel built in Harrisburg at Sylvan Heights

1814 Death of Bishop Egan; Philadelphia episcopacy remains vacant until 1820

1817 "Old Jesuit Mission," Saint Ignatius Loyola, Buchanan Valley, founded

1820 Most Reverend Henry Conwell, Vicar General of Armagh, Ireland, installed as second Bishop of Philadelphia

1823 Leo XII becomes pope; mission station at Millertown (now Immaculate Conception of the Blessed Virgin Mary, Fairfield), established

1827 Saint Patrick, Harrisburg, founded for Irish Catholics

1828 Saint Peter, Columbia, founded; Sisters of Charity open home for girls in Harrisburg

1829 Pius VIII becomes pope

1830 Sacred Heart of Jesus, Lewistown, founded; Sisters of Saint Clare establish school in McSherrystown; Reverend Francis Patrick Kenrick appointed coadjutor to Bishop Conwell with right of succession

1831 Gregory XVI becomes pope

1832 Diocesan seminary of Saint Charles Borromeo opens in the episcopal residence in Philadelphia

1833 Diocesan newspaper *Catholic Herald,* a predecessor of the *Catholic Standard and Times,* established in Philadelphia

1836 Saint Edward the Confessor, Shamokin, founded; Sisters of Saint Clare establish school in Pottsville

1840 Saint John the Baptist, New Freedom, founded

1842 Death of Bishop Conwell; Most Reverend Francis Patrick Kenrick named third bishop of Philadelphia; Saint Catherine of Siena, Quarryville, founded

1844 Anti-Catholic mob violence forces closing on Sunday, May 12, of all Catholic churches in Philadelphia

1846	Blessed Pius IX becomes pope
1847	Famine in Ireland brings many Irish immigrants to Pennsylvania
1848	Saint Columba, Bloomsburg, founded; Saint Joseph, Danville established as a parish
1849	Saint Joseph, Lancaster, founded as a German parish, the first ethnic parish in what is now the Diocese of Harrisburg
1850	Saint Patrick, Trevorton, founded; Saint Joseph, Dallastown founded; Saint Andrew, Waynesboro, founded
1851	Saint Patrick School, York, opens
1852	Immaculate Conception, York, founded for German Catholics; Immaculate Conception, New Oxford, founded; Immaculate Conception of the Blessed Virgin Mary, Fairfield, founded; Father (now Saint) John Nepomucene Neumann, C.Ss.R., installed as fourth bishop of Philadelphia, replacing Bishop Kenrick, who became Archbishop of Baltimore
1853	Our Lady, Help of Christians, Lykens, founded; Saint Francis Xavier, Gettysburg, founded
1854	Saint Joseph Academy, McSherrystown, opens; *Ineffabilis Deus* issued by Pope Pius IX, solemnly declaring the dogma of the Immaculate Conception of the Blessed Virgin Mary
1855	Seven Sorrows of the Blessed Virgin Mary, Middletown, founded; Immaculate Conception of the Blessed Virgin Mary School, York, opens

1857	Father James Frederick Wood appointed Coadjutor Bishop of Philadelphia
1859	Saint Joseph the Worker, Bonneauville, Gettysburg, founded; Saint Lawrence, Harrisburg, founded for German Catholics; Saint Hubert, Danville, founded for German Catholics; Assumption of the Blessed Virgin Mary School, Lebanon, opens
1860	Holy Trinity, Columbia, founded; death of Bishop John Nepomucene Neumann; The Most Reverend James Frederick Wood installed as fifth Bishop of Philadelphia
1861	Outbreak of the Civil War
1862	Immaculate Conception of the Blessed Virgin Mary School, New Oxford, opens
1863	Saint Michael the Archangel, Sunbury, founded; Battle of Gettysburg, July 1-3
1864	Saint Joseph, Hanover, founded
1865	Holy Trinity School, Columbia, opens; Saint Joseph School, Hanover, opens; Civil War ends with surrender of Robert E. Lee and his army on April 9; President Abraham Lincoln assassinated on Good Friday, April 14; all Confederate armies surrender by May 25
1866	Our Lady of Mount Carmel, Mount Carmel, founded; Saint Peter School, Columbia, opens
1867	Saint Aloysius School, Littlestown, opens

PART 1
THE EPISCOPACY OF JEREMIAH F. SHANAHAN, THE FOUNDER,
FIRST BISHOP OF HARRISBURG, 1868-1886

On March 3, 1868, Blessed Pius IX issued a decree establishing the Diocese of Harrisburg, made up of 18 counties in southcentral Pennsylvania, the 15 that comprise the diocese

Map of the Diocese of Harrisburg

today plus Fulton, Centre, and Clinton. Named as first bishop of this new diocese was 34-year-old Most Reverend Jeremiah F. Shanahan.

In 1868 the new diocese was home to about 25,000 Catholics in an area of 10,000 square miles. There were 61 worship sites, including churches, chapels, and stations. Of the 61, twenty were parishes with pastors in residence. Nineteen

Blessed Pius IX, who issued the decree establishing the Diocese of Harrisburg in 1868.

FATHER JOHN JOSEPH KOCH (1840-1917)

A native of France, Father (later Reverend Monsignor) John Joseph Koch came to the United States as a seminarian and upon his ordination in 1863 was appointed pastor of Saint Joseph Parish, Milton. At that time Saint Joseph, one of the very few Catholic parishes in the northern section of the diocese, encompassed an area 100 miles by 40 miles. Writing in 1918, the historian Father M. M. Hassett wryly observed that Father Koch, for the three years of his pastorate there, spent his days "mostly on horseback, attending to the spiritual wants of his widely dispersed flock." In 1866 Father Koch became the first pastor of the newly erected Saint Edward Parish in Shamokin, where he remained for a half century, ministering to the growing Catholic population attracted to the area to work in the anthracite coal mines. He celebrated his golden jubilee there in 1916, a record which Hassett called "nearly unique in the annals of the Church."

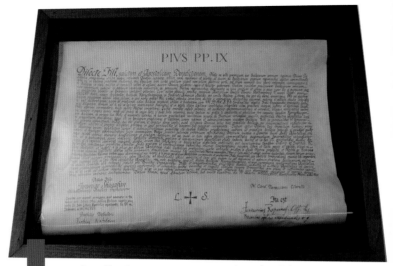

Papal Bull of Pope Pius IX erecting the Diocese of Harrisburg on March 3, 1868. Translated from Latin, the Bull states in part: "...Having consulted with Our Venerable Brothers, the Cardinals of the Congregation for the Propagation of the Faith, who have studied the matter carefully, We have determined to establish this new See. Wherefore, in keeping with the counsel of the aforementioned Cardinals, and exercising Our full Apostolic Authority, We hereby establish and constitute in the City of Harrisburg a new Episcopal See, under the care of its own Bishop, to be known henceforth as the 'Diocese of Harrisburg.'... Given at Rome, at Saint Peter's, under the ring of the Fisherman, on the Third day of March, 1868, in the twenty-second year of Our Pontificate."

diocesan priests and three Jesuit missionaries were serving in the diocese. There were seven parochial schools and one academy. Nuns from three orders—Sisters of Saint Joseph, Sisters of Saint Francis, and Sisters, Servants of the Immaculate Heart of Mary—were in residence.

Though the overall population of the new diocese was small, its establishment with Harrisburg as its center positioned it with advantage. Saint Patrick church, Harrisburg, located at the site of the present Cathedral, just about 200 yards from the capitol building, became the procathedral. Its location on the eastern bank of the Susquehanna river situated it along a major travel route in the state.

This site for Saint Patrick church had been chosen in the 1820s to serve the large population of Irish immigrants who had settled close to their work constructing the Pennsylvania canal along the Susquehanna river. When the church was selected as the procathedral, the name was retained, and Saint Patrick was named the patron of the diocese.

In the 1870s the church was enlarged to seat 700 and the bell was added.

Bishop Shanahan was keenly aware of the need for more priests. His background as a seminary rector prompted him to establish a seminary in the new diocese. To this end he purchased the Sylvan Heights property in eastern Harrisburg and in October 1883 opened a diocesan seminary, directed by Father Massimo Cassini, in the mansion on the estate. He also had the bishop's residence relocated there. Sadly, the cost of maintaining a seminary proved too great for the limited resources of the diocese, and in 1886, the year of Bishop Shanahan's death, the seminary closed.

The property continued to serve as the bishop's residence until 1901, when the orphanage for girls replaced it on the site.

Bishop Shanahan recognized the importance of having a formal Catholic presence in the burgeoning communities throughout his see. When the diocese was erected in 1868, of the 18 counties, 4 were without even a mission station:

Fulton, Juniata, Perry, and Snyder. Four more—Columbia, Cumberland, Mifflin, and Union—had only chapels or stations, which were attended by clergy only several times a year, some as few as 3 times a year.

Lancaster, the county with the largest Catholic population, had five parishes. Dauphin and Adams counties each had three; York and Northumberland each had two. The remaining counties — Lebanon, Franklin, Centre, Clinton, and Montour — each had just one.

Newly constructed Saint Patrick Cathedral, early 1900s

FIRST ORDINATION WITHIN THE DIOCESE OF HARRISBURG

On August 22, 1869, Bishop Jeremiah Shanahan celebrated the first ordination of priests within the year-old diocese. At ceremonies in the Saint Patrick Procathedral, he ordained Father Anthony Kaul, Father Aloysius Kuhlman, and Father Daniel Reilly.

Father Kaul was the first of the three to receive Holy Orders, thereby becoming the first priest to be ordained in the diocese. He was the founding pastor of Saint Anthony of Padua Parish in Lancaster, which was named in his honor, and set a national record for serving as pastor there for 65 years.

Bishop Jeremiah Shanahan's cathedra, now in the Bishop Dattilo Priests' Retirement Residence

MOST REVEREND JEREMIAH F. SHANAHAN, D.D.
FIRST BISHOP OF HARRISBURG
1868-1886

Serviam.
I will serve.

Jeremiah Francis Shanahan was born on July 13, 1834, at Silver Lake, Susquehanna county, Pennsylvania, to John and Margaret (Donovan) Shanahan. He was educated at Saint Joseph College, Binghamton, New York, and Saint Charles Borromeo Seminary, Overbrook, Philadelphia. Upon ordination by Bishop (now Saint) John Neumann on July 3, 1859, he was appointed rector of the newly established preparatory seminary at Glen Riddle. In the nine years in which he served as rector, more than 30 of the students from this new school proceeded on to the seminary at Overbrook. He remained in this position until he was appointed bishop of the newly established Diocese of Harrisburg. Only 34 years of age, he was consecrated on July 12, 1868, in Philadelphia by Archbishop James Frederic Wood.

Bishop Shanahan attended the first Vatican Council in Rome during 1869-1870 and the Third Plenary Council in Baltimore in 1884. During his tenure as ordinary, he worked untiringly to shepherd his flock. The new diocese enjoyed strong and rapid growth in the size of the Catholic population, the number of new parishes and missions, and the development of parochial education.

What must have been a great disappointment to him, however, was his failed attempt to establish a seminary in the diocese. In 1883 he oversaw the opening of a seminary at Sylvan Heights in Harrisburg, but its doors closed just 3 years later, in 1886, the year of his death.

Bishop Shanahan died on September 24, 1886. To say that his funeral, just 5 days later, was massive is an understatement, especially considering that in 1886 travel was by train, boat, and horse-drawn carriage. In addition to clergy from the Diocese of Harrisburg, his fellow priests in attendance included the Most Reverend Patrick J. Ryan, Archbishop of Philadelphia, plus 8 bishops, 24 priests from the Archdiocese of Philadelphia, 9 each from the dioceses Pittsburgh and Scranton, 4 from Erie, and representative clergy from as far away as Chicago, Michigan, and Vermont. He was buried in the cemetery adjacent to the pro-cathedral, but when the cemetery was relocated, his remains were moved to Mount Calvary Cemetery, Harrisburg. Included among his survivors was a younger brother and priest, Father John Walter Shanahan, who would become the third bishop of Harrisburg.

Procathedral choir, 1870s

Professor B. H. Strickland, choir director at the procathedral in the 1870s

Saint Anthony of Padua, Lancaster, founded in 1870.

In 1868 the churches also reflected the Irish and German backgrounds of the majority of their parishioners. Of the 20 parishes, three in Harrisburg, Lancaster, and Columbia had been established as German; all the others conducted their day-to-day affairs in English.

Bishop Shanahan devoted much effort to establishing a Catholic worship site in communities throughout the 18-county diocese. During

Bishop Jeremiah Shanahan lying in state.
The coffin was placed upon a platform constructed
over the front pews in the procathedral.

Saint Joseph Hospital, Lancaster, in 1905.
The hospital was incorporated in 1885 under Sisters
of Saint Francis of Glen Riddle.

the 18 years of his episcopacy, he opened 10 new parishes, elevated seven missions to the rank of parish, and appointed resident pastors to a number of missions.

One of the strong areas of growth in these years was the northern portion of the diocese, where, until the 1860s, the Catholic population had been extremely low. The sparseness of a Catholic population up until then is generally acknowledged to reflect the anti-Catholic sentiment of this staunchly Protestant area. In the 1870s and 1880s, many immigrants from eastern Europe, enticed by the promise of work in the coal mines, settled there, forming a number of ethnic parishes.

Catholic education was also a high priority in the new diocese. During Bishop Shanahan's episcopacy the number of schools more than quadrupled, increasing from 7 to 29, with an attendance of over 4,200 children in 1886. By 1886 there were eight orders of sisters in the diocese to guide the education of the children, the three already in the diocese in 1868 plus Sisters of Mercy, Sisters of Charity, Sisters of Christian Charity, Sisters of the Holy Cross, and Felician Sisters. Twenty-three of the schools were staffed by religious and six by lay teachers.

In the summer of 1886, at the age of 52, Bishop Shanahan suffered a reversal in his health. Despite guarded optimism for his recovery, his death followed quickly on September 25. In his 18 years as bishop, the diocese he shepherded with vigor and care had grown to 35,000 souls attended by 51 priests.

Letter written and signed by Bishop
Jeremiah Shanahan just months
after becoming the first bishop of
the Diocese of Harrisburg.

1868 Diocese of Harrisburg established on May 23 by Pope Pius IX with the Right Reverend Jeremiah Shanahan as the first bishop; Saint Patrick, Harrisburg, becomes procathedral; Saint Joseph School, Lancaster, opens

1869 Presentation of the Blessed Virgin Mary, Marietta, and Saint Ignatius of Loyola, Centralia, founded; Immaculate Conception of the Blessed Virgin Mary School, York, opens; first ordination within the Diocese of Harrisburg

1870 Saint Anthony of Padua, Lancaster, founded as a German parish; Saint Joseph, Locust Gap, founded

1871 Saints Peter and Paul church, Larue, blessed; Saint Anthony of Padua School, Lancaster, opens; Saint Charles Borromeo Seminary at Overbrook near Philadelphia opens with 128 students

1872 Saint Stanislaus Kosta, Shamokin, founded for Polish Catholics, the first Polish parish in Pennsylvania

1873 First school for the Cathedral Parish of Saint Patrick, Harrisburg, opens; Saint Joseph School, Bonneauville, opens

1874 Corpus Christi School, Chambersburg, and Saint Edward School, Shamokin, open

1875 Sacred Heart of Jesus, Williamstown, founded; Saint Joseph, Mount Carmel, founded as a Polish parish; Philadelphia erected an archdiocese with then Bishop James Frederic Wood as first archbishop

1877 Saint Francis Xavier School, Gettysburg, opens

1878 Saint James, Steelton, founded for Irish Catholics; Pope Leo XIII becomes pope

1879 Assumption of the Blessed Virgin Mary, Mount Joy, and Saint Joseph, Mechanicsburg, founded; Thomas Edison invents the electric light bulb

1880 Sacred Heart Academy for Girls, Lancaster, chartered; Seven Sorrows of the Blessed Virgin Mary School, Middletown, opens; First Provincial Council convenes

1881 First International Eucharistic Congress held in Lille, France

1882 Saint Stanislaus Kostka School, Shamokin, opens

1883 Sylvan Heights Seminary, Harrisburg, opens (closes in 1886); Saint Joseph Hospital, Lancaster, under Sisters of Saint Francis of Glenn Riddle, opens

1886 Sacred Heart of Jesus, Cornwall, founded; Sylvan Heights becomes Episcopal residence (until 1901); Bishop Jeremiah Shanahan dies

PART 2
THE EPISCOPACY OF THOMAS MCGOVERN, THE WELCOMER, SECOND BISHOP OF HARRISBURG, 1888-1898

Father Thomas McGovern was serving as pastor of Saint Joseph, Danville, when he was named the second bishop of Harrisburg. He was consecrated on March 11, 1888, at the age of 55 and set out immediately to continue the work begun by his predecessor.

One of his first projects was to convene the First Synod of the Diocese of Harrisburg. The assembly, meeting in August 1888, reaffirmed the acceptance of the acts and decrees of the 1884 Third Plenary Council in Baltimore, developed a code of laws for the diocese, and established a diocesan school board.

A major concern for Bishop McGovern was the need for parishes and priests to serve the growing number of immigrants from eastern Europe who were settling in the northern part of the diocese.

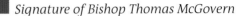

Signature of Bishop Thomas McGovern

The latter half of the 1800s saw a great influx of a new wave of immigrants drawn by the promise of abundant work in the anthracite coal mines. To accommodate this growing Catholic population, Bishop McGovern established 6 new parishes, all of which were ethnic—4 in Mount Carmel and 2 in Shamokin. A related challenge for this second bishop of the diocese was to provide priests to minister to this large population of non-English-speaking parishioners. He was successful in bringing clergy from Europe to augment the ranks of diocesan clergy, though, as parish records attest,

Much fanfare welcomed Bishop McGovern as the second bishop of Harrisburg.

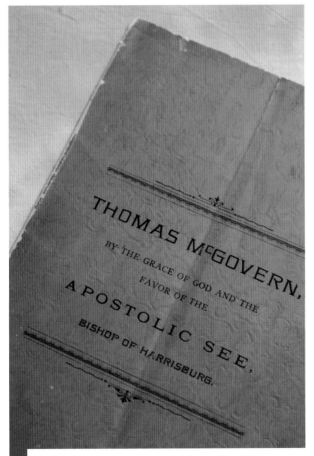

Bishop McGovern's Apostolic See book

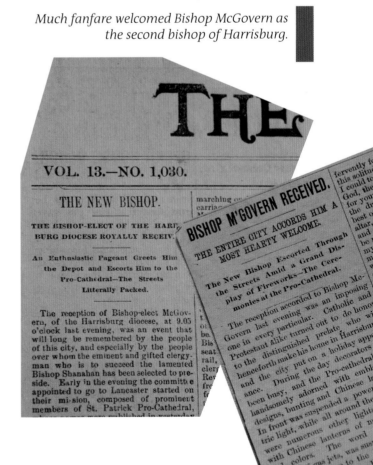

SYLVAN HEIGHTS

Sylvan Heights Home, Harrisburg

The Sylvan Heights Home for orphaned girls opened in 1901. In the first year of operation, the home, staffed by the Sisters of Mercy, welcomed 80 girls. The facility was enlarged in 1906 and renovated in 1915 following a disastrous fire. Throughout its history Sylvan Heights offered a home-like atmosphere to its residents.

In 1966 the home began to accept boys up to the age of 12, in particular, siblings of girls already in residence there.

The home remained in operation until 1979, when the facility closed and the residents were transferred. The property was subsequently sold, but the memories of the almost 2,000 residents who through the years were at home there will continue to endure for many more years to come.

---

their stays were many times short, resulting in frequent turnover of parish administration.

With a strong anti-Catholic sentiment already present in the northern portion of the diocese, the increased numbers of Catholics settling in the area served to intensify Protestant-Catholic friction and resulted in much debate. An accomplished debater, Bishop McGovern visited the area frequently and readily engaged in what were sometimes heated exchanges.

Students and teacher at Immaculate Conception School, New Oxford, 1889

The growth of the union movement, particularly as it involved the mining communities, contributed to tensions in the area. The large number of Catholics within the ranks of the workers caused the union issues to become intertwined with the religious differences.

Elsewhere in the diocese, growth also continued during Bishop McGovern's episcopacy. Steelton's Assumption of the Blessed Virgin Mary Parish was established as a mission for Eastern European Catholics. The missions in Hanover, Middletown, New Oxford, and Waynesboro were raised to the rank of parishes. The parishes already in existence continued to grow in both population and physical plant. It was a time in which many congregations renovated and enlarged their churches, rectories, and schools. Included in the construction were seven new church buildings.

From 1888 to 1898 the Catholic population in the diocese increased from 35,000 to 42,000, a sizable growth in just one decade. With the addition of the six new parishes and the elevation of four missions to parish status, the number of parishes grew to 47. Parish schools increased

The main altar and altar servers in the procathedral, 1897.

from 29 to 32. Even though only three new schools were opened, school enrollment increased dramatically from just over 4,300 to almost 6,000.

Sadly, Bishop McGovern became ill in the spring of 1898, and in July, with his compromised health made worse by the ravages of a heat wave, he passed away at Sylvan Heights on July 25, with his brothers and sisters at his side.

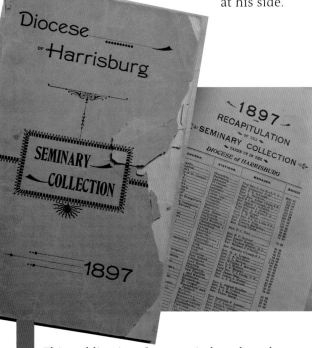

This publication, 64 pages in length and arranged by parish, lists the names of all individuals and the amounts they contributed to the 1897 seminary collection. It was the practice in the late 1800s and into the 1900s to publish lists such as this.

FATHER HENRY G. GANSS (1855–1912)

Reverend Doctor Henry G. Ganss, a native of Lancaster, studied for the priesthood at Saint Vincent Seminary, Latrobe, where he earned a doctorate in music. He was ordained in 1878. In August 1891 he became pastor of Saint Patrick, Carlisle, and immediately was active in the religious and cultural societies of the community. During his ministry there, he entered into scholarly debates with Protestant ministers, performed concerts at the Carlisle Opera House, and was one of the founders of the Todd Memorial Hospital. He worked closely with Saint Katharine Drexel in the apostolate of Indians and Blacks.

He enjoys international renown as a composer. Among his best-known works is the hymn "Long Live the Pope."

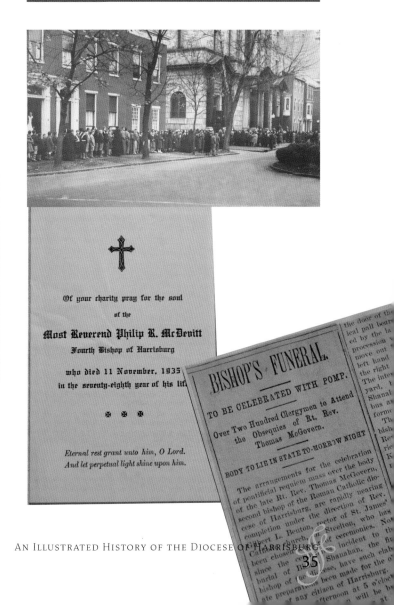

Of your charity pray for the soul
of the
Most Reverend Philip R. McDevitt
Fourth Bishop of Harrisburg
who died 11 November, 1935
in the seventy-eighth year of his life

✠ ✠ ✠

Eternal rest grant unto him, O Lord.
And let perpetual light shine upon him.

BISHOP'S FUNERAL.
TO BE CELEBRATED WITH POMP.
Over Two Hundred Clergymen to Attend the Obsequies of Rt. Rev. Thomas McGovern.
BODY TO LIE IN STATE TO-MORROW NIGHT

MOST REVEREND THOMAS MCGOVERN
SECOND BISHOP OF HARRISBURG
1888-1898

Forti salus in fide.
A strong faith in your salvation.

(1 PETER 5:9)

Thomas McGovern was born in 1832 in Swalinbar, County Cavan, Ireland, the son of Edward and Margaret (Gillece) McGovern. His family came to America when he was just one year old and, after a brief residence in Lancaster, the family settled in Bradford County.

From early on he enjoyed a reputation as a formidable debater. As a youth his distinguishing trait was his prowess in disputation, and decades later a newspaper article observed that "it was a bold man who, knowing his (Bishop McGovern's) powers in that direction, was willing to enter into a controversy with him."

This future bishop was educated at Saint Joseph College, Binghamton, New York; Mount Saint Mary's College and Seminary, Emmitsburg, Maryland; and Saint Charles Borromeo Seminary in Philadelphia. Upon ordination by then-Bishop James Frederic Wood on December 27, 1861, he was assigned pastoral duties in Philadelphia. Later he served at Saint Patrick, York, and Saint Joseph, Danville.

In years prior to the 1877 trial in Bloomsburg of the Molly Maguires, Father McGovern had ministered to all three of the men on trial for murder. As a clergyman, he preached and wrote with strong conviction about the dangers of secret oath-taking societies.

He was appointed bishop of Harrisburg on December 6, 1887, and consecrated by Bishop William O'Hara on March 11, 1888. As bishop he served with unrelenting dedication and energy that helped the diocese grow in strength in numbers in the last decade of the century. He died on July 25, 1898, and was buried in Mount Calvary Cemetery, Harrisburg.

Bishop McGovern's pyx, inscribed
"Dear Jesus, bless Thomas"

1887	Pennsylvania Railroad train station at Harrisburg opens; Catholic University of America founded in Washington, D.C.
1888	Most Reverend Thomas McGovern appointed second bishop of Harrisburg; Saint Joseph, Mount Carmel, founded; Saint James School, Steelton, and Saint Joseph School, Locust Gap, open; First Synod of the Diocese of Harrisburg convened
1890	Saint Joseph School, Danville, opens
1892	Assumption of the Blessed Virgin Mary, Shamokin, and Saint John the Baptist, Mount Carmel, founded for Slovak Catholics; Holy Cross, Mount Carmel, founded for Lithuanian Catholics; Saint Edward High School, Shamokin, and Saint Joseph School, Mount Carmel, open
1893	Second Synod of the Diocese of Harrisburg convened; Saint Edward, Shamokin, becomes first church in the United States to be lighted by electricity
1894	Saint Michael the Archangel, Shamokin, founded for Lithuanian Catholics
1895	Our Mother of Consolation, Mount Carmel, founded for Polish Catholics
1897	Saint Ignatius School, Centralia, opens
1898	Bishop McGovern dies; Very Reverend John Joseph Koch appointed interregnum administrator; Saint Stephen, Shamokin, founded as a Polish parish; Assumption of the Blessed Virgin Mary, Steelton, founded for Croatian Catholics; Spanish-American War, results in American occupation of Cuba (until 1909); United States annexes Puerto Rico, the Philippines, and Guam

PART 3
THE EPISCOPACY OF JOHN W. SHANAHAN, THE BUILDER
THIRD BISHOP OF HARRISBURG, 1899-1916

After a nine-month interregnum, the diocese welcomed as its third bishop, the younger brother of their beloved first bishop. On January 7, 1899, the Reverend John Walter Shanahan, then pastor of Our Mother of Sorrows in Philadelphia and superintendent of parochial schools in the Archdiocese of Philadelphia, was appointed the third bishop of Harrisburg. He was consecrated on May 1, 1899, at age 53 and installed several days later in ceremonies at the procathedral.

Altar servers, Conewago, 1901

Saint Patrick school, York, early 1900s

The Saint Patrick Procathedral and cemetery, on the site of the present Cathedral. When the Diocese of Harrisburg was established in 1868, Saint Patrick church, built in 1827, became the procathedral. The edifice continued in use until the Cathedral was built in 1904-07. Instead of simply being torn down, the church building was dismantled and shipped by rail to Burnham, where, reconstructed, it was the home of All Saints Chapel until 1951. The adjacent cemetery of the procathedral was relocated to Holy Cross Cemetery, Harrisburg.

His installation over, he immediately focused his attention on becoming acquainted with the see he would shepherd for the next 17 years. To this end he set out on a comprehensive visitation schedule which took him to almost every one of the 47 parishes in the diocese, inquiring at every stop about local needs and concerns.

The diocese had experienced rapid growth in the latter years of the 1800s, and in his visits Bishop Shanahan saw first hand the pressing need to establish new parishes as well as to divide some city parishes that had expanded to an unwieldy size. As many of these newcomers had brought with them

*Signature of
Bishop John W. Shanahan*

the language, traditions, and culture of their homeland, Bishop Shanahan established ethnic parishes to provide for their spiritual needs. Thus in the early part of the 1900s, ethnic parishes and missions were erected for Catholics whose backgrounds were Slovak, Slovenian, Hungarian, Polish, Italian, Greek-Ruthenian, Austro-German, Tyrol-Austrian, Lithuanian, and Croatian. To serve these non-English-speaking congregations, he enlisted the help of religious orders and welcomed foreign priests able to speak the tongues of what had become a polyglot population, especially in the northern counties of the diocese.

In his 17 years as bishop, the third bishop founded 21 new parishes, raised seven missions to the rank of parishes, erected three missions, and established a resident chaplaincy at the State Hospital for patients suffering from tuberculosis, located at Mount Alto in Adams County. This phenomenal growth under the leadership of Bishop Shanahan was the greatest the diocese has experienced in its history.

Another need evident to Bishop John Shanahan was a diocese-wide effort to care for orphaned children. Disease and accident all too often left children without parental care. Ironically, the very work that had drawn so many immigrants to the diocese with the hope of a higher living standard was by its nature so dangerous that work fatalities were not uncommon. The bishop successfully petitioned parishes to accept an assessment of one dollar per each member of the congregation to enable the diocese to open an orphanage. With the solid financial base, the diocese promptly transformed the former seminary at Sylvan Heights into an orphanage for girls. The facility, large enough to house up to 100 children, opened on November 21, 1901, under the care of the Sisters of Mercy.

In 1907 a second assessment throughout the diocese plus several individual generous gifts provided the means for the diocese to construct a home for boys. On September 1, 1911, the Paradise Protectory and Agricultural School, located on a 280-acre parcel of land near Abbottstown in York County, opened for orphan boys. The home was administered by the Sisters of Saint Joseph.

*Copper cornerstone box,
Saint John the Evangelist
church, Enhaut*

Paradise School, Abbottstown

Order of FORTY HOURS' Devotion
In the CHURCHES and CHAPELS of the DIOCESE of HARRISBURG, PA.
1900

HENRY G. GANSS, Chancellor.

MOST REVEREND JOHN W. SHANAHAN
THIRD BISHOP OF HARRISBURG
1899-1916

Non recuso laborem.
I will not refuse the burden.

John Walter Shanahan, was born on January 3, 1846, at Silver Lake, Susquehanna County, Pennsylvania. He was educated at Saint Joseph's College, near Binghamton, New York, and the Saint Charles Borromeo Seminary, Overbrook, Philadelphia, and on January 2, 1869, was ordained to the priesthood by his brother, Bishop Jeremiah F. Shanahan.

In addition to pastoral assignments, Father Shanahan served as superintendent of Catholic schools in Philadelphia from the time of his ordination until he was named the third bishop of Harrisburg on January 7, 1899. He was consecrated on May 1, 1899, in Philadelphia by Archbishop Patrick J. Ryan. Unlike his predecessor, who had arrived in Harrisburg amid much pomp, including a lengthy parade and fireworks, Bishop Shanahan slipped in quietly, entering, by his own dictate, "unheralded and unknown."

Thus Bishop John Shanahan became the shepherd of the same diocese in which his brother Jeremiah had served as the first bishop. Although it is not unusual for a family to have two of its sons become bishops, it is highly rare even to the present to have brothers serve as bishop within the same diocese.

During the years of his episcopacy, the diocese continued the same growth it had enjoyed under his two predecessor bishops. He erected parishes and missions, opened orphanages for girls and boys, and oversaw the construction of Saint Patrick Cathedral.

With the convenience of railroad travel, he became a champion of face-to-face meetings. He preferred to speak with others in person and to see his parishes first hand rather than rely on written communication.

This third bishop commanded great respect for his ability to handle financial matters. He apparently kept a tight rein on finances throughout his see, using his frequent parish visits to peruse record books with his characteristic attention to detail. He successfully solicited donations from throughout the diocese to fund such large ventures as the establishment of the two orphanages and the construction of the cathedral.

Bishop Shanahan died February 19, 1916, and was buried in Mount Calvary Cemetery, Harrisburg. The Right Reverend Monsignor Maurice M. Hassett, Vicar General of the Diocese, wrote that the third bishop "was a model of kindly aggressiveness, in the greatest cause to which a man may devote his life.... The diocese which was the fortunate domain of his labors is the best witness to the fact that the harvest of his episcopate has been abundant."

Bishop Shanahan also addressed the need for a permanent cathedral. For over a quarter of a century the diocese had used the former Saint Patrick's church as its temporary seat. The Diocesan Synod convened by the bishop in 1902 wholeheartedly approved the construction of a permanent cathedral for the diocese. The architectural firm of George L. Lovatt of Philadelphia was engaged, and to provide sufficient space for the new edifice, the adjacent cemetery was moved to Mount Calvary Cemetery in Harrisburg. Construction, by the McShane Company also of Philadelphia, began in 1904 and was completed in 1907.

Interior of Saint Patrick Cathedral, early 1900s

MARY MORIARITY BRINDLE

The early history of the faith in Mechanicsburg is largely the story of the living faith of a great Catholic woman aided by the interest and encouragement of Bishop John W. Shanahan. The chapel of Saint Joseph's Mission was built largely with the bishop's own personal funds. The project was inspired by Mrs. Mary Moriarity Brindle, who had determined that she and her children and a few scattered souls whom she rallied about her should not lose the faith.

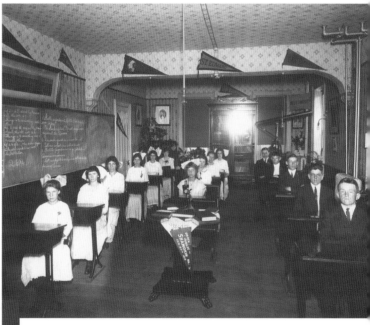

A class at Shamokin's Saint Edward's High School, the first high school in the diocese

St. Francis Xavier's School.

Certificate of Promotion

This certifies that *Edgar Hamilton*

has satisfactorily completed the course of study prescribed for the *Fifth* GRADE, and is therefore entitled to this testimonial, and to promotion to the *Sixth* GRADE.

Given at Gettysburg, Pa., this *19* day of *June*, *1903*.

Sisters of Charity. TEACHERS. *Rev. T) Crotty,* RECTOR.

_____ *Father Menwear* _____

St. Patrick's Cathedral, Harrisburg, will be dedicated on Tuesday, May 14, 1907. The ceremony will begin at 10 o'clock. You are respectfully invited to be present.

Devotedly yours in Christ,

J.W. Shanahan.

Bishop of Harrisburg.

Please return the enclosed postal card as soon as possible.

Invitation to the dedication of Saint Patrick Cathedral, May 14, 1907

As the diocese focused on constructing its cathedral, a change also occurred to alter the geographic area of the see. With the establishment of the Altoona diocese in 1906 three counties—Centre, Clinton, and Fulton—were reassigned from Harrisburg to the newly formed diocese. The result was a reduction of the diocese from 18 to its present 15 counties and a change in area from 10,000 to its current 8,000 square miles. Nonetheless, with the continued growth within the diocese, the number of churches, schools, and priests in the diocese all increased even in that year, despite the loss of one sixth of the counties and 20 percent of its land mass.

SERVICE AND SACRIFICE IN WORLD WAR 1

Over 3,150 parishioners of the Diocese of Harrisburg served in the armed forces during World War I. There were 164 fatalities. Saint Edward's in Shamokin suffered the greatest loss with the death of 13 of its members.

JOHN TIMON REILY (1856-1924)

John Timon Reily was a noted Catholic writer and historian from Conewago in the early years of the diocese.

His writing helped to preserve much of the history of Conewago. He described his work as "a humble effort to preserve some remembrances of those who have gone before, and by their lives, their labors and their sacrifices, secured for succeeding generations the enjoyment of happy homes, and all the blessings of our holy Catholic religion."

Today the John Timon Reily Historical Society in McSherrystown carries on his efforts.

JEDNOTA

Father Stephen Furdek organized the First Catholic Slovak Union in Cleveland in 1890 as a Catholic fraternal and beneficial society to meet the needs of Slovak immigrants. Through the years, this organization has contributed more than 20 million dollars to Catholic charities. Although Slovaks comprise only a small percent of the diocesan population, their presence has been much more visible due to the national institutions which they established within the diocese, mainly in Middletown and Danville. In 1909 Bishop John Shanahan and Monsignor Peter Huegel helped Father Furdek locate property, which eventually gave rise to the Jednota Home for Orphans, Immaculate Conception elementary school, the Jednota Printery, the Slovak Museum and Archives, the original motherhouse of the Sisters of Saints Cyril and Methodius, and Saint Anne Home for the Aged.

THE DIOCESE OF HARRISBURG

HARRISBURG PENNSYLVANIA

Pentecost Collection for the Orphans.

DEAR BRETHREN:—*To our Venerable Clergy and Beloved Children of the Laity.*

Again, we appeal to you in behalf of the destitute Orphan Children of the Diocese. This time, we include the orphan boys, as well as the orphan girls. The Paradise Protectory for Boys is ready for occupancy, and we need the means to support it.

We are all anxiously and immediately concerned about our destitute Catholic orphan children, children who have been baptized in the Faith, and, who, on that account, have a right to be brought up in the Catholic Religion. The various sects or denominations look after their own children ; we should look after ours. And while, in a broad spirit of Catholic charity, we stand ready, at all times, to assist the needy, irrespective of creed, or race, or color, we must remember that there is a special obligation resting upon us to safeguard the Faith of our own people, particularly the Faith of the little ones who have inherited it from saintly ancestors. This Pentecost Collection for the orphans should be the

One Great Collection of the Year.

It can yield to no other in importance ; for, it is intended to provide relief for those who are absolutely helpless—for those who are in imminent danger of being lost to Religion, to Society, and to God. Our Orphan Asylums are not intended to be an accommodation for worthless parents who want to be rid of the care of their children altogether, or who wish to have their children educated at the public expense. This must be constantly kept in mind by clergy and people who will not recommend for admission, or allow to remain in our orphan asylums, children who have responsible parents and suitable homes.

The Pentecost Collection for the Orphans must be announced in every church and chapel of the diocese on Pentecost Sunday, and be taken up at the residences of our people during the month of June. I respectfully request the Reverend Pastors to appoint, on Pentecost Sunday, trustworthy persons who will call on our Catholic brethren

At Their Homes,

receive their offerings and names, and on finishing the work, report to their respective pastors. All returns should be made to me by the 1st day of July. I shall publish the lists of contributors, and have the report distributed at an early day.

With fervent prayers for your temporal and eternal welfare, I remain,

Your devoted servant in Christ,　✠ J. W. SHANAHAN

Feast of the Patronage of St. Joseph.　　　　　　　　　*Bishop of Harrisburg.*
1911.

KNIGHTS OF COLUMBUS

The Knights of Columbus, a fraternal and insurance organization for Catholic men, was founded in New Haven, Connecticut, in 1882. The organization came to the Diocese of Harrisburg on October 28, 1899, in Shamokin, when 43 men obtained a charter as Council 458 with John Menahan as first Grand Knight. In addition to parish and diocesan-level activities, the Knights also serve the Church and its members with such public benefits as refurbishing the façade of Saint Peter's Basilica in Rome for the Great Jubilee Year 2000 A.D. and underwriting the broadcast in English of the Pope's Christmas Midnight Mass. At present there are 42 councils in the diocese.

HOLY NAME SOCIETY

The Holy Name Society in the Diocese of Harrisburg began on December 12, 1900, when the National Headquarters in New York City issued a charter to the parish society at Saint Joseph Parish, Locust Gap. Within the next 10 years a dozen more charters were issued in the diocese. In the following years more than 100 more were granted. The organization celebrates respect for the name of Jesus and organizes such activities as holy hours, retreats, and recognition banquets. Its blood bank program has benefited all parishioners. Nationally, the Society was instrumental in having the words "under God" added to the Pledge of Allegiance.

Children of Saint Francis of Assisi School, Harrisburg, ca. 1916

Early in 1898, the threat of war began to appear on the world stage. All through the first decade and a half of the 1900s tensions increased as battles were fought and alliances were forged. Then on July 28, 1914, with Austria-Hungary's declaration of war on Serbia, World War I, the war that was to end all wars, began. The conflict was still raging when on February 19, 1916, Bishop Shanahan passed away at Saint Joseph Hospital, Lancaster, following a sudden but critical illness.

Of the 10 synods of the Diocese of Harrisburg, the third through seventh were convened by Bishop John Shanahan between 1899, the year he became bishop, and 1914, just two years before his death. Bishop McGovern had convened the first and second, and Bishop Philip McDevitt would call the eighth in 1928, Bishop Leech, the ninth in 1943, and Bishop William Keeler, the tenth in 1988, a full century after the first gathering.

Saint Joseph, York, first church, rectory, and school, 1914

1899 Most Reverend John Shanahan appointed third bishop of Harrisburg; Annunciation of the Blessed Virgin Mary, McSherrystown, founded; First Knights of Columbus Council in diocese organized in Shamokin; Third Synod of the Diocese of Harrisburg convened

1900 Sacred Heart of Jesus, Lancaster, founded; Sacred Heart of Jesus Mission, Excelsior, opens

1901 Saint John the Evangelist, Enhaut, Steelton, founded for German-Hungarian Catholics; Saint Ann, Steelton, founded for Italian Catholics; Sacred Heart of Jesus, Harrisburg, and Saint Francis of Assisi, Harrisburg, founded; Saint Joseph, Locustdale, founded; Saint Katharine's Hall, Carlisle, opened by Mother Katharine Drexel for instruction of African-American and Native-American children; Sylvan Heights Orphanage, Harrisburg, opens; Centre, Clinton, and Fulton counties transferred from Harrisburg to Altoona Diocese

1902 Assumption of the Blessed Virgin Mary School, Steelton, and Sacred Heart of Jesus School, Conewago, open; Fourth Synod of the Diocese of Harrisburg convened

1903 Our Mother of Holy Purity, Wrightsville, founded; Saint Pius X becomes pope

1904 Sacred Heart of Jesus, Spring Grove; Our Lady of Perpetual Help, Marion Heights, founded for Polish, Slovak, Italian, and English-speaking Catholics; Saint Louis Mission Station (later Saint Matthew the Apostle and Evangelist, Dauphin) founded

1905 Saints Cyril and Methodius, Lebanon, founded for Slovak Catholics; Saint Vincent de Paul, Hanover, dedicated; Saint Peter, Mount Carmel, founded for Italian-speaking Catholics; Our Lady of Mercy, Roaring Creek, founded; Sacred Heart of Jesus School, Williamstown, and Saint Stephen School, Shamokin, open; Confraternity of Christian Doctrine established in all parishes worldwide

1906 Our Lady of the Blessed Sacrament, Harrisburg, founded; Immaculate Conception of the Blessed Virgin Mary, Berwick, elevated from a mission to a parish; Saint Gertrude, Lebanon, founded for Austro-Hungarian Catholics

1906 Our Lady Help of Christians School, Lykens, and Saints Cyril and Methodius School, Lebanon, open; Catholic population in Pennsylvania at 1.2 million of the total population of almost 7 million

1907 Queen of All Saints, Burnham, and Saint Rose of Lima, York, founded; Motherhouse for the Lithuanian Sisters of Saint Casimir established in Mount Carmel, with Venerable Maria Kaupas as first superior; Holy Cross, first Lithuanian parochial school in America, opens in Mount Carmel; Construction of Saint Patrick Cathedral, Harrisburg, completed

1908 Saint Mary's Grade and High School, McSherrystown, opens; Fifth Synod of the Diocese of Harrisburg convened

1909 Assumption of the Blessed Virgin Mary, Kulpmont, founded for Hungarian Catholics; Saint Peter the Apostle, Steelton, founded for Slovenian Catholics; Saint Peter the Apostle School, Steelton, opens; Most Holy Rosary Chapel, South Mountain, founded for tuberculosis patients; Sisters of Saints Cyril and Methodius founded

1910 Saint Gertrude School, Lebanon, opens

1911 Sisters of Saint Casimir move to the Archdiocese of Chicago; Paradise Protectory, Abbottstown, a school for boys, opens; Sixth Synod of the Diocese of Harrisburg convened

1913 Saint Joseph, York, founded; Assumption of the Blessed Virgin Mary School, Shamokin, opens

1914 Saint Casimir, Kulpmont, founded for Polish Catholics; Our Mother of Perpetual Help, Ephrata, founded; Saint Clement Mission House, Ephrata, established by Redemptorists; Saint Joseph School, Shamokin, opens; Saint Joseph School, York, opens; Saint John the Baptist School, Mount Carmel, opens; Immaculate Conception Jednota Home, Middletown, dedicated under the sponsorship of the First Catholic Slovak Union; Seventh Synod of the Diocese of Harrisburg convened; Benedict XV becomes pope; World War I begins (continues through 1918)

1915 Saint Rose of Lima School, York, opens; Saint Casimir School, Kulpmont, opens; Saint Ann School, Steelton, opens

Part 4
The Episcopacy of Philip R. McDevitt, the Educator
Fourth Bishop of Harrisburg, 1916-1935

After the death of Bishop John W. Shanahan, the Most Reverend Philip R. McDevitt, a 57-year-old priest from the Archdiocese of Philadelphia, was appointed the fourth bishop of Harrisburg on July 10, 1916, and was consecrated on September 21, 1916.

Bishop McDevitt came to Harrisburg with a background similar to that of his predecessor. Like Bishop Shanahan, he had served as superintendent of parochial schools in the Philadelphia archdiocese. His administrative methods served as models in Catholic school systems across the nation.

Early 20th-century monstrance from the former parish of Our Lady of Perpetual Help, Marion Heights. This ornate monstrance, used in the liturgy of Benediction, is richly decorated with enamel pictures of the apostles, Our Lord, Our Lady and Saint Peter. The flames shooting out around the circle suggest the "Sun of Righteousness" (Malachi 4:2). The adoring angels hold the instruments of the Sacred Passion.

Responding to the directives in the Code of Canon Law, which were promulgated the same year he became bishop, he set up a Chancery system for diocesan administration. Monsignor John C. Thompson was named the first chancellor of the diocese.

In the early months of his episcopacy, the fourth bishop turned his attention to Catholic secondary education in the diocese. One of his first acts was to set up a centralized administrative structure; accordingly, he appointed Father Peter M. Steif to the newly established position of superintendent of schools. He worked with local pastors to merge the individual parish high schools into regional, inter-parochial schools. This new office of superintendent of schools provided centralized assistance for these schools. During his

COUNCIL OF CATHOLIC WOMEN

The National Council of Catholic Women was established by the bishops of the United States in 1920. As an integral part of the United States Catholic Conference, the Council joined all existing organizations of women into a federation that enables them to retain their own particular purposes and autonomy. The Harrisburg Diocesan Council of Catholic Women was organized in 1924. The council provides a voice for Catholic women in those issues in which their faith requires unity and provides representation at national and international conferences of concern to women.

Saint Rita, Blue Ridge Summit, founded 1919

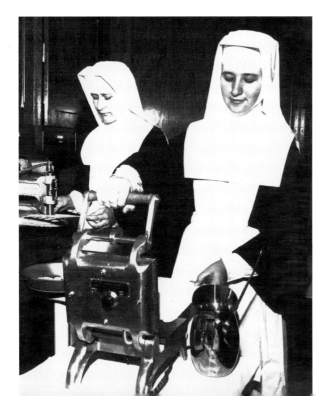

Dedication of Our Mother of Consolation School, Mount Carmel, by Bishop McDevitt on November 23, 1924.

orphanages at both Sylvan Heights and Paradise School underwent expansion.

During his tenure many programs were begun in the diocese, including the Legion of Decency, the Society for the Propagation of the Faith, the Diocesan Council of Catholic Women, and the Mission Board, which assisted parishes financially during the trying years of the depression.

administration eight inter-parochial high schools were established.

The bishop also encouraged the growth of parochial education in the parishes throughout his see. During his episcopacy, schools opened in 12 parishes, and a number of schools already in place updated and enlarged their facilities. He also encouraged religious vacation schools in parishes across the diocese.

In addition, the Slovak Girls' Academy at Danville opened under the governorship of the Sisters of Saints Cyril and Methodius, and the

A host baker from the 1920s. Each parish convent had a host baker, used by the sisters to make the hosts for Holy Communion. The batter was poured onto the bottom plate, the top was pressed down and locked; then the baked wafer was pried off and the hosts were cut out by hand with the cutters. Today almost all hosts are purchased commercially.

MOST REVEREND PHILIP R. MCDEVITT
FOURTH BISHOP OF HARRISBURG
1916-1935

Maria impende juvamen.
Mary, send your help.

Philip Richard McDevitt was born July 12, 1858, in Philadelphia, the son of Richard and Mary Ann (Dinneney) McDevitt. He was educated at La Salle College, from which he was the first priest alumnus, and Saint Charles Borromeo Seminary, Overbrook, both in Philadelphia, and was ordained to the priesthood in Philadelphia on July 14, 1885.

In addition to pastoral assignments, Father McDevitt was appointed superintendent of Catholic schools of Philadelphia in 1899. In this position, he gained a national reputation as a

Catholic educator and administrator. He was named a Domestic Prelate with the title of Right Reverend Monsignor on July 16, 1910.

He was appointed bishop of Harrisburg on July 10, 1916, and was consecrated on September 21, 1916. Bishop McDevitt served on the Committee of the National Catholic Welfare Conference and was chairman of the Catholic Press Department. He served three terms as president of the American Catholic Historical Society. He was a nationally recognized historian and writer. In 1925 he received an honorary doctor of laws degree from the University of Notre Dame.

In the years that Bishop McDevitt shepherded the diocese, the nation experienced World War I, the flu epidemic of 1918, and the 1929 crash of the stock market, which set off the worst economic depression of the nation's history. To help cope with the dismal economic situation during the depression, he established the Mission Board, directed by Monsignor Joseph Schmidt.

During his administration the parish high schools that had been founded throughout the diocese were merged into regional inter-parochial schools.

In 1935, just months before his death, he celebrated the golden jubilee of his ordination to the priesthood. It was a momentous occasion during which he received word from the Vatican that Pope Pius XI had appointed him an honorary assistant to the Papal Throne, a rare honor. It was at this time too that he announced the appointment of the Most Reverend George L. Leech as the first auxiliary bishop of the diocese. His death, caused by an attack of pneumonia, came on November 11, 1935. He was buried in Holy Cross Cemetery, Harrisburg.

Procession celebrating Saint Ann's Day, by members of Saint Ann's Parish, Steelton, during the pastorate of Father Michael O'Flynn, 1928.

In the 18 years of his administration, new communities of religious came to the diocese: Sisters of Saints Cyril and Methodius settled in Danville; Sisters, Adorers of the Blood of Christ, near Columbia; the Daughters of Mercy in York; and the Dominican Sisters, of the Perpetual Rosary in Enola.

The First Mission Sunday in the diocese, celebrated at Saint Patrick Cathedral, December 6, 1925. Bishop McDevitt is standing, fourth from the left. The Propagation of the Faith had been established in the diocese the preceding year.

Although a heart attack in 1930 caused the bishop to slacken his pace, he continued to fulfill his duties up to just days before his untimely death five years later. In 1934 he was centrally involved in the seventh Eucharistic Congress in Cleveland. His last official act as bishop was to confer the Sacrament of Confirmation at Saint Joseph, Berwick, just two weeks before his death.

By 1935 the Catholic population in the diocese stood at almost 89,000. There were 81 parishes, 24 missions, and 8 chapels served by 160 priests. Sixty parishes had parochial schools, with a total enrolment of almost 15,000, and the 12 diocesan high schools enrolled almost 1,600 students. The proportion of children enrolled in parochial schools in the diocese was higher than that in the majority of the dioceses in the United States.

Bishop McDevitt's death resulted from a cold that developed into pneumonia. Even the specialists summoned from Pittsburgh to treat him could not restore him to health. With relatives and fellow priests at his bedside, he died at the bishop's residence at 111 State Street on November 11, 1935. As part of the ceremonies, 1,300 parochial school children attended an early-morning Mass at the Cathedral on the day of the funeral. Bishop McDevitt is buried in the priests' circle in Holy Cross Cemetery, Harrisburg. Today there are high schools named for Bishop Philip R. McDevitt in Harrisburg and in suburban Philadelphia.

In the 1920s the Gonzaga Band from Paradise School, Abbottstown, traveled throughout the diocese, marching in local parades and performing at religious as well as civic functions.

The faithful wait in line to pay their final respect to Bishop McDevitt at the Cathedral on November 14, 1935.

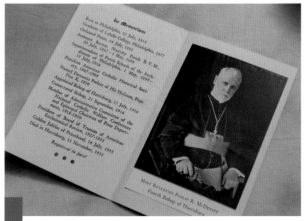

Bishop McDevitt's memorial card

THE MISSION BOARD

During the 1920s, Monsignor Joseph Schmidt, who served as Director of the Propagation of the Faith, took a bold step to assist our fledgling parishes when he established the Mission Board of the Diocese of Harrisburg. Msgr. Schmidt, with his infinite wisdom and faith in Christ, traveled the diocese and asked the faithful to lend money for the good of the whole diocese. With the funds he obtained, he was able to purchase all outside financial obligations that were owed throughout the diocese. This heroic effort enabled him to provide the diocese with financial security during the Great Depression. His valiant effort is the cornerstone of the Diocesan Savings and Loan. Through this effort, the diocese is able to lend parishes and schools the financial support they need to renovate or construct new buildings at a considerably lower interest rate than can be offered by any outside financial institution. Many persons from throughout the diocese continue to invest their monies with this program, receiving interest, and helping our parishes to remain self-sufficient.

TIMELINE

1916   Bishop John Shanahan dies; Most Reverend Philip McDevitt named fourth bishop of Harrisburg

1917   The Blessed Virgin Mary appears to three children at Fatima, Portugal

1918   Fiftieth anniversary of the Diocese of Harrisburg celebrated; Saint John the Evangelist Mission (later Saint Joan of Arc), Hershey, founded; flu epidemic kills over 500,000 Americans; Code of Canon Law, promulgated in 1917, goes into effect;
World War I ends on November 11.

1919   Saint Anthony of Padua, Ranshaw, and Saint Rita, Blue Ridge Summit, founded; Our Lady of Lourdes, New Holland, founded; Sacred Heart of Jesus School, Harrisburg, opens; Harrisburg Catholic High School (later Bishop McDevitt High School), Harrisburg, opens;
Sisters of Saints Cyril and Methodius establish motherhouse in Danville

1920   Saint James, Lititz, founded; National Council of Catholic Women established; League of Nations formally established

1922   Saint Cyril Academy, Danville, opens; Sacred Heart of Jesus High School, Williamstown, opens; Pius XI becomes pope; 19th Amendment to the Constitution gives all American women the right to vote

1923   Saint Anne, Lancaster, founded; Saint Vincent de Paul School, Hanover, opens

1924   Saint Anne School, Lancaster, opens; Assumption of the Blessed Virgin Mary School, Kulpmont, opens; Father Joseph Schmidt named first director of the Society for the Propagation of the Faith in the diocese; Harrisburg Diocesan Council of Catholic Women established

1925   Saint Andrew School, Waynesboro, opens; Dominican Nuns of Perpetual Rosary establish a monastery at Enola (later to move to suburban Lancaster); Adorers of the Blood of Christ establish motherhouse in Columbia

1926   Our Lady of Lourdes, Enola, and Saint Mary, Gate of Heaven, Myerstown, founded; Saint Anthony of Padua School, Ranshaw, opens; Franciscan Fathers' Croatian Mission Commissariat staff Assumption of the Blessed Virgin Mary, Steelton

1927   Saint Joan of Arc School, Hershey, and Saint Joseph School, Dallastown, open; Saint Mary's High School, York, opens; Saint Anne's Home, Columbia, established by the Sisters, Adorers of the Blood of Christ

1928   Saint Joseph, Berwick, founded as an Italian parish; Saint Paul Chapel, Atlas, founded; Saint Theresa of the Infant Jesus, New Cumberland, founded; Saint Paul the Apostle, Annville, founded; Our Lady of Perpetual Help School, Marion Heights, opens; Eighth Synod of the Diocese of Harrisburg convened; Presidential election with Catholic Alfred ("Al") Smith on the ballot foments wave of anti-Catholicism throughout the country

1929   Saint Mary's High School, York, renamed York Catholic High School; Saint Mary's High School, Lebanon, renamed Lebanon Catholic High School

1930   Lancaster Catholic High School opens; Harrisburg Catholic High School, Harrisburg, opens

1933   Saint Edward High School renamed Shamokin Catholic High School

1934   Sacred Heart of Jesus, Lewisburg, founded

ETHNIC GROUPS WITHIN THE DIOCESE OF HARRISBURG

Although the Diocese of Harrisburg encompasses the Pennsylvania Dutch Country and is usually associated with it, the rich mosaic of peoples who make up the diocese did not really develop until after the Civil War. From the Colonial period until the time of the Civil War the Catholic population drew mainly from the Irish and Germans.

IRISH

From Colonial days the Irish who settled in what is now the Diocese of Harrisburg were mainly Protestant Scots Irish; Catholics from the southern counties of Ireland were also present in great numbers. However, because they were Catholic, they experienced considerable prejudice and discrimination. Nevertheless, because these Irish Catholics came to this country speaking the English language, they had an advantage over the non-English-speaking Catholic immigrants and were able to establish themselves and assimilate more quickly. Thus, they often claimed first place among the Catholic population. Not surprising, then, four early parishes were dedicated to Saint Patrick in Harrisburg, Carlisle, York, and Trevorton.

GERMANS

Immigrants from Catholic parts of Germany settled in Pennsylvania from Colonial times onward, becoming part of the sub-strata of the diocese. Theirs were among the first of the diocese's early parishes, and they formed the bulk of parishioners in

Saint Joseph, Lancaster, the first ethnic (German) parish in what is now the Diocese of Harrisburg.

Lancaster, Lebanon and York counties especially. Holy Trinity in Columbia and Saint Joseph and Saint Anthony in Lancaster were founded as German parishes. The influx of German-speaking Austrians, who had been relocated by the Hapsburgs into the Balkans during the late 18th century and differed in culture from those who originated in Germany, created the need for the bishop to erect the German-Hungarian parishes of Saint Lawrence in Harrisburg, Saint John in Enhaut and Saint Gertrude in Lebanon.

EASTERN AND SOUTHERN EUROPEANS

Immigrants from Eastern and Southern Europe began arriving in our area in the 1850s and 1860s, only a few years before the Diocese of Harrisburg was established in 1868. A combination of political oppression and unfavorable economic conditions was the impetus behind the major wave of immigration to America. Lured by the advertisements of coal and steel companies promising jobs in the booming coal regions and steel towns as well as letters from earlier immigrants hearing enthusiastic reports about their new lives, thousands of new immigrants came to build a better future for themselves and for their children. These poorest of the poor helped America to develop into the superpower it is.

Eager for work, these newcomers accepted wages, which they considered high enough but which those already established in the mining and steel industries considered low. Initially this economic disparity along with their foreign languages and Catholic religion earned them considerable resentment in their new communities.

The Church was by far the strongest influence in the lives of these immigrants, and the parish was the hub around which their lives revolved.

The church bound the faithful spiritually by liturgical events and devotional services. Christmas and Easter, Lent and Advent remained the highlights of the immigrants' social and religious year.

These immigrant parents laid great stress on the value of education. This is attested to by the fact that every one of the ethnic parishes in the diocese had a parochial school.

ITALIANS

Italians came into the diocese at the end of the 19th century and settled primarily in Harrisburg, Lancaster, York, and Hershey. Some came as skilled stonemasons and found employment in the quarries. Those who settled in Marysville built the Rockville railroad bridge over the Susquehanna, reputed to be the longest stone arch bridge in the world. Others, especially those from the impoverished south of Italy, came as unskilled workers and sought employment wherever they could. Italian ethnic and language parishes were established in Mount Carmel, Steelton, and Berwick. The Daughters of Mercy established Holy Child Nursery and Misericordia Nursing Home in York.

POLISH

The Polish immigrants were the largest and earliest East European group to settle in the diocese, coming in 1854, and in 1872 Bishop Jeremiah Shanahan established Saint Stanislaus in Shamokin, the first Polish parish in Pennsylvania. Saint Stephen in Shamokin, Saint Joseph and Our Mother of Consolation in Mount Carmel, and Saint Casimir in Kulpmont were established to serve their pastoral and liturgical needs. Polish immigrants also made up a majority of the parishioners in the parishes of Marion Heights, Ranshaw, and Roaring Creek.

Saint Stanislaus, Shamokin, the first Polish parish in Pennsylvania.

SLOVAKS

The Slovaks, even by national statistics, were second in number. They settled in Mount Carmel in 1875, where Bishop Jeremiah Shanahan established Saint John the Baptist parish. Other Slovak parishes were Saint Mary in Shamokin and SS. Cyril and Methodius in Lebanon. The major contributions of the Slovak Catholics to the diocese include the basilica, motherhouse and other institutions of the Sisters of SS. Cyril and Methodius in Danville and the Jednota Estates and Printery in Middletown.

LITHUANIANS

The Lithuanians hold a prominent place among the small ethnic groups instrumental in developing the diocese, with the parishes of Holy Cross in Mount Carmel and Saint Michael in Shamokin. Venerable Mother Maria Kaupas established the first religious community of Lithuanian women in the United States, the Sisters of Saint Casimir, in Mount Carmel in 1907.

Pysanky eggs are decorated for Easter using a centuries-old East European method of applying melted beeswax in the etching of elaborate designs onto the eggshells. This art of egg decorating is representative of the many traditions honored and preserved by ethnic groups within the diocese.

CROATIANS

The Croatians arrived in Steelton beginning in the 1890s to work in the steel mills. To address the influx of Croatians and other immigrants, in 1898 Bishop John Shanahan established Saint Mary parish in Steelton for East European Catholics. Saint Mary Parish would come to be the largest Croatian parish in Pennsylvania.

The Eastern province of the Adorers of the Blood of Christ, which worked among the Croatians at Saint Mary in Steelton, established their provincial house, retirement village and academy at Columbia.

SLOVENIANS

The first Slovenian immigrants came to Steelton in 1883 and, loyal to their Catholic faith, by 1909 Bishop John Shanahan established Saint Peter parish for their needs in their newly adopted town.

AUSTRIANS AND HUNGARIANS

Austrians and other German-speaking immigrants from the province of Banat in lower Hungary (which later was ceded to Yugoslavia) also immigrated at the turn of the century.

For their special pastoral care, Saint John in Enhaut, Saint Gertrude in Lebanon, and Saint Lawrence in Harrisburg were established. Hungarian-speaking immigrants were also present in goodly numbers in the parishes in Berwick and Kulpmont.

UKRAINIANS AND RUTHENIANS

Ukrainian and Ruthenian immigrants also had parishes of the Byzantine Rite established for them in Mount Carmel, Centralia, Marion Heights, Shamokin, Berwick, Williamstown, and Harrisburg. These, however, were subject to their own Ordinaries.

Perhaps the most enviable record attesting to the solidity of these faith communities is the fact that the East European parishes in the diocese have contributed over 100 priests and almost 300 nuns to the service of the Church.

The descendents of these European immigrants are now in every parish in the diocese. They have long become an integral part and an honored mainstay of the greater community. While becoming good Americans, they have remained good Catholics, true to the tradition of their forefathers.

PART 1
THE EPISCOPACY OF GEORGE L. LEECH, THE ORGANIZER, FIFTH BISHOP OF HARRISBURG, 1935-1971

On February 17, 1935, at age 45 the Reverend Monsignor George L. Leech was consecrated as Titular Bishop of Mela and Auxiliary Bishop of Harrisburg, the first auxiliary bishop in the diocese. Sadly, the ailing Bishop Philip McDevitt was too weak to attend the consecration. Following the death of Bishop McDevitt just three weeks later, Auxiliary Bishop George L. Leech became administrator and on December 19, 1935, was installed as the fifth Bishop of Harrisburg. The growth and forward movement of the diocese under Bishop McDevitt continued during Bishop Leech's episcopacy, which extended to 35 years, the longest of the first eight bishops of the diocese.

When Bishop Leech was consecrated, the diocese was comprised of 81 parishes, 24 missions, and 8 chapels served by 130 diocesan priests plus 30 priests from Religious Orders. There were 60 parochial schools with a total enrollment of 14,500 children. In addition 12 high schools enrolled almost 1,600 students. The Catholic population stood at over 88,000. One of every 12 residents of the counties within the diocese was Catholic.

From 1939 to 1945 the world was at war for the second time in less than a quarter century. No new parishes were erected during those war years, though high schools did continue to open across the diocese. With the end of the war came the founding of a record number of parishes and missions, 16 within a decade, and new schools also opened across the diocese. By the end of his episcopacy, Bishop Leech would open more places of Catholic worship in the diocese than any of his fellow bishops of the Harrisburg See.

Cardinal John Joseph Krol and Bishop Leech at Sylvan Heights

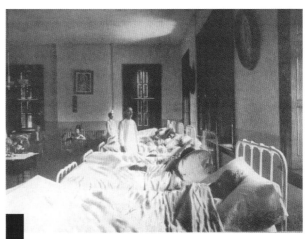

Ward of Saint Joseph Hospital, Lancaster

MOST REVEREND GEORGE L. LEECH
FIFTH BISHOP OF HARRISBURG
1935-1971

Non Nobis Domine.
Not to us, O Lord.

(PSALM 113)

George Leo Leech was born May 21, 1890, at Ashley, Pennsylvania, the son of William Dillon and Helen Mary (Fitzsimons) Leech. He was educated at the Saint Charles Borromeo Seminary, Overbrook, Philadelphia.

After his ordination in 1920, he pursued postgraduate studies at the Catholic University of America and was awarded a doctorate in Canon Law.

As a young priest, Father Leech served as secretary at the Apostolic Delegation in Washington, a position that provided him with the opportunity to visit every diocese in the United States. Later he became pastor of Saint Patrick's Church, Pottsville. In 1935, at age 45, he was consecrated as Titular Bishop of Mela and Auxiliary Bishop of Harrisburg. On October 17, 1935, after the death of Bishop McDevitt, he was appointed fifth bishop of Harrisburg.

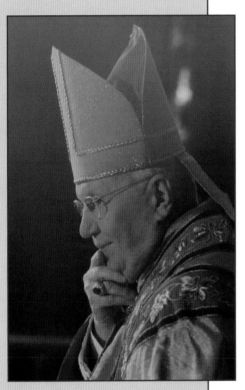

In 1956 Auxiliary Bishop Lawrence F. Schott was appointed to assist with the administration of the diocese. The next year, on May 12, 1957, Bishop Leech received the honor of being named assistant at the papal throne.

Bishop Leech served longer than any other bishop of the Harrisburg Diocese, a total of 35 years. During his tenure he shepherded his flock through the last years of the Great Depression, World War II, the technological developments of the 1950s, and the theological changes of the 1960s. He participated in all four sessions of the Second Vatican Council.

During the quarter century after World War II, the southcentral area of Pennsylvania was among the fastest growing in the nation. In response the diocese added thirty-five new parishes during Bishop Leech's episcopacy to accommodate the growth in Catholic population.

Bishop Leech retired in 1971 and received the appointment of Titular Bishop of Allegheny. He continued to reside at the Bishops' Residence until his death on March 12,1985. He is buried at Holy Cross Cemetery, Harrisburg.

From the beginning of his episcopate, Bishop Leech recognized the importance of a network of support systems for the diocese. Already in place was the Mission Board, which had been established during Bishop McDevitt's tenure to provide financial support to the many parishes placed in dire financial straits during "The Great Depression." In 1938, Bishop Leech fostered the establishment of Catholic Charities as the official social service agency of the diocese to address needs at the individual, family, and community level. Monsignor Charles J. Tighe served as the first director.

Paradise School, 1940s

Less than a decade later the diocesan Catholic Youth Office was established, and in 1949 Catholic Charities opened Madonna Center in Harrisburg to provide special services for African-Americans. Facilities for unwed mothers and for children needing special attention were opened under the auspices of Catholic Charities. Villa Vianney in Lebanon, a residence for retired priests, opened in 1955, the same year an Apostolate was formed for migrant workers. An Apostolate for Spanish-speaking Catholics in the diocese followed just six years later.

APPOINTMENT IN SAMARRA

Bishop Leech was possibly a prototype for the character Monsignor Creedon in John O'Hara's novel *Appointment in Samarra.*

Literary scholars note a similarity between Bishop Leech and the fictional Monsignor Creedon in the 1935 novel. Novelist O'Hara typically created his characters from composites of real people, usually individuals he knew personally, and he set the novel in Gibbsville, the fictional town based on his native Pottsville, PA. O'Hara was acquainted with then-Father Leech, who had been pastor of Saint Patrick Church in Pottsville, the home parish of the O'Hara family.

Saint Gregory Hymnal, mainstay hymnal used throughout the diocese in the first half of the 1900s

ANNA DILL GAMBLE

Anna Dill Gamble was a prominent lay leader, writer and historian who campaigned for women's suffrage. Miss Gamble was an adult convert to the Catholic faith, having been received into the Church by Cardinal James Gibbons of Baltimore in 1917. She founded the Catholic Women's Club of York and was elected the first president of the Harrisburg Diocesan Council of Catholic Women in 1924. In 1932 she represented Catholic Women at the Geneva Disarmament Conference in Switzerland.

She also attended the International Eucharistic Congress in Buenos Aires in 1934 as the NCCW delegate and later received the *Pro Ecclesia et Pontifice* award for her contributions to the Church as a lay person.

Miss Gamble died January 22, 1956, and was buried from Saint Patrick Church, York, after a Mass celebrated by Bishop Leech.

FATHER PHILIP J. GERGEN (1899-1961)

During World War II, Father Philip J. Gergen (1899-1961) attended to the spiritual needs of Catholic German prisoners of war held at Olmsted Air Force Base, Middletown, Pennsylvania. Among the prisoners were three seminarians who remembered Father Gergen's kindness and, after the war, sent him this hand-sewn stole from Germany.

Father Gergen used the stole until his death. It is now preserved in the Archives of the Diocese of Harrisburg.

Hand-sewn stole from Catholic German Prisoners of War

Members of the Youth Ministry of Saint Joseph, Coal Township, form a snow shovel brigade to clear the walkway near the church in the mid1900s.

In 1956 Monsignor Lawrence Schott was consecrated as auxiliary bishop of Harrisburg to assist Bishop Leech with the administration of the diocese. In 1958 the radio and television apostolate was established in the diocese.

In 1958 the universal church entered an especially significant period with the election of Blessed John XXIII as pope. He issued his encyclical *Mater et Magistra,* addressing social and economic matters worldwide and in 1962 convened the Second Vatican Council, which would inaugurate significant change within the Catholic Church. Auxiliary Bishop Schott attended the first session of the Council; Bishop Leech and then-Auxiliary Bishop Joseph T. Daley, all four sessions. Also attending all the sessions was the Very Reverend William H. Keeler, whom the Pope appointed as *peritus,* or special advisor, to the Council.

The Blessed Mother was the focus of much attention in the 1950s. In 1950 Pope Pius XII proclaimed the Dogma of the Assumption of the Blessed Virgin Mary. In that year August 15, the Feast of the Assumption, became a holy day of obligation in the United States. In 1954, to celebrate the 100th anniversary of the Dogma of the Immaculate Conception, Bishop Leech founded the Legion of Mary in the diocese.

Ninth Diocesan Synod, 1943

Baptismal font from Saints Cyril and Methodius church, Lebanon
(Diocesan Archives Collection)

CATHOLIC CAMPUS MINISTRY

To Father (later Auxiliary Bishop) Lawrence Schott goes the credit for establishing the forerunner of the Catholic Campus Ministry in the diocese. When assistant pastor at Saint Patrick Church, Carlisle, in the 1930s, he established a bulletin for the Catholic students attending Dickinson College and Dickinson School of Law. Within a few years the bulletins were being distributed to all the colleges in the diocese, and Father Schott was named Diocesan Moderator of the Catholic Student Centers on college campuses.

In 1964 the program became part of the national Newman Apostolate, and in the same year the first building in the diocese dedicated specifically to be a Newman Center opened at what was then Millersville State Teachers College. Full-time and part-time chaplains were appointed as the program expanded and Newman Centers were established on campuses throughout the diocese. In 1970 the name changed from Newman Apostolate to Catholic Campus Ministry.

Today the Diocese of Harrisburg has a Catholic Campus Ministry presence on 14 campuses. Catholic Campus Ministry provides a wide variety of spiritual, liturgical, educational, service and social opportunities for college and university communities to foster faith and friendship.

Zucchetto worn by Pope Pius XII, December 5, 1950 (Diocesan Archives Collection)

THE CATHOLIC WITNESS

In 1966, Bishop George L. Leech established the diocesan newspaper, *The Catholic Witness*. The name of the paper draws upon Jesus' last words spoken on earth: "You shall be witnesses for me ..." Published 24 times a year, with a circulation of 78,000, the newspaper, now in its fifth decade of publication, continues true to its mission defined by Bishop Leech to be "of personal and practical help, as we try to be loyal and true witnesses for Christ in our daily living, spiritual and temporal, in private and in public."

The Catholic **WITNESS**
VOL. 41 - NO. 22   NOVEMBER 11, 2005
DIOCESE OF HARRISBURG, PA.

Catholic Witness founded in 1966

Bishop Leech with Pope Paul VI

Professor Bernard Wert's "Missa Pro Fidelibus"

BERNARD WERT

Bernard Wert served as organist-choirmaster at Saint Patrick Cathedral for 45 years, from 1921 to 1966. His involvement with music extended much beyond the cathedral. He was the director of music and instructor in Gregorian Chant at College Misericordia, Dallas, PA, and teacher of singing at Sylvan Heights Home, Harrisburg, as well as instructor for a number of choirs throughout the diocese and a private teacher of piano, organ, and voice.

He taught theory and composition and was himself the composer of a number of Masses, motets, and other pieces of sacred music. His church music, published by the Gregorian Institute of America, was known and used nationwide. In the 1960s, in the early days of the congregation's active participation in the Mass, his "Missa Pro Fidelibus" was, by Bishop Leech's directive, sung by all congregations in the diocese. The stacks of beige cards on which the Mass was printed were a common sight at the ends of pews and on tables at the rear of churches throughout the diocese.

Bishop McDevitt, in his letter offering the cathedral position to Wert in 1921, had written, "... My only condition is that you should provide music that conforms to the laws of the Church." Throughout his 45 years of service, Wert was known and respected for his strict adherence to this dictum.

The decade of the 1960s was a time of growth and change. Following Bishop Schott's death in 1963, Father Joseph T. Daley, Vice-Rector of Saint Charles Seminary, Overbrook, in Philadelphia was named auxiliary bishop. The Newman Apostolate was formally established in the diocese in 1964 to provide for the intellectual, religious and spiritual development of college students enrolled in colleges and universities within the territory of the diocese. Communication within the diocese expanded in 1966 with the founding of the diocesan newspaper, *The Catholic Witness*.

Professor Bernard Wert and one section of the Academy Choir from Danville during the Pontifical Jubilee Mass on October 17, 1945.

Centennial Mass of the Diocese of Harrisburg, celebrated at Hersheypark Arena, 1968

MOST REVEREND LAWRENCE F. SCHOTT
AUXILIARY BISHOP
1956-1963

Diligite Alterutrum.
Love one another.

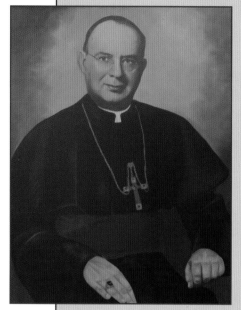

Lawrence Francis Schott was born in Philadelphia on July 26, 1907, the son of Thomas and Emma (Hofer) Schott. Following the death of his father, his mother married Adam Mayan of Danville. The family resided in Danville, where they belonged to the German parish of Saint Hubert's.

Lawrence Schott was educated at Saint Vincent Preparatory School, College and Seminary, Latrobe, Pennsylvania. He was ordained to the priesthood in Harrisburg by Bishop McDevitt on June 15, 1935.

Father Schott served as assistant pastor at Holy Trinity, Columbia, and Saint Patrick, Carlisle. To him goes the credit for establishing the Newman Apostolate, the forerunner of the Catholic Campus Ministry, in the diocese.

He also served as principal of Harrisburg Catholic High School and pastor of Our Lady of Mount Carmel, Mount Carmel. Father Schott was made a Domestic Prelate (Monsignor) on November 18, 1952.

He was appointed Auxiliary Bishop of Harrisburg on March 1, 1956, and was consecrated by Bishop Leech at Saint Patrick Cathedral later in the year. Bishop Schott attended the first session of the Second Vatican Council. Following a rapidly progressing illness, he died on March 11, 1963, and was buried in Holy Cross Cemetery, Harrisburg. Bishop Schott Museum at Our Lady of Mount Carmel, Mount Carmel, is named in his honor.

The year 1963 brought with it the death of Blessed John XXIII and the election of Paul VI as pope. Under Pope Paul VI the Vatican II Council continued its work, which would have far-reaching effects on the Church and Catholicism throughout the world. In 1970 the *novus ordo*, or New Liturgy of Mass, was introduced throughout the diocese.

In the 35 years under the leadership of Bishop Leech, the diocese had experienced tremendous growth. When he retired in 1971, the diocese had 102 parishes plus 18 missions and 21 stations. In addition, there were 108 chapels, 16 of which had resident chaplains. The diocese had a record 252 priests, including those from religious orders, and 1,040 women religious.

By 1971, even with mergers to establish inter-parish schools, the number of parochial schools had grown to 63, with almost 18,000 children enrolled. As a result of several consolidations, there were seven diocesan high schools, with an enrollment that had quadrupled since 1935 to over 6,400. In addition, Catholic education in the diocese included three private elementary schools and four private high schools.

During Bishop Leech's tenure, the number of Catholics in the diocese more than doubled to over 186,000 souls: by 1971 one out of every eight residents within the geographic boundaries of the diocese was Catholic.

HOWARD FETTERHOFF (1924-1996)

Born in Scranton in 1924, Howard Fetterhoff served as executive director of the Pennsylvania Catholic Conference for 27 years. Part of his work was to monitor legislation in all areas of justice for the benefit of all Pennsylvanians. He was widely respected by the Legislature and Governor's office throughout his tenure for his integrity, diplomacy, and commitment to all the citizenry of the state. Pope John Paul II named him a Knight of Saint Gregory the Great, and he held honorary doctorates from three Pennsylvania Catholic Universities. Cardinal Keeler returned to the diocese to preside at his funeral at Saint Patrick Cathedral.

VATICAN COUNCIL II

The twenty-first ecumenical council, which became known as Vatican Council II, met in Rome between 1962 and 1965. One of the most important councils in Church history, it was only the second such assembly since the Council of Trent (1545-1563). Blessed John XXIII is given the singular credit for summoning the gathering, proclaiming that it was convened through the

inspiration of the Holy Spirit. The Blessed Pope died after the close of the first session, and his successor, Paul VI, continued the work in the Johannine Tradition.

Vatican II had far-reaching effects on the Church and throughout the world. One change growing out of the Council was the more active involvement of the laity in church matters. Lay members began to serve on parish and diocesan councils to address administrative and pastoral matters. Parish ministries and organizations flourished. In 1968 the permanent diaconate was approved in the diocese.

Liturgical changes were the most noticed. The front altar, enabling the priest to celebrate Mass facing the congregation, became the altar of sacrifice in churches across the diocese and around the world. Lectors, cantors and extraordinary ministers of Holy Communion began to take part in parish masses, and within many churches altar rails were removed and hymn boards installed. Musical instruments in addition to the organ accompanied the congregation's sung worship, and contemporary music took a place with Gregorian chant as part of the music of Catholic worship.

Paul VI solemnly closed the Council on December 8, 1965. Since that time, the Church has benefited from a deepening understanding of the theology of the Council documents and its spirit of continuing renewal.

ETHNIC GROUPS WITHIN THE DIOCESE OF HARRISBURG

If the period from Colonial times to the Civil War belonged to the Irish and the Germans, and if the period from post-Civil War to World War I belonged to the East and Southern Europeans, the period from post-World War II to the present belongs to the African-Americans, Hispanics, and Asians.

AFRICAN-AMERICANS

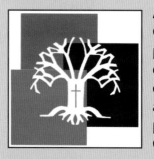

African-American Catholics have been present in the territory of the diocese since colonial times. Though a relatively small percentage of the total Catholic population, African-American parishioners are present and active throughout the diocese, especially in Harrisburg, Lancaster, York, and Chambersburg, and in many of our Catholic schools. Black Catholic Ministry in the diocese provides greater awareness and celebration of the dynamic presence of the African-American community in our midst.

HISPANICS

Shortly after World War II Hispanics began to come in great numbers to work in the farmlands of the Susquehanna Valley. Farm workers from Puerto Rico and Mexico, from Central and South America began to settle here and by the middle of the 1990s Lancaster, Lebanon, York, and Benderville all had Hispanic parishes. In 1995 all except one of the ethnic parishes were suppressed during the parish consolidation program. At present,

San Juan Bautista in Lancaster is the only ethnic parish in the diocese. However, Saint Benedict in Lebanon, Saint Mary in York, Saint Francis of Assisi in Harrisburg, Saint Francis Xavier in Gettysburg, and Saint Joseph in Hanover serve the needs of our growing Hispanic Catholic population. Hispanic ministry has also recently begun in York Springs.

ASIANS

The period after the Vietnam War saw a great influx of Asian Catholics into the diocese, especially Vietnamese and Filipinos. Later there came many Koreans, Cambodians, Laotians, Thais and Burmese. Although there is a ministry to these Asian Catholics, no ethnic parishes have been established for them. They seem to fit well into the territorial parishes in which they live and they become actively involved in these parishes. Bishop Rhoades encourages ethnic, cultural, and religious celebrations with which they can identify.

Kính mừng Maria, dầy ơn phúc. Đức Chúa Trời ở cùng Bà. Bà có phúc lạ hơn mọi người nữ, và Giêsu. Con lòng Bà, gồm phúc lạ. Thánh Maria Đức Mẹ Chúa Trời, cầu cho chúng con. là kẻ có tội Khi này và trong giờ lâm tử. Amen.

"The Hail Mary" in Vietnamese

1935	Bishop McDevitt dies; Most Reverend George L. Leech appointed fifth Bishop of Harrisburg
1937	Saint Bernard, New Bloomfield, founded
1938	Catholic Charities established in the diocese; Saint Peter School, Mount Carmel, opens
1939	Pius XII becomes pope; World War II begins (ends 1945); Blessed Martin de Porres House, Harrisburg, founded by Mary Frecon
1940	Mount Carmel Catholic High School, Mount Carmel, opens; Delone Catholic High School, McSherrystown, opens; the first section of the Pennsylvania Turnpike opens
1941	Saint Joseph Academy, Columbia, opens for girls
1943	75th Anniversary of the Diocese of Harrisburg; Misericordia Convalescent Home, York, established by the Daughters of Our Lady of Mercy; Our Lady, Help of Christians School, Lykens, closes; Ninth Synod of the Diocese of Harrisburg convened
1945	World War II ends
1946	Saint Bernard, New Bloomfield, founded; Saint Francis Preparatory School moves from Loretto, Pennsylvania, to Spring Grove; Saint Mark the Evangelist, Greencastle, founded as a mission; Saint Luke the Evangelist, Mercersburg, founded as a mission
1947	Diocesan Catholic Youth Office established
1948	Saint Catherine Laboure, Harrisburg, founded; Saint Margaret Mary Alacoque, Harrisburg, founded; Holy Infant, York Haven, founded; Diocese of Harrisburg consecrated to the Immaculate Heart of Mary
1949	Saint Catherine Laboure School, Harrisburg, opens; Saint Margaret Mary School, Harrisburg, opens; Saint Theresa School, New Cumberland, opens
1949	Madonna Center opened by Catholic Charities to provide assistance to African Americans
1950	Our Lady of the Visitation, Shippensburg, founded; Queen of the Most Holy Rosary, Elysburg, founded; Our Lady of Good Counsel, Marysville, founded; Saint Eleanor Regina Chapel, built for vacationers at Pine Grove Furnace, opens; Dogma of the Assumption of the Blessed Virgin Mary proclaimed by Pope Pius XII
1951	Seven Sorrows of the Blessed Virgin Mary School, Middletown, opens; Good Shepherd, Camp Hill, founded
1952	Polio outbreak forces schools and churches to close until the crisis passed; Queen of Peace, Millersburg, founded; Saint Joseph, Mechanicsburg, founded; Saint Joseph School, Mechanicsburg, opens; Our Lady of Lourdes High School, Shamokin, opens
1953	Our Lady of Fatima, Jonestown, founded; Saint John the Evangelist School, Enhaut, opens; Dominican Monastery moves from Enola to Lancaster; Carmelite Nuns establish monastery in Mount Carmel; Good Shepherd School, Camp Hill, opens
1954	Saint Bernadette, Duncannon, founded; Saint Columba School, Bloomsburg, opens; Sacred Heart of Jesus School, Lewistown, opens; mission of the Blessed Virgin Mary, Queen of Apostles, Newville, organized; Legion of Mary established in diocese by Bishop Leech to celebrate the 100th anniversary of the Church's dogma on the Immaculate Conception
1955	Saint Thomas More, Northumberland, founded; Holy Spirit, Palmyra, founded; Immaculate Conception of the Blessed Virgin Mary School, Berwick, opens; Villa Vianney, Lebanon, founded as a retirement residence for priests; Apostolate for migrant workers formed

1956 Msgr. Lawrence Schott named auxiliary bishop of Harrisburg; Saint Jude Thaddeus, Apostle, Mifflintown, founded; Our Mother of Perpetual Help School, Ephrata, opens

1957 Holy Family, Harrisburg, founded; Saint Richard, Manheim, founded; Holy Spirit Hospital, Camp Hill, incorporates; Harrisburg Catholic High School renamed Bishop McDevitt High School

1958 Blessed John XXIII becomes pope; Holy Family School, Harrisburg, opens; Saint Peter School, Elizabethtown, opens; radio and television apostolate established in diocese; Sacred Heart Academy, Lancaster, closes

1959 New Lebanon Catholic High School opens; Saint Joseph School, Locust Gap, closes; inauguration of David Lawrence, first Catholic governor of Pennsylvania

1960 Holy Name of Jesus, Harrisburg, founded; Saint Hubert, Danville, closes; John F. Kennedy elected, the first Catholic to attain the U.S. Presidency

1961 Encyclical *Mater et Magistra,* addressing social and economic matters, issued; Christ the King, Benton, founded; Holy Name of Jesus School, Harrisburg, opens; Apostolate for Spanish-speaking Catholics established in diocese; Our Lady of Perpetual Help School, Marion Heights, closes; Carmelite Nuns move to Elysburg

1962 Second Vatican Council convened by Pope John XXIII, continues through 1965; Sacred Heart of Jesus, Conewago, elevated to rank of minor basilica; Maria Joseph Manor, Danville, completed by Sisters of Saints Cyril and Methodius; Saint Martin de Porres canonized

1963 Paul VI becomes pope; Auxiliary Bishop Schott dies; Bishop John Nepomucene Neumann beatified by Pope Paul VI; Trinity High School, Camp Hill, opens; President John F. Kennedy assassinated on November 22

1964 Most Reverend Joseph T. Daley appointed Auxiliary Bishop of Harrisburg; Saint Leo the Great, Rohrerstown, founded;

1964 Saint Pius X, Selinsgrove, founded; schools in Mount Carmel merge into Holy Spirit School, Mount Carmel, becoming the first consolidated inter-parochial elementary school in the United States; high schools in Shamokin and Mount Carmel merge to form Our Lady of Lourdes Regional High School, Coal Township; Newman Apostolate (later Catholic Campus Ministry) established

1965 Saint Gregory the Great, Lebanon, founded; Saint Philip the Apostle, Millersville, founded; Saint Leo the Great School, Rohrerstown, opens; first Concelebrated Mass in the diocese celebrated at the Cathedral on Holy Thursday

1966 Diocesan newspaper, *The Catholic Witness,* begins publication

1968 Auxiliary Bishop Joseph T. Daley appointed Coadjutor Bishop of Harrisburg with right of succession to Bishop Leech; diocesan school board formed; Sacred Heart School, Williamstown, closes, and its students sent to Lykens-Williamstown Consolidated Catholic High School; Saint Ann and Saint James schools, Steelton, consolidated into Bishop Neumann School; Sacred Heart, Excelsior, closes; Martin Luther King, Jr., assassinated on April 4

1969 Apollo 11 lands on the moon and Neil Armstrong becomes first person to walk on the moon, July 20

1970 Vatican II's *novus ordo* liturgy for Mass introduced throughout the diocese; trial of the "Harrisburg Seven" involves priests and sisters from the diocese

1971 Bishop Leech retires; Coadjutor Bishop Joseph T. Daley appointed sixth bishop of Harrisburg; the faithful granted permission to receive Holy Communion under both forms; Saint Edward Church, Shamokin, ravaged by fire

PART 2
THE EPISCOPACY OF JOSEPH T. DALEY, THE PLANNER,
SIXTH BISHOP OF HARRISBURG, 1971-1983

The transition from the episcopacy of Bishop Leech to that of Bishop Daley was especially smooth, as Bishop Daley had served as auxiliary bishop and then coadjutor bishop with the right of succession during the 8 years prior to becoming, at age 55, the sixth bishop of the Diocese of Harrisburg upon the retirement of Bishop Leech in 1971.

Bishop Daley endorsed and wholeheartedly encouraged the expanded involvement of the laity that grew out of the mandates of Vatican II. During the 1970s the laity's active role in liturgical celebrations and the daily workings of the church at all levels increased dramatically. Lay members now not only served on boards and committees but were named to positions of leadership as well. By the end of his episcopacy, all the parishes in the diocese had councils composed of religious and lay members.

He appointed a diocesan commission of sacred liturgy, music, and art to implement programs approved by the Ecumenical Council in the Vatican and American Council of Bishops.

During his episcopacy the diocese continued to grow. New parishes and apostolates were established. The annual observance in the diocese of Catholic School Week began in 1973, focusing community-wide attention on the value of Catholic education.

Bishop Daley viewed parish buildings as concrete symbols of faith and, accordingly, encouraged parishes to complete construction and renovation. In the 1970s almost half of the parishes and missions of the diocese either built or improved their church buildings, educational facilities, parish centers, and rectories. Further, the diocesan offices, which had been located at various sites in the Harrisburg area, were brought together in 1975 at the newly constructed Diocesan Center at 4800 Union Deposit Road, Harrisburg. A separate building in the complex serves as the Bishops' Residence.

During Bishop Daley's tenure, the diocesan construction program amounted to more than $21.5 million.

In the 1970s Project H.E.A.D. (Help Experienced Adults Develop), renamed Senior Adult Ministry in 2001, was launched diocese-wide for parishioners over the age of fifty. Individual parish groups, such as "Saint Joseph Golden Hills Club" (Lancaster), "Saint John's Jewels" (New Freedom), "The Harvest Club" (Gettysburg), and "Sunflower Club" (Shamokin) began to form across the diocese.

Diocesan Center as it appeared in 1975

Ciborium manufactured by the Wilton Armetale Company, Columbia, for the 41st International Eucharistic Congress held in Philadelphia 1976 to celebrate the American Bicentennial.

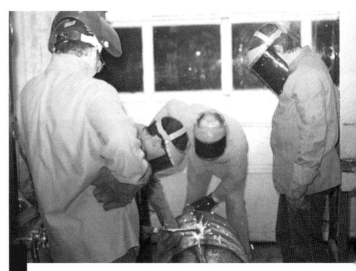

Welding class at Paradise School, Abbottstown, 1980s.

The diocesan Lenten Appeal was inaugurated in 1974. In its first ten years more than $14 million was pledged in support of diocesan ministries and other programs.

The Trinity Spiritual Center, Shiremanstown, opened in 1974. Bishop Daley, who prior to coming to the diocese had served as vice-rector of Saint Charles Borromeo Seminary in Overbrook, Philadelphia, was keenly aware of the importance of nurturing vocations. He began vocation discernment programs at the Center for both men and women to learn and pray about their vocations.

It was also under Bishop Daley that the summer evangelization program began in the diocese in 1975. The program, which became a model for the United States, gives diocesan seminarians the chance to devote their summers to working in parishes, as well as in other sites, such as hospitals, to receive specialized training in spreading the word of God.

Also in 1975 Conewago Chapel, the cradle of Catholicism in the diocese, was named a National Historic Site. As the nation's bicentennial approached, other historic church buildings in the diocese also received local and county recognition as historic sites.

In the nation's bicentennial year, the 41st International Eucharistic Congress was held in Philadelphia. Through the efforts of Bishop Daley, Protestant clergy from the area took part in the ecumenical day of the conference, during which Archbishop Fulton J. Sheen spoke.

Priests and sisters from the diocese ministered to the Vietnamese and Cambodian refugees who lived temporarily at Fort Indiantown Gap in the 1970s until they settled into a new life in the United States. Bishop Daley formed the diocesan Apostolate to the Vietnamese and named as its head Father Nguyen Van Hoa, the first Vietnamese priest ordained in the United States.

Under Bishop Daley's leadership the Religious Education Resource Centers were established to train catechists; also, ministries for the separated, divorced, and widowed were initiated, and Harrisburg joined with a handful of other dioceses in the country in the Catholic Communications Television Network.

In 1978, a decade after the forming of a permanent diaconate in the diocese, the first class of permanent deacons was ordained.

Intinctorium, a ciborium with a well in the center for the consecrated wine. During the 1960s and 1970s, Holy Communion was given under both species by "dipping" the sacred host into the precious blood.

Nineteen seventy-nine is remembered as the year of the nuclear accident at Three Mile Island, situated in the middle of the diocese and only 11 miles from the cathedral. Bishop Daley made national headlines in the Catholic press for authorizing priests in parishes close to the site to grant general absolution.

In July of the same year, Monsignor William H. Keeler was named auxiliary bishop of the diocese. In October, Pope John Paul II celebrated Mass at Yankee Stadium in New York and in Philadelphia.

Like the 1970s, the 1980s were also years of growth in the diocese. Worshipping communities were formed for the two largest Hispanic communities in the diocese, Cristo Salvador in York and Saint Juan Bautista in Lancaster. Bishop Daley conferred the Sacrament of Confirmation in Spanish for both congregations.

After a three-year struggle with cancer, Bishop Daley succumbed to the disease in the fall of 1983. During his episcopate the Catholic population of the Harrisburg See had grown to almost 200,000 in 110 parishes, 47 missions and stations, and 100 chapels. There were 10 Catholic high schools, 3 of them private, and 57 Catholic elementary schools, including 4 that were private. The community service offered by Catholic Charities had grown immensely; ministries and services such as pastoral planning, Parish Pastoral Councils, campus ministry, and consolidated financial services had expanded broadly.

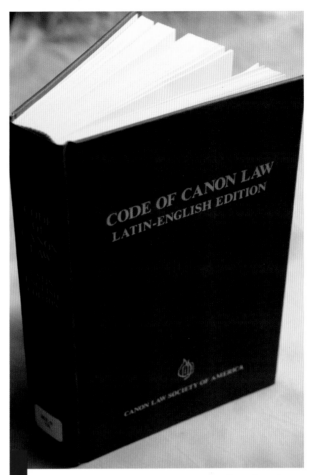

Latin-English edition of the revised Code of Canon Law, which took effect in 1983. The effort to revise the Code was begun under Pope John XXIII and completed under Pope John Paul II. The revised code replaces the Code of Canon Law promulgated in 1917 during the papacy of Pope Benedict XV.

THE PENNSYLVANIA CATHOLIC CONFERENCE

The Pennsylvania Catholic Conference is the public affairs arm of Pennsylvania's Catholic bishops and the eight Latin Rite and two Byzantine Rite dioceses in the state. The Board of Governors of the Conference meets annually to establish the principles and determine its policies, and the staff continues its work throughout the year. The objective of the PCC is to formulate policy positions with reference to state government programs, legislation and policies that affect the common good and the interests of the Church. Almost one third of the total population of Pennslyania is Catholic, and Catholic Charities is the largest private provider of human services in the Commonwealth.

PART 3
THE EPISCOPACY OF WILLIAM H. KEELER, THE ECUMENIST
SEVENTH BISHOP OF HARRISBURG, 1983-1989

With the death of Bishop Daley, Auxiliary Bishop Keeler was elected Vicar Capitular of the diocese. One of his first official duties was to carry out Bishop Daley's wish that the diocese be dedicated to the Blessed Mother. Bishop Daley, in the last months of his life, had expressed this wish, following the example of Pope John Paul II's consecration of the world to the Immaculate Heart of Mary. On October 23, less than a month after Bishop Daley's death, the diocese was formally dedicated to Our Lady under the title "Mary, Queen of Peace." Together with Saint Patrick, Mary serves as co-patron. The ceremony began with a procession from City Island to the cathedral. Participants from throughout the diocese carried banners and recited the rosary en route. Bishop Keeler, as interregnum administrator, presided at the cathedral liturgy.

Pope John Paul II and Cardinal William Keeler.

Reliquary holding a relic of Saint Patrick.

MOST REVEREND WILLIAM H. KEELER
(NOW CARDINAL WILLIAM KEELER)
SEVENTH BISHOP OF HARRISBURG
1984-1989

Opus fac evangelistae.
Do the work of an evangelist.

(II TIMOTHY 4:5)

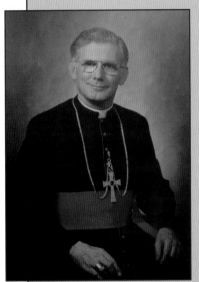

William Henry Keeler was born March 4, 1931, in San Antonio, TX, the son of Thomas L. and Margaret T. (Conway) Keeler. Reared in Lebanon, PA, he attended Saint Mary School and Lebanon Catholic High School. He earned a B.A. from Saint Charles Borromeo Seminary in Overbrook, Philadelphia, in 1952, and a Licentiate in Sacred Theology from Pontifical Gregorian University, Rome, in 1956.

After ordination to the priesthood in 1955, he served as assistant pastor and later pastor at Our Lady of Good Counsel, Marysville, and as secretary and later Defender of the Bond of the Diocesan Tribunal. In 1961 he received his doctorate in Canon Law.

As secretary to Bishop Leech during Vatican Council II (1962-1965), Father Keeler was appointed *peritus*, or special advisor, to the Council by Pope John XXIII. He also served on the staff of the Council Digest, a daily communication service sponsored by the United States Bishops.

In 1965, he was named Papal Chamberlain, with the title of Monsignor, and in 1970, Prelate of Honor.

Monsignor Keeler became Vice Chancellor of the Harrisburg Diocese in 1965, Chancellor in 1969, and later Vicar General. A decade later he was appointed Auxiliary Bishop of Harrisburg and Titular Bishop of Ulcinium (Dulcigno).

On January 4, 1984, he was installed as the seventh Bishop of Harrisburg. After leading the diocese for seven years, he was appointed Archbishop of Baltimore and, on May 23, 1989, became the fourteenth archbishop of the nation's oldest See.

An influential participant in national and international issues involving the Church, he was elected President of the National Conference of Catholic Bishops (NCCB) in 1992. He is well known for his work in Catholic-Jewish dialogue. He serves on the Pontifical Commission for Promoting Christian Unity and the Pontifical Council for Inter-Religious Dialogue. On November 28, 1994, His Eminence Cardinal William Keeler was named to the College of Cardinals by Pope John Paul II.

In 2005 he celebrated the 50th anniversary of his ordination to the priesthood and the 25th as bishop.

Cardinal Keeler, named to the College of Cardinals by Pope John Paul II, 1994.

Beretta worn by Cardinal Keeler during studies in Rome.

THE RED MASS

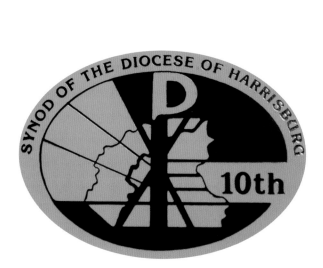

The Red Mass of the Saint Thomas More Society

St. Thomas More Society of Central Pennsylvania

The Red Mass began in 13th-century England, when King Edward I opened each term of court with a votive Mass invoking the guidance and blessing of the Holy Spirit upon the work of justice in society. The name "Red Mass" derives from the red-trimmed robes worn centuries ago by judges and public officials.

During the days of (now-Saint) Thomas More, this Mass was opened to the public. The tradition was brought to the United States in 1928, and since then has been celebrated annually in many cities throughout the nation.

The Saint Thomas More Society of Central Pennsylvania was founded in 1989 when the late Honorable Genevieve Blatt, Judge of the Commonwealth Court of Pennsylvania, gathered a small band of Catholic lawyers to bring this time-honored tradition to the Capital Region. The society is dedicated to the memory of Saint Thomas More, the patron saint of statesmen and politicians and an exemplar of personal and legal integrity. The Red Mass is celebrated annually at the cathedral.

Laity and clergy meet for the 10th Synod, convened by Bishop Keeler.

Also in 1988 Bishop Keeler granted permission for a Sunday Latin Tridentine-rite Mass, using the 1962 sacramentary, to be celebrated monthly at Trinity High School, Camp Hill. The same year the newly formed Foundation of Catholics United in Service (FOCUS) established an endowment fund in the diocese to provide scholarships and grants to help families send their children to Catholic schools.

In 1989 Bishop Keeler accepted the call to become Archbishop of Baltimore. His last gift to the diocese was to raise the chapel of the motherhouse of the Sisters of Saints Cyril and Methodius, Danville, to the rank of minor basilica, making this minor basilica the only one in the world honoring the co-patrons of Europe and giving Harrisburg distinction as the only diocese in Pennsylvania to have two minor basilicas.

On January 4, 1984, Bishop Keeler, at age 53, was installed as the seventh bishop of the diocese. During his episcopacy, programs emphasizing active participation in parish life continued, along with renewed commitment to ecumenism and inter-religious activities and to evangelization. The 10th Synod of the Diocese of Harrisburg, which outlined these programs, culminated on June 5, 1988. Appropriately, laity, along with clergy and religious, participated in the synod.

1985   Bishop Leech dies

1986   Coordinator appointed for ministry to diocese's Black Catholics; remaining Steelton schools consolidated into Saint John Neumann School; Immaculate Conception and Saint Joseph schools, Berwick, consolidated into Holy Family School

1987   Blessed Sacrament School, Harrisburg, closes

1988   Tenth Synod of the Diocese of Harrisburg convened; Saint (orginally Blessed) Katharine Drexel, Mechanicsburg, founded; Nuestra Senora de Guadalupe (Our Lady of Guadalupe), Lebanon, founded for Hispanic Catholics; Saint Francis of Assisi School closes; monthly celebration of Latin Tridentine-rite Mass at Trinity High School, Camp Hill, commences; FOCUS endowment fund established for children attending Catholic schools

1989   Saint Thomas More Society of Central Pennsylvania formed; Assumption of the Blessed Virgin Mary Consolidated School, Lebanon, renamed Our Lady of the Valley; Motherhouse Chapel of Saints Cyril and Methodius, Danville, raised to the rank of minor basilica; Bishop Keeler named Archbishop of Baltimore

Chapel of the motherhouse of Saints Cyril and Methodius, Danville, newly erected as a minor basilica, 1989

THE SISTERS OF SAINTS CYRIL AND METHODIUS

This Congregation was founded in Scranton in 1909 by Father Matthew Jankola to provide teachers for schools in Slovak parishes. Pope Saint Pius X approved the new congregation, and the first three Sisters made their profession in 1909. The Sisters of Saints Cyril and Methodius came to the Diocese of Harrisburg in 1913 when they assumed charge of Saint John the Baptist School, Mount Carmel. In 1917 the Jednota Estates, Middletown, became the site of the Community's temporary motherhouse.

With the purchase of the Castle Grove estate of 190 acres in Danville in 1919, the Community acquired a permanent motherhouse known as Villa Sacred Heart, where they established an academy for girls in 1922. The academy and motherhouse were expanded with a new building in 1921 and a magnificent chapel in 1939, which was designated as a minor basilica in 1989. A generalate and residence hall were added in 1957 and a home for the aged in 1962. In these developments and in all their progress, the Sisters benefited from the guidance of the Bishops of Harrisburg. They continue in their apostolate of education and health care for the elderly.

THE DISCALCED CARMELITE NUNS

On March 31, 1953, Bishop Leech invited Mother Marguerite Marie, prioress of the Carmelite monastery in Loretto, Pennsylvania, to found a monastery in Northumberland County. On September 18, 1953, six nuns under the leadership of Mother Marguerite Marie of the Divine Heart came to the Diocese of Harrisburg and took up their residence in a temporary monastery at 21 East Avenue, Mount Carmel. To supplement the alms, by which, according to their

Rule, they are maintained, the nuns made altar breads and altar linens.

The community doubled in size in eight years, and a new monastery was built in Elysburg on land donated by Monsignor Paul D. Weaver. The nuns moved to the new convent on June 1, 1961. The nuns observe the primitive rule of Carmel, which was restored in 1562 under Saint Teresa of Avila, with the help of Saint John of the Cross. Under this rule the nuns observe strict cloister, poverty, perpetual abstinence, frequent fasts and a love of solitude and silence.

DOMINICAN SISTERS OF THE PERPETUAL ROSARY

The Institute of the Dominican Sisters of the Perpetual Rosary is a cloistered contemplative branch of the Order of Preachers. The Sisters have all monastic observances, including choral recitation of the Liturgy of the Hours. The chief purpose of the institute, after the sanctification of its members, is to assure the perpetuity of the Most Holy Rosary. Hourly throughout the day and night, the Sisters succeed each other in praying the rosary for Our Holy Father the Pope, for Holy Mother Church, for our Bishop and our diocese, and for all intentions recommended to them.

The Harrisburg monastery at Enola was founded from Baltimore in 1925 under the leadership of Mother Mary of the Crown. The monastery at Enola was damaged by fire in 1952. A new property was purchased on Lititz Pike near Lancaster, and the Sisters moved there on January 22, 1953. Cardinal Amleto Giovanni Cicognani blessed a new monastery and chapel on May 22, 1955.

THE SISTER ADORERS OF THE MOST PRECIOUS BLOOD

The Sister Adorers of the Most Precious Blood sent a group of sixteen sisters from Croatia to establish a motherhouse in Alton, Illinois, in 1906. The opening of Saint Mary's School, Steelton, by four of these Sisters in 1913 marked the entry of the Sister Adorers into the Diocese of Harrisburg. Later in 1925, with the permission of Bishop Philip R. McDevitt, they transferred their motherhouse to the East, locating it on the old Quay Farm near Columbia. The renovated mansion on the grounds became Saint Joseph Convent. A new motherhouse and academy were construction in 1941, and Saint Anne's Home for the aged was built to accommodate 110 guests.

In 1964 a new building, called Marian Hall, was erected and now functions as a retreat center for the Diocesan Council of Catholic Women and occasional student and adult groups.

PART 1
THE EPISCOPACY OF NICHOLAS C. DATTILO, THE CONSOLIDATOR, EIGHTH BISHOP OF HARRISBURG, 1990-2004

After Bishop William Keeler's appointment as Archbishop of Baltimore in 1989, Bishop Nicholas Dattilo, at age 57, became the eighth bishop of the Diocese of Harrisburg. In January 1990 the faithful throughout the diocese witnessed his ordination and installation Mass on live television.

From the beginning of his episcopacy, Bishop Dattilo often observed that Vatican II focused on lay

Opening and dedication of Nia Center, headquarters of the Black Catholic Apostolate, at Saint Francis of Assisi, Harrisburg, in 1992. Bishop Rhoades (then pastor of Saint Francis) is on the left.

SAINT MARTIN DE PORRES

In 1939 Mary Frecon established Blessed Martin de Porres House, known also as The House of Hospitality, on North Seventh Street, Harrisburg. There, she ministered to the poor and the sick, offering them food and shelter. The center was honored with a visit by Dorothy Day and Peter Maurin, founders of the Catholic Worker movement. In 1950 Mrs. Frecon's failing health forced the center to close.

In 1996 the Saint Martin de Porres Catholic Worker House on Allison Hill in Harrisburg opened to offer food, housing, and spiritual guidance to sufferers of alcohol and drug abuse and those recently released from prison. A number of volunteers assist at the mission.

The mission is named for Saint Martin de Porres (1579-1639), who grew up in poverty in Lima, Peru. Trained as a barber-surgeon, he ministered to the less fortunate and subsequently became a Dominican Friar. He was canonized on May 6, 1962.

Catholic Worker House, Harrisburg, opens in 1996 under the patronage of Saint Martin de Porres.

BISHOP NICHOLAS C. DATTILO
EIGHTH BISHOP OF HARRISBURG
1990-2004

Love life and do good.

Nicholas Carmen Dattilo, was born March 8, 1932, in New Castle, Pennsylvania. His parents were Frank Dominick Dattilo and Emma M. (Nocera) Dattilo. He completed his seminary studies at Saint Vincent Seminary in Latrobe and the Saint Charles Borromeo Seminary, Overbrook, Philadelphia.

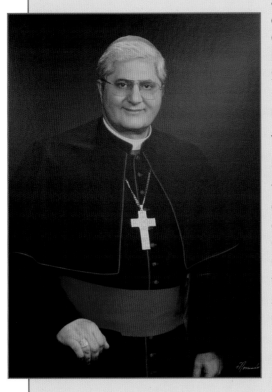

Ordained a priest for the Diocese of Pittsburgh in 1958, Father Dattilo was parochial vicar at Saint Patrick, Canonsburg, and pastor of Madonna del Castello, Swissvale, and later Saint Vitus, New Castle. He served the Diocese of Pittsburgh as Vicar for Religious Women, Secretary for Clergy, General Secretary, and Vicar General.

He was named the eighth Bishop of Harrisburg in November 1989 and was ordained to the episcopacy on January 26, 1990.

A number of initiatives and events defined Bishop Dattilo's tenure: the Ecclesial Lay Ministry, re-organization of the diocesan administrative structure, the diocese's 125th anniversary celebration, parish mergers, establishment of San Juan Bautista as a parish and Saint George as a mission, construction of the Cardinal Keeler Center and the Priests' Retirement Residence, policies for the protection of minors, including the mandate of zero-tolerance of abuse, and the First Eucharistic Congress of the diocese.

In his preaching, he was known for the humor he interjected to emphasize his message. At Confirmation ceremonies, even as his listeners chuckled at his wit, he challenged confirmands to live their faith and reminded parents and sponsors of their obligation to nurture the spiritual lives entrusted to their care.

In addition to serving as president of the Pennsylvania Catholic Conference and co-chair of the Pennsylvania Conference on Interchurch Cooperation, he was a member of visitation and evaluation committees for several Catholic seminaries and served on the Board of Regents for Saint Vincent Seminary in Latrobe.

Bishop Dattilo died on March 5, 2004, and is buried at Saint Lucy's Cemetery of Saint Vincent de Paul Parish, New Castle. In 2005 the Priests' Retirement Residence was named in his memory.

The Salvation Ring, presented by Pope John Paul II to Bishop Dattilo for his Episcopal Ordination.

SAINT KATHARINE DREXEL 1858–1955
Feast Day: March 3

Born into the wealthy Drexel family of Philadelphia, Saint Katharine Drexel dedicated her life and inheritance to the care of the poor. Initially, as a lay person she financed Indian missions in the western part of the country. When she asked Pope Leo XIII for assistance from missionaries, he urged her to become a missionary. She completed her novitiate at the convent of the Sisters of Mercy, Pittsburgh and, in 1891, founded the Sisters of the Blessed Sacrament, an order dedicated to work among the Native-American and African-American poor.

Within the Diocese of Harrisburg, the Order provided religious training for the Catholic children at the Carlisle Indian School, the first off-reservation school for Native-Americans. Pupils there included the outstanding athlete Jim Thorpe. Saint Katharine Drexel visited Carlisle many times.

Saint Katharine was canonized by Pope John Paul II in October 2000.

"Gather Up the Fragments": mural depicting the history of the Diocese of Harrisburg, painted by Tuoc Than, Holy Family Parish, in 1996.

Twelve new parishes were formed from the mergers in 1995. In the list below, the year of founding and the ethnic roots of the merged parishes are noted. Asterisks indicate the worship sites of the new parishes established as a result of the mergers.

Our Lady of Hope, Coal Township, Shamokin
*Saint Joseph 1913
Saint Stephen 1898 - Polish

Cathedral Parish of Saint Patrick, Harrisburg
*Saint Patrick 1826 - Irish
Sacred Heart of Jesus 1901
Saint Lawrence 1859 - German

Holy Angels, Kulpmont
*Assumption of the Blessed Virgin Mary 1909 - Hungarian
Saint Casimir 1915 - Polish
Our Lady of Perpetual Help (Marion Heights) 1905 – Polish, Slovak, Italian, and English

Saint Benedict the Abbott, Lebanon
*Saints Cyril and Methodius 1905 - Slovak
Nuestra Senora de Guadalupe 1988 – Hispanic

Saint Cecilia, Lebanon
*Saint Gertrude 1906 - German, Austrian, Hungarian, and Serbian
Saint Gregory the Great 1965

Our Lady of Mount Carmel, Mount Carmel
*Our Lady of Mount Carmel 1886
Saint Ignatius of Loyola (Centralia) 1869
Saint Joseph 1875 (Mount Carmel) - Polish
Saint Joseph (Locust Gap) 1870
Saint Joseph (Locustdale) 1913

Divine Redeemer Parish, Mount Carmel
*Our Mother of Consolation 1895 - Polish
Holy Cross 1892 - Lithuanian
Saint John the Baptist 1892 - Slovak
Saint Peter 1905 – Tyrolean Italian
Saint Paul Chapel (Atlas) 1928

Mary, Mother of the Church, Mount Joy
*Assumption of the Blessed Virgin Mary 1979
Presentation of the Blessed Virgin Mary (Marietta) 1869

Mother Cabrini Parish, Shamokin
Assumption of the Blessed Virgin Mary 1892 - Slovak
*Saint Edward the Confessor 1866
Saint Stanislaus Kosta 1874 - Polish
Saint Michael the Archangel 1894 - Lithuanian
Saint Anthony of Padua (Ranshaw) 1919

Prince of Peace, Steelton
*Assumption of the Blessed Virgin Mary 1898 - Croatian
Saint Ann 1901 - Italian
Saint James 1878 - Irish
Saint Peter the Apostle 1909 - Slovenian
Saint John the Evangelist (Enhaut) 1902 – German-Hungarian

Saint Monica, Sunbury
*Saint Michael the Archangel 1863
Saint Thomas More (Northumberland) 1955

Church of the Immaculate Conception, York
*Immaculate Conception of the Blessed Virgin Mary 1852 - German
Cristo Salvador 1980 – Hispanic

The Pilgrim Millennial Cross, which traveled to each parish in the diocese during Jubilee Year 2000.

Signing for the hearing impaired, Saint Patrick Cathedral, 2001

involvement in the life of the church, "like a laser beam." He urged the diocese to work to make each parish "a center of worship, service, and education," and a major focus of his work was to strengthen parish life.

He oversaw the development of the Ecclesial Lay Ministry to prepare laity to serve their parishes as pastoral staff, RCIA coordinators, directions of religious education, and youth ministers.

One of the first actions of Bishop Dattilo was to re-organize the diocesan administrative structure by moving from the chancery system to the secretariat system. With this new structure seven secretariats were established to encompass all areas of diocesan administration.

In 1993 the diocese commemorated its 125th anniversary with celebrations culminating in Mass at the cathedral. The same year area clergy formalized their resolve to work together as they signed the Lutheran, Anglican, Roman Catholic Covenant (LARC).

The most-remembered date during Bishop Dattilo's ordinary is July 1, 1995, for on this day 38 parishes and missions were merged to establish 12 new parishes. The consolidations followed an intensive diocese-wide consultation process that studied population shifts within the diocese along with availability of clergy and parish resources. Most of the mergers involved ethnic parishes in the northern tier of the diocese, where job losses in the mining industry had caused many parishioners to move from the area.

In 1999 ground was broken for the Cardinal Keeler Center and the adjacent Priests' Retirement Residence at the Diocesan Center, Harrisburg.

The new millenium brought with it Jubilee Year 2000, declared by Pope John Paul II to celebrate the Eucharist throughout the world. The Millenium Cross traveled to each parish in the diocese, and the first Eucharistic Congress of the diocese gathered faithful from across the diocese to celebrate Christ's presence in the Eucharist.

In October 2000 Saint Katharine Drexel was canonized, making her the third American saint with direct ties to the diocese. She had traveled to Carlisle many times to visit the Carlisle Indian School, which she had been instrumental in founding.

The diocese, led by Bishop Dattilo, was recognized across the nation for its firm stand in the wake of the 2002 scandals, in particular for its policy of zero-tolerance of abuses by clergy.

In 2003 San Juan Bautista Parish, Lancaster, received parish status, thus becoming the first Spanish parish in the diocese.

The next year, following a gradually debilitating illness, Bishop Dattilo passed away at Holy Spirit Hospital, Camp Hill.

Souvenir statue of Saint Patrick, commemorating the 125th anniversary of the Diocese of Harrisburg

1990	Bishop Nicholas C. Dattilo ordained eighth bishop of Harrisburg;
1991	Catholic schools in Lancaster consolidated into Resurrection School
1992	Archbishop Keeler named a cardinal; diocesan renewal process, "Growing Together in Faith," begins; consultation process for parish consolidation begins
1993	125th Diocesan Anniversary Mass celebrated at Saint Patrick Cathedral; new Catechism of the Catholic Church approved; LARC (Lutheran, Anglican, Roman Catholic) covenant signed
1995	Parish realignments merge 38 parishes to form 12 new parishes
1996	The first Diocesan Catholic Cultural Heritage Day celebrated
1998	Ecclesial Lay Ministry Program inaugurated in the diocese; Holy Trinity and Saint Peter schools, Columbia, consolidate into Our Lady of the Angels School; 3,200 young people and adults confirmed in a diocese-wide ceremony at Hershey Park Arena
1999	Groundbreaking for Cardinal Keeler Center and Priests' Retirement Residence on Diocesan Center Campus, Harrisburg; Saint George Mission, Mifflinburg, founded; Saint Cyril Academy, Danville, closes; Holy Doors at Saint Patrick Cathedral, Harrisburg, opened to launch Jubilee Year
2000	Saint Katharine Drexel canonized by Pope John Paul II; Jubilee Year 2000 celebrates the Year of the Eucharist; first Eucharist Congress of the diocese convenes
2001	Priests' Retirement Residence opens; Cardinal Keeler Center dedicated; World Trade Center and the Pentagon attacked and United Airlines Flight 93 downed by terrorists on September 11
2003	San Juan Bautista, Lancaster, becomes first Spanish parish in the diocese

PART 2
THE EPISCOPACY OF KEVIN C. RHOADES, THE EVANGELIZER
NINTH BISHOP OF HARRISBURG, 2004 TO THE PRESENT

Bishop Kevin C. Rhoades was ordained as the ninth Bishop of Harrisburg on December 9, 2004, at Saint Patrick Cathedral by Cardinal Justin Rigali, Archbishop of Philadelphia.

Immediately after his ordination and installation, he began his episcopacy with a vigor and energy that bespoke his youth. At age 47 he was the youngest diocesan bishop in the country.

He has set as his top priority the mission of evangelization. Another central priority is vocations. In the early months of his episcopacy, he initiated a pre-seminary Quo Vadis program, introducing young men to the possibility of a priestly vocation. Within his first year vocations rose significantly. He is likewise encouraging vocations to the consecrated life.

Bishop Rhoades has placed great emphasis on Catholic schools, catechesis and youth ministry. He established a commission on Catholic Social Doctrine proclaiming and serving the Gospel of Life. He also has expanded the role of the Diocesan Pastoral Council and has begun to reinstitute the permanante diaconate formation program in the diocese.

Ordination of Bishop Rhoades

Dedication of Priests' Retirement Residence in memory of Bishop Dattilo, 2005

YEAR OF THE EUCHARIST

Bishop Rhoades' episcopacy began during the special Year of the Eucharist, proclaimed by Pope John Paul II (October 2004 to October 2005). Throughout the year, Bishop Rhoades delivered dozens of homilies and talks throughout the diocese on the theme of the Eucharist, encouraging renewed appreciation of and devotion to the Blessed Sacrament, as well as emphasizing the link between the Eucharist, evangelization, and charity.

In response to his appeal for help after the disastrous tsunami in Asia and the destruction by Hurricanes Katrina and Rita along the Gulf coast, the parishes throughout the diocese contributed over a million dollars for Catholic Charities USA to send to this ravished area. The diocese responded also by donating chalices and ciboria plus lectionaries and sacramentaries to replace those destroyed in the flood and its aftermath. The contributed items came from parishes closed in the 1995 consolidations.

Statue of Saint Benedict
(Diocesan Archives Collection)

MOST REVEREND KEVIN C. RHOADES, NINTH BISHOP OF HARRISBURG 2004-THE PRESENT

Veritatem in Caritate
Truth in Charity

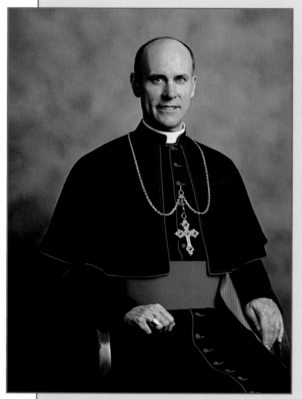

Most Reverend Kevin C. Rhoades was born November 26, 1957 in Mahanoy City, Pennsylvania. The son of Charles and the late Mary Rhoades, he grew up in Lebanon, a member of Assumption B.V.M. parish, and in 1975 graduated from Lebanon Catholic High School, also the alma mater of Cardinal William Keeler. He enrolled in Mount Saint Mary's College (now University), Emmitsburg, Maryland, and studied for two years there; and in 1977 entered Saint Charles Borromeo Seminary in Overbrook, Philadelphia, where he earned a bachelor's degree in philosophy. He did his theological studies at the North American College and the Pontifical Gregorian University in Rome.

After his ordination as a priest of the Harrisburg diocese in 1983, he served as parochial vicar in York and also ministered to the Spanish-speaking Catholics in the York area. In 1985 he returned to Rome, where he earned licentiate degrees in dogmatic theology and canon law.

In 1988 he returned to Harrisburg to serve as assistant chancellor under then-Bishop Keeler and to minister to Spanish-speaking Catholics in Dauphin, Cumberland, Perry, and Lebanon counties. He was appointed pastor of Saint Francis of Assisi Parish, Harrisburg, in 1990. In 1995 he accepted a faculty position at Mount Saint Mary's Seminary and in 1997 became the rector there, a role he fulfilled until his appointment by Pope John Paul II as Bishop of Harrisburg on October 14, 2004.

He was ordained Bishop on December 9, 2004, the Feast of Saint Juan Diego. On that date, he began his ministry as bishop of over 250,000 Catholics in this 15-county Diocese of Harrisburg.

In October 2005 over 5,000 diocesan faithful followed Bishop Rhoades in a Eucharistic Procession in a final celebration of the Year of the Eucharist. The procession began at Annunciation BVM Church, McSherrystown, and finished at the Basilica of the Sacred Heart of Jesus, Conewago, the earliest mission site in the diocese. The event marked the closing of the Year of the Eucharist, which had been designated by the late Pope John Paul II.

RELIGIOUS ORDERS OF WOMEN WHO HAVE WORKED IN THE DIOCESE

Bernardine Sisters
Carmelite Sisters of the Poor Sick
Daughters of Our Lady of Mercy
Discalced Carmelite Nuns
Dominican Sisters of the Perpetual Rosary
Dominican Sisters, Third Order of St. Dominic
Felician Sisters
Franciscan Sisters of Saint Joseph
Missionary Servants of the Most Blessed Trinity
Religious of the Holy Union of the Sacred Hearts
School Sisters of Notre Dame
Sisters Adorers of the Most Precious Blood
Sisters of Charity of Mount Saint Vincent
Sisters of Charity of Saint Vincent de Paul
Sisters of Christian Charity
Sisters of the Holy Cross
Sisters of Mercy
Sisters of Saints Cyril and Methodius
Sisters of Saint Casimir
Sisters of Saint Francis of Christ the King
Sisters of Saint Francis of Glen Riddle
Sisters of Saint Joseph, Chestnut Hill
Sisters, Servants of the Immaculate Heart of Mary, Immaculata
Sisters, Servants of the Immaculate Heart of Mary, Marywood

RELIGIOUS ORDERS OF MEN WHO HAVE WORKED IN THE DIOCESE

The various religious orders of men have played a significant role in the history of the territory now known as the Diocese of Harrisburg. Jesuit missionaries from Canada and Maryland were the first priests to traverse the length of the diocese along the Susquehanna River.

Later Jesuit missionaries founded the first parishes of the diocese. Trappists and Sulpicians served for a brief time in Adams County.

The Conventual Franciscans and the Holy Ghost Fathers brought peace and the consolations of religion to the harassed and troubled immigrants of the coal regions. The Croatian Franciscans later served the same purpose in Steelton. Thriving parishes in Lancaster County are evidence of the missionary zeal of the Redemptorist Fathers.

The Benedictines trained so many of our priests at Saint Vincent Seminary and now staff parishes in Lebanon County. The Oblates of Mary Immaculate did yeoman service throughout the diocese. The Precious Blood and Augustinian Fathers will be remembered for much-needed help in the parish ministry. Capuchins served at Abbottstown and now serve in York and Harrisburg.

The field of secondary education was strengthened by the work of the Third Order of Saint Francis, the Oblates of Saint Francis de Sales, and the Brothers of the Christian Schools.

Many others rendered great assistance in various diocesan offices of the Harrisburg See. For the work of all these servants of the Lord the diocese is grateful.

2004   Bishop Dattilo dies; Reverend Kevin C. Rhoades becomes ninth bishop of Harrisburg; "Year of the Eucharist," extending from October 2004 to October 2005, declared by Pope John Paul II

2005   Pope John Paul II dies, April 2; Pope Benedict XVI becomes pope, April 19; Priests' Retirement Residence named for Bishop Dattilo; 11th Synod of Bishops convened at the Vatican on the theme: "The Eucharist: Source and Summit of the Life and Mission of the Church"; in response to hurricanes Katrina and Rita, which ravished the southern gulf coast, the collection taken up throughout the diocese for relief efforts was the largest in diocesan history; diocesan procession closes "Year of the Eucharist"

Bishop Dattilo Retirement Residence for Priests

Cardinal Keeler Center

Bishop Rhoades and Pope Benedict XVI, 2005

In 2005, the twelve parishes established in the 1995 mergers celebrated their tenth anniversaries. Their celebrations reflect and affirm the resiliency, cooperation, and love of the thousands of parishioners who are a new part of these new faith communities.

Under the leadership of Bishop Rhoades, the faithful of his see are looking ahead with optimism and renewed faith as they peer into the future toward the milestone of the 150th anniversary of the Diocese of Harrisburg.

CATHOLIC SCHOOLS IN THE DIOCESE OF HARRISBURG

SECONDARY SCHOOLS

Camp Hill, Trinity High School
Coal Township, Our Lady of Lourdes Regional High School
Harrisburg, Bishop McDevitt High School
Lancaster, Lancaster Catholic High School
Lebanon, Lebanon Catholic School
McSherrystown, Delone Catholic High School
York, York Catholic High School

ELEMENTARY SCHOOLS

Berwick, Holy Family Consolidated
Bloomsburg, Saint Columba
Camp Hill, Good Shepherd
Carlisle, Saint Patrick
Chambersburg, Corpus Christi
Columbia, Our Lady of Angels
Dallastown, Saint Joseph
Danville, Saint Joseph
Elizabethtown, Saint Peter
Ephrata, Our Mother of Perpetual Help
Gettysburg, Saint Francis Xavier
Hanover, Sacred Heart
Hanover, Saint Joseph
Hanover, Saint Vincent de Paul
Harrisburg, Holy Family
Harrisburg, Holy Name of Jesus
Harrisburg, Saint Catherine Laboure
Harrisburg, Saint Margaret Mary
Harrisburg, The Cathedral Consolidated
Hershey, Saint Joan of Arc
Lancaster, Resurrection
Lancaster, Sacred Heart
Lancaster, Saint Anne
Lancaster, Saint Leo the Great
Lebanon, Lebanon Catholic
Lewistown, Sacred Heart
McSherrystown, Annunciation B.V.M.
Mechanicsburg, Saint Joseph
Middletown, Seven Sorrows B.V.M.
Mount Carmel, Holy Spirit Consolidated
New Cumberland, Saint Theresa
New Oxford, Immaculate Conception
Shamokin, Queen of Peace
Steelton, Prince of Peace
Sunbury, Saint Monica
Thomasville, Saint Rose of Lima
Waynesboro, Saint Andrew
York, Saint Joseph
York, Saint Patrick

PRIVATE SCHOOLS

Danville, Saint Cyril Pre-School and Kindergarten
McSherrystown, Saint Joseph Academy Pre-School
New Freedom, Saint John the Baptist Pre-School

EPILOGUE

From the seventeenth century, when Jesuit missionaries from Canada paddled down the Susquehanna through primeval Indian lands, to the twenty-first, when the Pride of the Susquehanna paddles past the skyscrapers of Pennsylvania's capital city, a long line of history has flowed down the central waterway of William Penn's Holy Experiment.

From a post-Civil War missionary diocese of 25,000 Catholics to the beginning of the third millennium, when nearly 300,000 Catholics form the largest church body in the mid-state, the diocese of Harrisburg finds itself, as one of the mid-sized dioceses in our country, evangelizing middle America.

Inspired by Saint John Neumann, Saint Elizabeth Ann Seton, and Saint Katharine Drexel, may we continue to make God's Name known in our part of His world.

The Pride of the Susquehanna Riverboat, *an authentic paddlewheel riverboat, sails the Susquehanna River in Harrisburg each year during the summer months.*

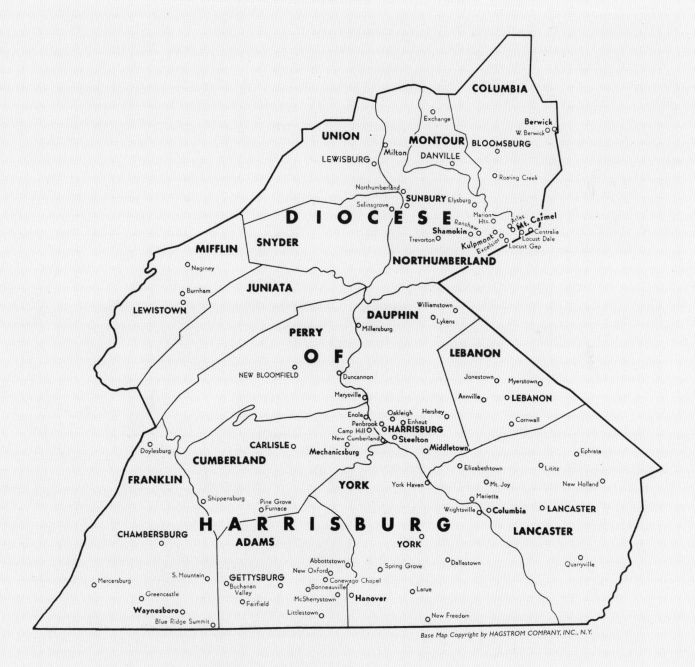

Base Map Copyright by HAGSTROM COMPANY, INC., N.Y.

Abbottstown
IMMACULATE HEART OF MARY

*I*n 1809 Frederick Brandt, a Bavarian immigrant, bought 237 acres of land just north of Abbottstown and built a large stone house with a sizable room to use as a worship space called Paradise Chapel. This evolved into what is now known as Immaculate Heart of Mary Parish. Generous donations from prominent families enabled parishioners to

build a new church with an adjoining cemetery in 1845. The structure is believed to be the first in the United States dedicated to the Blessed Mother under this title.

Traveling Irish friars took up residence in the church after 1900, using the parish as a central locale for their work spreading the Gospel. In a 1949 renovation, a stone memorial tower with the inscription "Heart of Mary, Pray for Us" was erected. Over time, parishioners added other buildings, including a Religious Education Center in 1980, a center that became the forefront of religious education within the area. Today more than 195 children study under the guidance of the Sisters of Saint Joseph.

Annville
SAINT PAUL THE APOSTLE

Christmas 1987

*C*atholicism began to flourish in the Annville area in the 1920s, when Italian immigrants, seeking work in stone quarries and a new life in this country, settled there. Families met in homes to provide religious education for their children, and Saint Gertrude Church in Lebanon provided pastoral care to this fledgling mission named for Saint Paul the Apostle. The acquisition of a church building in 1928 elevated the mission to parish status. While language barriers created a challenge, as most Italian worshippers spoke little English, strong pastoral leadership overcame the hurdles, and the church grew steadily over the next seventy-five years.

The church again reached out to immigrants in the 1970s, when nearby Fort Indiantown Gap served as a resettlement camp for Vietnamese refugees. Opening its doors to them, parishioners sponsored families and provided assistance with food, shelter, and medical services. Today, more than 680 families strong, the church continues its outreach to the needy, embracing in 1990 a mission in Haiti, called Saint Marc's.

*C*onstruction of the North Branch Canal, which began July 4, 1828, brought workers of the Catholic faith to the Berwick area. Mass was celebrated in private homes by Reverend John Fitzpatrick, who attended to the religious needs of Catholics along the Susquehanna River. On August 26, 1828, he purchased property on Mulberry Street, which was used

as a cemetery for the many who died working on the canal. It was in use until 1904, when the cemetery was relocated to its present site at Briar Creek Township. The property later became the site of the first and second Saint Mary's churches.

The first resident pastor was Father John O'Donnell, appointed in October 1906. A period of industrialization and the great immigration increased the parish population with newcomers from Central, Southern and Eastern Europe. A parish school was opened in 1954 and continued in operation until 1987. In 1975 a consultative decision was made to purchase thirteen acres in northeast Berwick and rebuild the parish complex there.

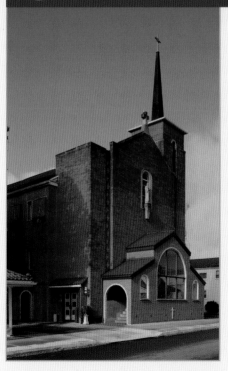

*O*ne hundred years before there was Saint Joseph's in Berwick, the first organized Catholic activity led to the development of Immaculate Conception parish. In 1917, aware of the need of a church to serve the growing number of Italian-speaking Catholics in West Berwick, Father Leonard Baluta, pastor of Saint Mary's, asked Bishop McDevitt to organize Saint Joseph parish. The tremendous spiritual work of this man of God began to have its effect on the Catholics of east and west ends of town.

Father Francis Albanese was appointed first pastor in 1928, and the good work of the growing parish continued through the pastorate of Father Francis Mongelluzzi. In January 1955 the church was destroyed by fire but was quickly rebuilt. A parish school was begun in 1957 staffed by the Daughters of Mercy. During the pastorate of Father Dominick Mammarella the parish properties were greatly enhanced with religious pieces of art. In 1995 with the suppression of all ethnic parishes Saint Joseph's became the district parish for West Berwick.

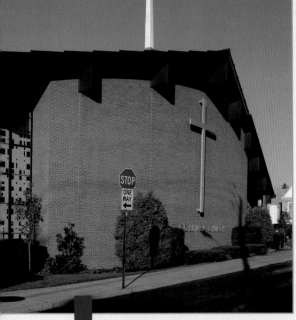

Saint Columba, Bloomsburg

Saint Columba Parish, founded as a mission under Saint Joseph Parish, Danville, traces its roots to Irish and German immigrants who worshiped in private homes during the 1840s. Saint Columba became a parish with the appointment of the first resident pastor, Father Andrew O'Brien, in October 1882. Under the guidance of long-time proactive leadership, Saint Columba thrived.

In the late 1930s, pastoral leaders, noticing a decline in Catholic youth involvement, founded the "Columbian Club" for Catholic students attending Bloomsburg State Teachers College (now University). Today, this group continues to meet and celebrate liturgies.

Dedication 1970

In 1961, after extensive census work, the mission of Christ the King was opened for the 165 Catholics of the Benton area and is affiliated with Saint Columba. Many improvements have been made to accommodate the growing population, and the campus minister of Bloomsburg College now serves the mission.

In 1994 Saint Columba launched an outreach program to aid the needy; through its food bank, which is now sponsored by the Bloomsburg Ministerium, and a monthly Good Neighbor Collection, the parish supports an array of local charities. Saint Columba has just completed a $2 million building/renovation project in which a new parish center was built, a firehouse was converted into a food bank and pre-school, and the rectory interior was restored.

Christ the King, Benton

Buchanan Valley
SAINT IGNATIUS LOYOLA

Situated on a scenic hillside in Buchanan Valley, Saint Ignatius Loyola began as "The Mountain Church." Although the early church records were destroyed by fire, the existence of a chapel is clearly remembered in tradition; along the mission trail from Conewago to Chambersburg, Jesuit missionaries celebrated Mass in a farmhouse owned by the Irwin family. When a modest church, built by parishioners in 1817, came under threat from a land dispute, Father Louis DeBarth secured the future of the parish by purchasing the land outright for the church in 1819.

For 90 years the church welcomed priests from Gettysburg, Conewago, and Chambersburg until it became an official parish with a resident priest in 1911. Today, the parish serves more than 150 families scattered over this mountain region. With the church structure still well-preserved, parishioners have added a rectory, cemetery, dining pavilion, and a picnic grove, a fitting setting for the annual church picnic, an event that has taken place for more than 165 years.

Camp Hill
GOOD SHEPHERD

In 1951 the parish of the Church of the Good Shepherd, Camp Hill, was formed from the western part of Saint Theresa Parish in New Cumberland. Father Thomas J. Simpson was appointed the first pastor. The new congregation celebrated its first Mass on May 31, 1951, in the home of parishioners Daniel and Genevieve Crowley. From 1951 until the first church was completed in 1953, weekend Masses were celebrated in The Hill Theatre on Market Street in Camp Hill. Initially, Sisters of Mercy from Saint Theresa Parish conducted religion classes on Sundays in the theater after Masses.

In 1952 ground was broken at Thirty-fourth and Market Streets in Camp Hill for construction of a church and school, and on September 13, 1953, the new edifice was dedicated. The same year the school opened, staffed by the Sisters, Servants of the Immaculate Heart of Mary, from Immaculata, Pennsylvania.. By the 1970s the congregation had grown so much that Masses had to be celebrated in the auditorium of Trinity High School, in addition to the Masses at the church. Eventually, the present church was constructed on Trindle Road and was dedicated on November 5, 1978.

1954

Fiftieth anniversaries were celebrated for the founding of the parish and the opening of the school in 2001 and 2003, respectively.

Saint Patrick, Carlisle

The historic parish of Saint Patrick dates from 1779, when Father Charles Sewall, S.J., from Conewago, bought a small lot in Carlisle for "the first foundation of Catholicity, west of the Susquehanna." The log chapel built there was replaced by a larger brick structure in 1806. Between 1835 and 1857, now Saint John Neumann visited Saint Patrick 12 times to administer the sacrament of confirmation.

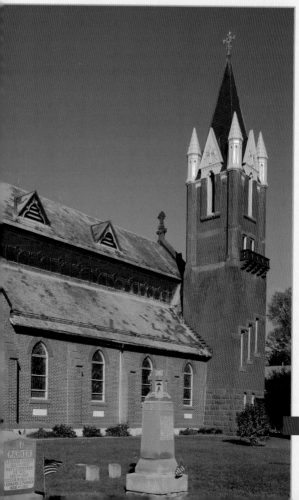

The brick chapel served the congregation until 1894, when a new building, designed and erected by Reverend Dr. Henry Ganss, was dedicated. Contributions by parishioners and now-Saint Katharine Drexel, who later established a mission school in Carlisle for Blacks and Indians, as well as proceeds from the musical and oratory talents of Father Ganss, enabled the church to be built debt free.

Fire damaged the church in 1923. Father Francis Welsh rebuilt it and started a school, staffed by the Sisters of Mercy. Today, this parish, the first in America to be named after Ireland's patron saint, is home for over 2,300 hundred families and provides a comprehensive education for 400 students each in Saint Patrick School and the CCD Program.

Interior of Saint Patrick Shrine Church

To accommodate vacationers at Pine Grove Furnace, the summer chapel of Saint Eleanor Regina was built in 1950, while Msgr. Joseph Schmidt was pastor of Carlisle. Its name was stipulated in a designated gift which aided in establishing the mission.

Exterior of Saint Patrick Shrine Church

Chambersburg
CORPUS CHRISTI PARISH

*D*uring the late 1700s, the Irish-born missionary Father Dennis Cahill, finding the people of Chambersburg "exemplary and pious," purchased a plot of land on which he built a log structure that he named Christ's Church. Beginning in 1795 Chambersburg was a mission of Conewago and was attended by the prestigious Russian prince, Father Demetrius Gallitzan. In 1812 a stone church, named Corpus Christi, was erected to serve the area's growing Catholic population, and in 1820 the parish welcomed its first pastor, Father Charles Kearns. Mass was celebrated in the 1812 church throughout the 19th century; in 1907 the present church was dedicated by Bishop John Shanahan.

Pupils began studying in the church basement in 1874, and through the years the parish school has prospered under the Sisters of Saint Joseph and now under lay teachers.

The parish has seen a number of its young women enter religious communities, and its young men, the priesthood, notably the Very Reverend John Hughes, the first Archbishop of New York. Corpus Christi Parish has founded a number of missions and parishes, including Waynesboro, Shippensburg and Greencastle.

Confirmation 1946

Coal Township
OUR LADY OF HOPE

*T*he parish communities of Saint Joseph and Saint Stephen merged in 1995, giving rise to Our Lady of Hope, a new parish that marked the beginning of a new era for Catholics in the western part of Shamokin, Pennsylvania. The former Saint Joseph church structure functions as the worship space, and the former Saint Stephen church has been converted to a parish center.

With more than 1,500 parishioners, Our Lady of Hope has built a reputation for its compassion and outreach to the needy. In addition to its array of outreach ministries, including, among others, a bereavement committee and prayer circles, the parish regularly earmarks ten percent of its income for the Mother Teresa Circle of Hope outreach, an initiative that began in 1998 to aid the needy, both locally and internationally.

1997

The tithe from this outreach supports a local food pantry, a sister church in Haiti, and Catholic Charities with monthly monetary donations. Parishioners aim to be witnesses to and bearers of hope.

Columbia
HOLY TRINITY

When German immigrants began flocking to Columbia between 1840 and 1860, and Saint Peter's, the first and only Catholic church in the area was overcrowded, then-Bishop of Philadelphia, Saint John Neumann, suggested the group erect their own. Planning began in 1856 with liturgies held in Saint Peter's basement and in private homes until 1860, when the Holy Trinity parish was formally established and the cornerstone of a new structure laid. Although completing the building proved to be a slow process, the dedicated group formed a school and invited Franciscan nuns to direct it. Within a decade, Holy Trinity grew into the largest parish in the community.

Annual Fastnacht Bake

The parish burgeoned and by 1924 needed a bigger church. To raise funds, the parish's Altar Rosary Society held its first Fastnacht Bake at the beginning of Lent, an event that in the ensuing 80-plus years evolved into an annual tradition and a major fundraiser attracting nearly 116 volunteers who mix, roll, fry, and sell the yeast-raised deep-fried potato pastries, an event that, now famous, draws local and even national media to the church.

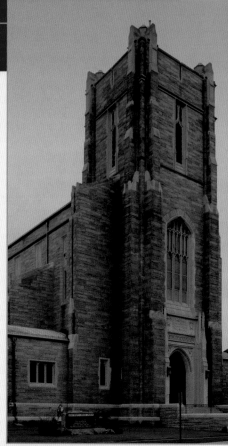

Cornwall
SACRED HEART OF JESUS

Sacred Heart of Jesus Parish, Cornwall, traces its beginning to 1848 when Bishop, now Saint, John Neumann granted permission for a mission station to be established near Colebrook. In 1852 a handful of Catholics, workers in the nearby ironworks, built a small chapel, named Saint Laurence. The priest from Saint Peter, Elizabethtown, ministered to the mission. When the ironworks closed in the early 1860s, the Catholic population dwindled and the chapel closed. As years passed, priests from Saint Mary's, Lebanon, ministered to the Catholics in the area.

Church in 1910, before it was moved to its present site

Finally, in 1886 Sacred Heart of Jesus was established as a parish, and a church was built along the old Cornwall-Lebanon Pike. Monsignor Adam Christ from Saint Mary's, Lebanon, oversaw the construction. Father Charles McMonigle, appointed in 1889, was the first resident pastor of the new parish. By 1914 the congregation wanted to see the church in a more-central location with room for expansion. As a result, the church was dismantled, moved piece by piece, and re-erected at its present location.

Through the years, adjacent parcels of land have been acquired, and new buildings as well as renovations have provided space and facilities for the congregation to grow and prosper. The most-recent major renovation was in 1997. Today the parish is home to over 500 families.

Saint Peter Church, Columbia

ounded in 1829 to minister to a dozen Catholic families, Saint Peter Church grew so fast that its original church structure had to be expanded by 1850. Rapid growth occurred into the 1880s, and parishioners were soon envisioning another expansion. More than 3,000 visitors came to celebrate the laying of the cornerstone of a new church in 1895.

For 177 years, Saint Peter, supported by the faith and dedication of its parishioners— now nearly 700 families strong— has continued the prodigious growth of its early days. The parish funds a Saint Vincent de Paul

Saint Peter Church, Columbia

outreach ministry to the area's needy, and its annual Lenten Friday Fish Fry boasts an army of volunteers who cook and serve full dinners, homemade soups, and sandwiches to the large number of patrons. Loretta Stone, 94, a life-long parishioner and volunteer, comments, "I practically lived at the church. I love going to church, hearing Mass. I used to clean and cook for the nuns and do whatever was needed at the church."

Catholic activity in the Wrightsville area began in 1871 when land was purchased for a school and cemetery. The school opened in 1874 with lay teachers but closed its doors several years later. The chapel of Our Mother of Holy Purity was constructed in 1903 and is administered from Saint Peter Parish, Columbia.

Our Mother of Holy Purity, Wrightsville

Dallastown
SAINT JOSEPH

The early settlers of the Dallastown area arrived from various provinces of Germany in the early part of the nineteenth century. The Catholics among them journeyed faithfully to York or New Freedom for the consolations of religion, for there is no record or tradition of visits of priests until the erection of the first church in 1853. The first priests who attended the parish were Redemptorists from Saint Alphonsus Church, Baltimore, and Jesuits from Conewago. Saint John Neumann conducted a canonical visitation in 1853 and returned for Confirmation in 1857. Later the parish was served by clergy from New Freedom and Saint Mary, York.

The first resident priest was Father Augustus Reudter. Bishop McDevitt dedicated the parish school in 1927, a further evidence of the staunch faith and sacrificial generosity of this small parish. The present church, dedicated in 1963, is a striking monument to the zealous interest, generosity and sacrifice of the parishioners, and, above all, to the glory of God.

Danville
SAINT JOSEPH PARISH

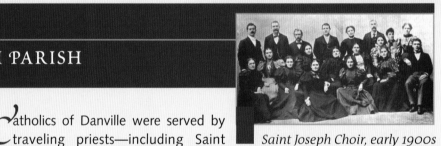

Saint Joseph Choir, early 1900s

Catholics of Danville were served by traveling priests—including Saint John Neumann— from 1806 until 1848, when the parish was officially established. The first church, built in 1848, served until the construction of the present building in 1868; the parish school, founded in 1890, expanded over the years, now educating children in grades 1 through 8.

Two additional parishes had been established in Montour County—Saint Hubert, Danville, to serve those of German descent, and Saint James, a mission parish in Exchange for outlying rural areas. These parishes were subsequently incorporated into Saint Joseph and have been commemorated in the Saint Hubert Chapel, added to the church in 1990, and the Saint James annex, added to the school in 2003.

A tithing parish, Saint Joseph established "Tithe the Tithe" in 2000. Through this program, its 1,269 families regularly support local, national and international outreach efforts. In 2004 alone the parish contributed $36,000 to a soup kitchen, a clothing and food distribution, and hospice care locally; to pro-life efforts and troubled adolescents on a national level; and toward a hospital in Africa, a mission to the poor in Jamaica, and a parish in Honduras on an international level.

The history of Saint Matthew, the Apostle and Evangelist, Dauphin, began in the 1700s when missionaries from Conewago and Lancaster visited the area. In the 1820s and continuing for almost a century, priests from Saint Patrick, Harrisburg, attended the mission station there. Through the years the mission had

First Mass, March 31, 1968

several names, including Stony Creek and, beginning in 1904, Saint Louis in Dauphin. Mass was celebrated in a rented storeroom and in private homes until 1912, when the number of Catholics in the area became too few to sustain the mission.

Finally, in 1955, with its numbers increased, Dauphin became a mission of Our Lady of the Blessed Sacrament, Harrisburg, and Mass was again celebrated at rented sites. In 1968 the building formerly used by the Dauphin Presbyterian Church was purchased for the growing congregation, which took the name Saint Matthew, the Apostle and Evangelist. Just eight years later the mission was raised to parish status, with Father Joseph Kelly, O. Praem., as the first pastor.

The new parish grew steadily and in the following years built a combined rectory, office, and classroom wing and, later, a parish center. In 2001 the parish celebrated its 25th anniversary and in this new century continues to grow and flourish.

Doylesburg
OUR LADY OF REFUGE

In 1790 a priest from Ireland, Father Dennis Cahill, celebrated Mass at the Timmons homestead in Amberson Valley, Franklin County, and organized a congregation there and at the Doyle homestead in Path Valley. The two groups communicated by walking "The Catholic Path" over Concocheague Mountain. The

Doyles built a log church in 1802 in their family graveyard, which they deeded to the Diocese of Philadelphia in 1815. The congregation replaced it in 1852 with the present brick church. It has been a mission of nine larger parishes and is now a mission of Corpus Christi, Chamberburg.

One hundred people in 39 households in four counties constitute membership, held together by their devotion to the Mass. Very few parochial activities are possible, but the people, like leaven, strive to influence many secular organizations and to live in harmony with the 99 percent of the population who are not Catholic. For several years the congregation has distributed tons of free baked goods to nursing homes and, through other churches, to the poor. "The works of religion" are carried out by strong families rather than by committee and ministries.

Elizabethtown
SAINT PETER

Historic Saint Peter Church, 1799

*I*n 1752 the first Mass for what would become Saint Peter Parish, Elizabethtown, was celebrated by Jesuit missionary Father Ferdinand Farmer at the farm of Henry Eckenroth a mile east of Elizabethtown. In the 1860s Eckenroth constructed a log chapel on his property. Known as the "Donegal Mission," this site was visited regularly by missionaries from Saint Mary's, Lancaster.

In 1799, the mission congregation laid the cornerstone for Saint Peter Church in Elizabethtown. In 1840 Saint Peter's became a parish with Father Francis Marshall as its first pastor.

Interior, Historic Saint Peter Church

The school, which currently includes K-3 through grade 5, opened in 1956, staffed initially by the Sisters, Servants of the Immaculate Heart of Mary, and now by a lay principal and faculty.

In the last quarter of the 1900s the parish experienced rapid growth and in 1998 broke ground for a new church just outside the town border. The new Saint Peter Church was blessed in September 1999. The now historic 1799 church continues in use for daily Mass and special liturgies. The parish, which celebrated its 250th anniversary in 2002, has grown from a single household in 1752 to almost 1,000 families.

New Saint Peter Church, 1999

Elysburg
QUEEN OF THE MOST HOLY ROSARY

Lenten fish dinners, 2000

*P*rior to 1950 the Catholics in the then-rural area of Elysburg traveled to the other nearby towns to attend Mass. On August 22, 1950, Queen of the Most Holy Rosary, Elysburg, the "church in the valley," was established as a parish with Father Thomas Eovacious as the first pastor. The home of Richard and Betty Fraily was purchased to serve as the rectory and temporary church until the church was completed. In 1951, on the Feast of Christ the King, the church and social center were dedicated. Sadly, the first funeral in the newly opened church was that of the first pastor, who died just four days after the dedication. Through the years the parish grew and additional land was purchased. Father Charles Slough became pastor in 1976, and in 1981 the thriving congregation, under his leadership, dedicated a new church and large social hall. The original church, renamed "Eovacious Education Building," was renovated to include a chapel for daily Mass and classrooms for Religious Education.

In the year 2000 the parish celebrated its 50th anniversary with a special Mass of celebration in its newly renovated church. Through the years of Father Slough's thirty years as pastor, the parish has grown to over 550 households.

Enola
OUR LADY OF LOURDES

The parish church of Enola is located only a few miles across the Susquehanna from the Cathedral, yet, for many years, it was literally a mission outpost of the faith. In the vast area to the north and west of Enola, there were scores of small towns lacking a Catholic church, the services of a priest and, in many instances, any known Catholics. The same conditions continue to some extent today.

The history of Catholicism in the area began about 1903 when Father F.M. Negroni, pastor of Saint Anne Church, Steelton, visited the area on a number of occasions to give pastoral care to the Italian Catholic workers employed at the Enola yards of the Pennsylvania Railroad. Mass was later celebrated on occasion by priests of the Cathedral.

In 1925 the Dominican Nuns of the Perpetual Rosary established a cloistered monastery in Enola. The priests of the Cathedral provided religious services, and Catholics of the area were invited to attend Mass in the chapel.

The monastery was badly damaged by fire in 1952, so a new property was purchased on the Lititz pike near Lancaster, and the Sisters moved from Enola on January 22, 1953.

Father Francis Dinkel was appointed administrator in 1938 and was the first resident priest in the parish. In 1980 a new church was built, adding to the growing parish complex.

Ephrata
OUR MOTHER OF PERPETUAL HELP

1998

The Redemptorists purchased the 80 acre Clare Point Farm in Ephrata on August 6, 1914. It was prime property. They took over the seller's home, the Willson Mansion, and celebrated their first public Mass in the Mansion, having hastily converted the dining room into a chapel. Thirteen people attended. The dining room served as the area's first Catholic Church from 1914-1925.

In 1925, the Redemptorist moved into the newly built Mission House opposite the mansion, and used its chapel as parish church from 1926-1940.

In May 1940, ground was broken for a church dedicated to Our Mother of Perpetual Help on the corner of Church and Pine Streets. Its seating capacity was 200, adequate at the time. In 1956, the school was built, and opened in 1957, staffed by the Bernardine Sisters, a group noted as quality educators.

With significant growth in the area, the church, having served so well for many years was now too small and Sunday Masses had to be celebrated in the gymnasium. A snow storm in 1993 caused the roof of the gym to collapse. The disaster provided the opportune moment for a new church. Construction began almost immediately and the building was consecrated on December 8, 1995.

Today, OMPH consists of more than 1500 families, with 300 children in its school and 390 children in its Religious Ed Program. The parish has 25 outreach ministries that include evangelization programs like RCIA and Alpha; Scripture Studies; a Benevolent Society; an active K of C; a Youth Group; a Bereavement Support Group and several athletic programs.

Presently, there are two Redemptorists assigned to the parish who receive steady assistance from three others for all parish activities.

Immaculate Conception of the Blessed Virgin Mary, Fairfield

1966

*I*mmaculate Conception of the Blessed Virgin Mary, "Saint Mary's," of Fairfield traces it beginning to the early years of the 1800s when Catholics in Millerstown, the original name of Fairfield, were under the pastoral care of priests from Saint Joseph in Emmitsburg, Maryland. Beginning in the 1850s priests from Conewago, Gettysburg, and Waynesboro, as well as from Mount Saint Mary's Seminary, tended the mission there. The cornerstone for a church was laid in 1852, and Saint John Neumann (then Bishop) confirmed 29 on a visit there in 1855.

The first permanent pastor arrived in 1910, and in 1914 a new rectory was constructed and the cemetery was relocated. Parishioners painstakingly moved the dead, one by one, by wagon to the new burial site.

In 1920 the church of Saint Rita in Blue Ridge Summit was founded and shares a pastor with Immaculate Conception in Fairfield. It has considerable importance because of its strategic proximity to Camp David, Maryland, the "Summer White House" of the U.S. President.

In these early years the parish began the tradition of holding a summer picnic, a yearly event that continued until World War II, when gas shortages and a ban on pleasure driving forced it to be cancelled.

Missionaries of the Sacred Hearts of Jesus and Mary assumed charge of the parish in 1993, and the present church was dedicated in 2000.

Original Saint Rita Chapel

Saint Rita, Blue Ridge Summit

Gettysburg
SAINT FRANCIS XAVIER

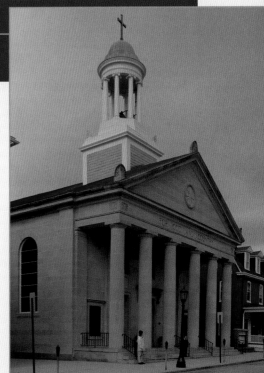

*ather Matthew Lakieu, S.J., established Saint Francis Xavier Parish in 1831 to serve Gettysburg's German immigrants. It flourished, requiring a larger church, built just 20 years later and dedicated by the Right Reverend John Neuman. Parishioners met the first of many challenges during the Civil War years when the Battle of Gettysburg pressed larger buildings in the area to serve as field hospitals. Saint Francis shut its doors to parishioners in July 1863 so that severely wounded soldiers could be treated there. Masses were celebrated in homes until they resumed at the church in January 1864.

During a period known as "the quiet years" after the Civil War, the parish added a rectory and a cemetery, and opened Gettysburg's first Catholic school, served first by the Sisters of Charity and now by the Sisters

of Mercy. After an 1894 fire damaged the church, parishioners remolded and expanded the facility. During World War I the parish again housed soldiers, this time suffering from the flu epidemic. In 1920 the first structure in the diocese built expressly for convent purposes of the Sisters of Mercy was built in Gettysburg.

Today, Saint Francis is multi-cultural, serving its German roots and the community's growing Hispanic population.

Gettysburg (Bonneauville)
SAINT JOSEPH THE WORKER

*atholics around Gettysburg date back to 1806 when worshippers traveled to Conewago, Gettysburg, or Littlestown for services. In 1859 Father Basil Shorb accepted a donation of land from his brother for a church in Bonneauville, just five miles outside of Gettysburg. The same year then-Bishop Neumann laid the cornerstone for Saint Joseph the Worker church; the church was dedicated and the first Mass celebrated on February 26, 1860.

Parishioner John McMasters donated land for a school that opened in 1873, and for more than 100 years, several communities of nuns directed it, among them, the Sisters of Charity of Mount Saint Vincent, the Sisters, Servants of the Immaculate Heart of Mary, and the Sisters of Saint Joseph of Chestnut Hill. The parish joined several other local churches in 1939 to establish Delone Catholic High School. Although the parish school closed in 1981, the Sisters of Saint Joseph of Chestnut Hill continue to educate parish children at area Catholic schools.

In addition to an annual church picnic and golf tournament, the parish holds fundraisers and special collections to honor the charities of Pope Benedict XVI. The church will celebrate its 150th anniversary in 2009.

*F*ather Thomas Johnson celebrated the first Mass in Greencastle in 1946 in the community room at a Citizen's National Bank. The 12 original Catholic families moved their worship space first to a Protestant-owned funeral home and then to the dining room at the McLaughlin Hotel. In 1960, the congregation of about fifty families purchased a home and transformed the first floor into a chapel and the second into an income-producing rental apartment. Proceeds form numerous bake sales and chicken dinners supported this first permanent worship site. Bishop Leech dedicated and consecrated Saint Mark's on August 18, 1965; parish status was granted in 1968.

Saint Mark the Evangelist, Ground breaking for the parish center, 1977.

The parish now boasts a larger church structure, a Catechetical school, and an active women's council involved in an array of outreach programs to help the needy and homebound and to serve the community. In 1995 Bishop Dattilo designated the administration and responsibility of Saint Luke the Evangelist Mission, formerly attached to Corpus Christi, Chambersburg, to Saint Mark's.

In 1967 Mr. and Mrs. Frank Gayman donated land for construction of a worship site in Mercersburg, and the next year Bishop Leech dedicated Saint Luke the Evangelist Mission church. Today, the mission counts about 92 families, who have developed a home-based religious education program for their children. With the area's recent developments, the mission is poised to grow within the next several years.

Saint Mark the Evangelist, Greencastle

Saint Luke the Evangelist, Mercersburg

The eminent York historian, Anna Dill Gamble, says there is reason to believe that English Jesuits established a mission post in the Conewago region as early as 1637. Father Joseph Greaton, S.J., the first priest whose name we know, attended the early Catholic settlers there. He arrived in Maryland in 1719 and was assigned to the mission territory of Northern Maryland and Southern Pennsylvania.

Conewago Chapel was a combination log dwelling and chapel built in 1741 by Father William Wappler, S.J., a priest sent to minister to the German Catholic immigrants who began to settle there in the 1730s. Father James Pellentz, S.J., who arrived in 1758, served as pastor there. A man of vision and ability, he was a close friend of John Carroll, America's first Bishop, and became his Vicar General in 1791.

By 1784 the Conewago congregation had grown to over a thousand members, the largest Catholic parish in early America. With the active help of parishioners, a new church, the largest Catholic church structure within the new nation, was started in 1785 and completed in 1787. The Sacred Heart of Jesus is the name Father Pellentz gave this imposing edifice. It became the first church in America dedicated to the Sacred Heart and probably the first parish church in the Western Hemisphere bearing this title. Today, it is the oldest Catholic church building in the United States built of stone.

The Russian prince, Demetrius Galitzin, spent his early years in the priesthood at Conewago. In 1799 he set out to evangelize west of the Susquehanna and found the Catholic settlement of Loretto, Pennsylvania, where he became known as "the Apostle of the Alleghenies."

The talented Father Louis de Barth, son of a German count, became pastor at Conewago in 1804. From 1814 to 1820 he was administrator of the vacant Philadelphia diocese and twice declined to become its bishop.

Conewago is the Mother Church of Pennsylvania west of the Susquehanna. It has given to the clergy dozens of its young men, including Monsignor John Timon, Bishop of Buffalo, and to many religious communities a large representation of its young women.

Pope John XXIII raised this church to the rank of a minor basilica on July 11, 1962, numbering it among the great churches of the world.

Hanover
SAINT JOSEPH

Hanover's Catholics traveled to Conewago chapel for services until 1785, when Father James Pellentz and six trustees purchased land for a worship space. Masses were celebrated in this space and in private homes until 1865, when a former Protestant church was purchased. In 1880 the first resident pastor, Father John Emig, S.J., built and dedicated a new Saint Joseph church.

A new parish school, built in 1950 to replace the old school established in 1873, has served the children's educational and religious needs, and from 1963 until 1975 Mass was celebrated in the school auditorium due to the church building's structural damage. A new church was completed in 1975 for the 7,000 parishioners.

The Monsignor Gribbin Parish Center, completed in 1996, houses a gymnasium, social hall, meeting rooms, and classrooms for the school of religious instruction and for the middle school. A new parish administrative center-priests' residence was dedicated in 2001. Established in 2004 and staffed by volunteers, a thrift shop was opened in the former rectory.

Just a few of the many parish organizations include the Caring Visitors Support Group, whose purpose is to meet the needs of concerned caregivers and their families; Council of Catholic Women; the Holy Name Society; and Pro-Life Committee.

The Baptistery with Tree of Life, 1975

Hanover
SAINT VINCENT DE PAUL

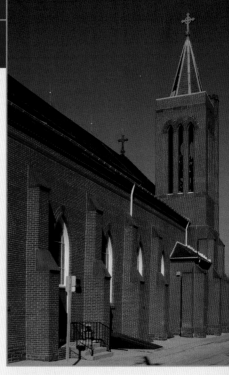

A century ago, Vincent O'Bold, a wealthy banker who lived in Hanover and worshipped at Conewago Chapel, dreamed of building a church. Upon his death, his sister, Gabriella O'Bold Smith, made his wish a reality. With their generous donation, Bishop John Shanahan sanctioned the construction of a church to be named Saint Vincent de Paul, honoring the saint and the church's benefactor. Dedicated in 1905, it had the honor of being consecrated, a unique ceremony done only when a church is debt free.

In 1924 parishioners opened a school that educated 200 pupils yearly. Donations from Mrs. Smith's estate funded the construction in 1925 of an adjoining convent for use by the Sisters of Saint Joseph, who staffed the school until 1988. Over the years the church has undergone three major renovations, added a rectory and auditorium/gymnasium, and purchased forty acres for a cemetery. The former convent houses a Thrift Shop, staffed by volunteers. In 2005 the church celebrated its 100th anniversary.

CATHEDRAL PARISH OF SAINT PATRICK

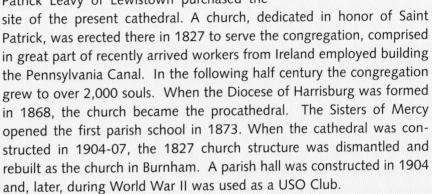

Missionaries from Conewago and Saint Mary's, Lancaster, visited Harrisburg in the 1700s and early 1800s. In 1824, Father Patrick Leavy of Lewistown purchased the site of the present cathedral. A church, dedicated in honor of Saint Patrick, was erected there in 1827 to serve the congregation, comprised in great part of recently arrived workers from Ireland employed building the Pennsylvania Canal. In the following half century the congregation grew to over 2,000 souls. When the Diocese of Harrisburg was formed in 1868, the church became the procathedral. The Sisters of Mercy opened the first parish school in 1873. When the cathedral was constructed in 1904-07, the 1827 church structure was dismantled and rebuilt as the church in Burnham. A parish hall was constructed in 1904 and, later, during World War II was used as a USO Club.

The parish of Saint Lawrence was founded in 1859 for the German-speaking Catholics of the Harrisburg area, and in 1901 Sacred Heart of Jesus parish was founded in the southern section of the city.

The Cathedral Parish of Saint Patrick was established in 1995 upon the merger of Sacred Heart of Jesus and Saint Lawrence with the original Saint Patrick Cathedral parish. Saint Patrick Cathedral is the worship site for the congregation, with the Saint Lawrence church building now serving as the cathedral chapel. The school is now an inter-parochial school used by the Cathedral, Enola, and Marysville parishes.

First Communion Mass at Saint Lawrence Chapel 1996

Watercolor by Nick Ruggieri, 1971

Statue of saint Patrick above the center door to the Cathedral

Holy Family, the sixth parish established in Harrisburg, evolved from the post-war resurgence in religious life. Even as suburban living took hold, the baby-boomer generation turned to spiritual enrichment, overcrowding city parishes. In response, Bishop Leech formed a new school and parish, reassigning over 1,000 parishioners from Saint Francis and Saint Catherine Laboure parishes. Father Frederick Bradel celebrated the first Mass at Bishop McDevitt High School in 1958.

The church building, blessed in 1959, also houses the parish school, attended by The Sisters, Servants of the Immaculate Heart of Mary, of Philadelphia. When Hurricane Agnes struck in 1972, parishioners donated money, clothing, and food to those devastated by severe flooding in the city. That summer, parishioners held the first parish festival, three nights of games, food and entertainment to support community outreach ministries.

1985

In the 1990s the parish added a wing housing a social hall, kitchen, classroom, meeting room, and library. Through its fundraising efforts, the parish supports many outreach groups such as the Legion of May. In the new millennium this vibrant parish, rich in spiritual life, continues to grow and prosper.

1962

To accommodate the steadily growing Catholic population in Harrisburg, Bishop Leech established Holy Name of Jesus Parish in 1960. Located in Lower Paxton Township, the new parish welcomed the first resident pastor, Father George Rost, who over the next eight years built a church building, social hall, and convent and purchased land for a rectory.

Eight Sisters of Saint Joseph of Chestnut Hill arrived in 1961 to open the doors of the parish school. Father Daniel Mahoney, pastor from 1968 until 2002, continued church expansion with a gymnasium, an education center, and rectory. Monsignor Robert Lawrence became pastor in 2002 and furthers the priestly ministry within the church, celebrating Sacraments, visiting the sick and dying, and distinguishing himself as a gifted administrator.

To generate funds for the church, parishioners host an annual summer festival, and every Christmas the congregation holds "The Giveaway," collecting gifts and food to aid needy families within the community. The parish now serves 3,400 families, and the school educates over 500 children from kindergarten through eighth grade.

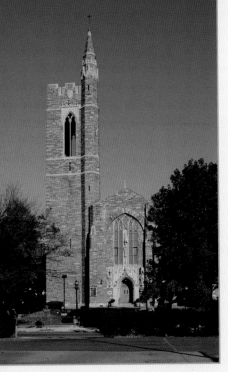

Our Lady of the Blessed Sacrament Parish began as a mission in 1900, attended by the Cathedral. Parish children attended school at Saint Genevieve's Convent until Bishop Shanahan approved the construction of a church and school in 1907. Parish membership grew rapidly, and construction of a new church structure began in 1929, coinciding with the Great Depression. The project, which exceeded a half million dollars, faltered because many of the donors could not fulfill their payments, leaving the church in debt for decades.

Set three blocks from the Susquehanna River, the parish suffered heavy losses due to the flooding of Hurricane Agnes in 1972, with 500 of the parish's 700 families affected. During the 1970s the size of the congregation lessened as many parishioners moved to the suburbs. The school closed in 1987, and students from the parish now attend the neighboring Saint Margaret Mary and the Cathedral Consolidated schools.

This resolute church currently counts 556 registered families, comprising a multi-racial and multi-socioeconomic congregation who attend Masses celebrated in English and Vietnamese.

Harrisburg
SAINT CATHERINE LABOURE PARISH

When the rapidly growing population of Saint Francis of Assisi Parish overburdened that church, Bishop Leech established Saint Catherine Laboure Parish—the first in the world dedicated to this saint—in 1948. The congregation's first Masses were celebrated at the Paxtang Municipal Auditorium. Plans for the construction of a temporary church building began immediately, and the first Mass was celebrated on Christmas Day 1948 in the partially completed structure.

Five Daughters of Charity arrived in 1949 to manage the parish school. By the time the nuns moved into a new convent in 1955, two hundred pupils had been enrolled in the school. Two decades later, the Sisters of Saints Cyril and Methodius assumed responsibility for the school and continue to operate it today. A permanent church replaced the temporary one in 1976, and parishioners also built a large parish center and expanded the school building to meet the needs of this growing parish, which today has more than 5,000 weekly worshippers.

An Illustrated History of the Diocese of Harrisburg

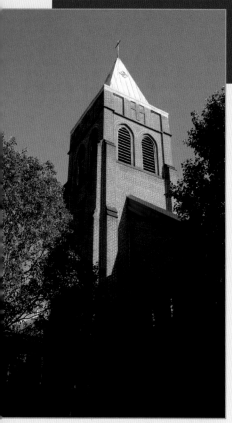

Bishop John W. Shanahan founded Saint Francis of Assisi in 1901 in Harrisburg's Allison Hill section; the church was dedicated in 1902. A fire in 1905 nearly destroyed it, but the parish rebounded and rededicated a refurbished church in 1906. The parish grew at such an astounding rate that by 1948, it became the Mother Church to Saint Catherine Laboure and Saint Margaret Mary. Saint Francis's more than 4,000 weekly worshippers prompted the Diocese to redraw parish boundaries, canonically erecting Holy Family Parish from parts of Saint Francis and Saint Catherine in 1958.

The parish school closed in 1988. In 2001, The Nativity School, a private, preparatory middle school for low-income boys, opened in the former school building. The parish has operated a soup kitchen since 1981 and participates in an array of social justice ministries, including The Joshua House, a resource center for inner city boys; The Silence of Mary Home, providing interim housing for teenagers/young adults; and The Catholic Worker House. Also, Saint Francis is the Hispanic Apostolate for Harrisburg. For the first time in its history, Saint Francis is under the pastoral care of Capuchin Franciscans from the Saint Augustine Friary in Pittsburgh, who arrived in July 2005.

Living Stations of the Cross

In 1948 Bishop George Leech drew parishioners from the overflowing church of Saint Francis of Assisi to form Saint Margaret Mary Alacoque Parish for the 800 Catholics living east of the city of Harrisburg. Initially, Sunday Masses were celebrated in Camplese's automobile show room, which also provided a temporary office for the new parish, and weekday Masses were celebrated in a private home. Eager parishioners worked hard to build a new parish and its support systems for the Catholics of this area. Ground was broken for a church, school, and cafeteria-social hall.

In 1949 the church was dedicated, and the school, under the School Sisters of Notre Dame, opened. The sisters staffed the school through 1985. From 1970 to 1995 the parish was under the care of the Oblates of Mary Immaculate.

Today more than 1400 families comprise this faith community. Parish ministries and activities give witness to the spirituality which draws new members and nourishes long-time members. Priority areas include: education, evangelization, pastoral care, liturgy, social justice and ecumenism. Significant growth and blessings have led to plans to build a new church in the near future.

Hershey
SAINT JOAN OF ARC

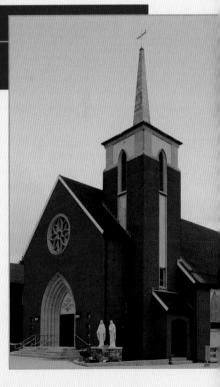

*W*hen Hershey and its Catholic population burgeoned in 1913, Mass was celebrated first at Saint Lucy's Chapel in Waltonville and then at Saint John the Evangelist mission. The congregation had grown by 1918 to more than 130, and a need for a church became evident. Milton S. Hershey donated land in 1920 for this purpose. After a groundbreaking the same year, a church was built on Chocolate Avenue to accommodate the congregation of about 300. Dedicated in May 1922 and named for Saint Joan of Arc, the new church featured a beautiful bell, also donated by Hershey to honor his late wife, Catherine.

Sisters from the Daughters of Our Lady of Mercy, frequent visitors to the Hershey area, accepted an invitation to oversee religious education for the parish and opened a school in 1927. The present church was constructed in 1962. In the ensuing years the parish added a parish office, a new and larger school building, and a gymnasium. The growing church celebrated its 85th anniversary in 2005 with a congregation of nearly 2,000 families, who participate in a wide offering of outreach ministries.

Kulpmont
HOLY ANGELS

*A*t the beginning of the 20th century, the Scott Colliery drew immigrants of many nationalities to Kulpmont. This small town, about midway between Mount Carmel and Shamokin, was a cosmopolitan metropolis. Among the immigrants were 150 Hungarian Catholic families, who built a church where they and their children could hear the word of God in their own language. As people of other backgrounds attended this church, unrest arose because of the language problem. There was great confusion until 1920 when Rev. Dr. Joseph J.C. Petrovits, a priest of the diocese, resigned his post on the faculty of the Catholic University in Washington to assume the pastorate of Kulpmont.

Catholics of Polish background came in large numbers to Kulpmont in about 1907. Father Vincent Wojno was appointed the first pastor of Saint Casimir Parish in 1915. The good people of this sturdy parish made a substantial contribution to the community and to the diocese. The Holy Ghost Fathers first served Catholics in the Marion Heights area from Our Mother of Consolation Parish in Mount Carmel. Mass was first offered in 1904. The mission cared for the Polish, Slovak, Italian and English speaking Catholics in the area. In 1906 a church was dedicated in honor of Our Lady of Perpetual Help with Father Leonard Baluta as first pastor. All three of these parishes maintained parochial schools until dwindling student populations forced them to merge.

In July 1995 these three parishes were combined into Holy Angels Parish, with Saint Mary Church as the worship site.

*F*ounded by Jesuit missionaries in 1741, Assumption of the Blessed Virgin Mary in Lancaster, or "Historic Saint Mary's," is the second oldest place of public Catholic worship in what is now the diocese of Harrisburg, preceded only by the "Conewago Mission" (now the Basilica of the Sacred Heart) outside of Hanover. In the colonial period, besides serving the Catholic population of Lancaster, missionaries from Saint Mary's traveled to mission stations in Lancaster, Lebanon, and western Chester counties.

A log chapel, called the "mission of Saint John Nepomucene," was built in 1742 but was destroyed by arson in 1760, a victim of the strong anti-Catholic sentiment fomented by the French and Indian War. Sadly, the sacramental and historical records of the missionaries were destroyed along with the building.

The congregation responded to the fire by building a stone church, named Assumption of the Blessed Virgin Mary, which served the congregation for 120 years. Through the colonial period and into the first half of the 1800s, the Catholic population, primarily a mix of German and Irish heritage, grew steadily. In 1849 a second Catholic church in Lancaster, Saint Joseph, was founded for the German Catholics, and Saint Mary's remained the church for the Irish Catholics. In 1852, a new Saint Mary's church was built adjacent to the old one, which remained in use as a hall until 1881.

In the 1880s and 1890s extensive renovation and expansion took place, giving the church its present appearance. A school, staffed originally by the Sisters of Charity from New Jersey, opened in 1886. The Sisters of Mercy came in the 1920s and continued to educate the children of the parish until the late 1980s. Saint Mary was one of three parochial schools of Lancaster merged into Resurrection Catholic School in the early 1990s.

Through the years the church and other buildings underwent a series of renovations and additions, and the congregation flourished. Included among the long list of pastors shepherding this historic parish are Father Bernard Keenan, a member of Lancaster's first school board and a trustee of Franklin and Marshall College; Father Peter J. McCullagh, who was responsible for nearly all of the fine works of art that grace Saint Mary's today; Father Henry Ganss, known worldwide as a composer of hymns and Masses; and Father Thomas Crotty, a Columbia native who established Saint Mary's high school, a forerunner of Lancaster Catholic High School.

In 1991 this history-rich congregation marked its 250th anniversary with a year-long celebration that included spiritual, social, and historical festivities. In the new millennium Saint Mary's continues its long tradition begun in the humble log chapel where its first generation of parishioners gathered in worship.

SACRED HEART OF JESUS

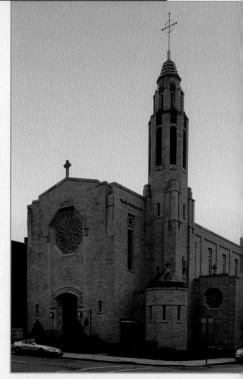

Near the end of the 19th century, the need for an additional Catholic church on the west side of Lancaster was apparent. On November 20, 1900, Bishop John Shanahan appointed Father Clement Berger as pastor, and the first Mass was celebrated on November 25, 1900 in the chapel of Saint Joseph Hospital. On December 3, Bishop Shanahan gave the name "Sacred Heart of Jesus" to the new parish.

Property was purchased on the corner of Nevin and West Walnut Streets, and ground was broken for a church on April 19, 1901; the structure was dedicated on September 22, 1901. The current church, designed mainly by the fifth pastor, Father John Kealy, was dedicated by Bishop Leech on November 15, 1953. The main altar mural gives a synopsis of devotion to the Sacred Heart. The unique stained glass windows depict the patron saints of various professions of parishioners. Additional renovations were completed in 1997.

Sacred Heart of Jesus Parish continues to share the love of Christ with members and the local community through many organizations and activities, including the parochial school, a quarterly newsletter, monthly socials, semi-annual socials to welcome new members, a parish health ministry, a local food bank, participation in community meals for the needy, and various charitable drives.

SAINT ANNE

Saint Anne's became a parish in November 1923, after 200 Catholics in Lancaster presented a petition to Bishop Philip McDevitt for a church. That same month, parishioners purchased properties on North Duke Street for a chapel and a rectory. A year later, a school was opened with the help of three Sisters of Mercy, who came to teach 72 children. Though financially challenging, the debt was alleviated within five years, and plans to build a new church and auditorium were announced. The economic downturn of the Great Depression brought financial hardship; the debt for the new buildings proved so onerous that the pastor and

parishioners thought the parish could not continue. However, the Mission Board of the diocese provided a plan under which the parish was able to honor its obligations.

In 2002 the church interior was completely renovated, brightening the sanctuary and meeting all criteria of liturgical norms. The thriving church of more than 1,400 parishioners runs a unique brown-bag lunch program out of the rectory that daily feeds sixty to seventy people—anyone who comes to the door hungry.

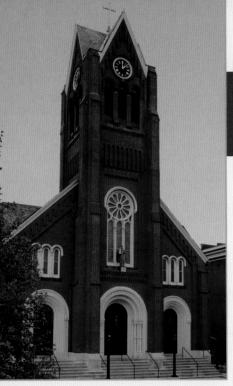

Lancaster
SAINT ANTHONY OF PADUA

Lyceum Group, 1912

On August 22, 1869, Father Anthony Kaul was the first priest ordained for the Diocese of Harrisburg. In 1870 he founded the parish of Saint Anthony of Padua to serve German immigrants in eastern Lancaster. Reverend Monsignor Kaul served as pastor for sixty-five years, the longest-known recorded term in the nation.

The church was completed and dedicated in 1877. In the early years, sermons at Masses were preached in High German, a practice discontinued after World War I. When Bishop McDevitt organized the Italian Mission of Lancaster in 1919, Monsignor Kaul provided the basement chapel for the regular celebration of Mass with the Italian immigrant community.served by Father Michael O'Flynn.

In 1974, Father Michael Vassallo was assigned the pastoral care of the Spanish-speaking Catholics, who used the lower level of the church to celebrate Holy Mass in Spanish. The practice continued until the founding of San Juan Bautista Catholic Center. Father Hoa Nguyen of the Diocese of Harrisburg has been celebrating Mass weekly in that same chapel in the Vietnamese language since 1986.

Today about 1,000 families participate in numerous outreach activities, especially in social justice ministry and by frequent visits to the elderly, the sick, and shut-ins, in their homes, hospitals, and local skilled-care facilities.

Church interior, 1895

Lancaster
SAINT JOHN NEUMANN

Youth ministry food collection

Dedicated in 1978, Saint John Neumann was established after Saint Anne Parish exceeded its capacity. Father John Acri was the founding pastor. Until the church was completed, Masses were celebrated at Lancaster Catholic High School and the Eden Theater. Although one of the newest parishes in Lancaster county, Saint John Neumann quickly became one of the largest. Under Father Patrick Devine, pastor from 1980 to 1994, the church structure was enlarged. Msgr. Richard Youtz, pastor since 1994, has assumed the pastoral duties of the mother parish of Saint Anne as well. With nearly 2,400 families, Saint John Neumann has expanded its ministries to include a thrift shop, food bank, and nursing ministry that enables a registered nurse to visit the elderly and shut-ins. More than 1,000 children are enrolled in religious education programs, and the active youth group continues to expand. The parish shares a school with Saint Anne's.

The parish's mission statement states, "We are a Catholic Community of disciples of Jesus Christ called to holiness and nourished by Word and Sacrament. Empowered by the Holy Spirit, we witness the kingdom of God in ourselves, in our community and in our world. We seek to accomplish this through these ministries: Liturgy and Worship, Faith Formation, Pastoral Care, Evangelization, Social Justice, Wellness, Stewardship, Fellowship and Community Life, Ecumenism, and Celebrating the Third millennium of Christianity."

Lancaster
SAINT JOSEPH

aint Joseph Parish, Lancaster, was established in 1849 for the German-speaking Catholics of Saint Mary Parish in Lancaster. The 200-member congregation was one of the first ethnic parishes in the United States. The church

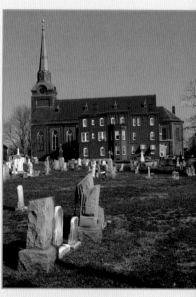

was built the next year. In the 1860s the first parochial school in Lancaster opened in the basement of the church, staffed initially by a lay teacher and then by the Franciscan Sisters from Glen Riddle, Pennsylvania. In the 1880s a new school and convent were constructed, and a new church was built, incorporating the existing church in its center. The parish continued to grow and in 1939 opened a new school, named Father Christ Memorial School, in memory of the parish's pastor of forty years.

In 1964 in response to the growth in the congregation, priests from Saint Joseph began to celebrate weekend Masses in the Manor Shopping Center auditorium for the faithful who would become Saint Philip the Apostle parish.

In 1995 with the merger of the Lancaster parochial schools, Saint Joseph school ended its 135-year history. The former convent is now used for CCD classes. Today Saint Joseph Parish continues to be faithful to its ethnic roots, serving the new immigrants and new cultures that have made their homes in the parish.

Lancaster (Rohrerstown)
SAINT LEO THE GREAT

parish with a long history of enthusiastic and dedicated volunteerism, devotion, and pride, Saint Leo the Great began as a mission of Lancaster's Sacred Heart of Jesus in 1963, and early Masses were celebrated in a rented barn (now affectionately known as the "Rustic Barn") until a worship space could be built. Members immediately formed the Men of Saint Leo and the Women of Saint Leo, two major fundraising groups still in existence today. They established a school, a convent, and a worship space, all by 1988.

In the 40 years since its inception, Saint Leo has grown from a small, dedicated parish to a thriving community 1,700 families strong. Still known for their enthusiasm, parishioners have founded a number of outreach ministries and social committees, including a Friendship Club that promotes physical, mental, and emotional health of those over age 50; the Love for Life outreach that educates parishioners about abortion alternatives; and an annual Mardi Gras celebration.

Christmas 1972

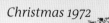

Lancaster (Millersville)
SAINT PHILIP THE APOSTLE

*E*ven before Saint Philip the Apostle Parish was founded in May 1965, dedicated Catholics attended Mass in the Manor Shopping Center Auditorium, a Mass instituted to accommodate the overflow of Lancaster's Saint Joseph and which attracted more than 1,000 worshipers. In 1965 the diocese purchased 18 acres at the intersection of Millersville Pike and Millersville Road as the future worship site for the congregation, and parishioners built the church, which was dedicated in 1968. Many parish organizations were formed in the early years of the parish, including the Men's Club, the Women's Auxiliary, the Legion of Mary, the Mothers' Group, and Guys and Dolls for senior citizens.

For 21 years, the parish's 1,000-plus families have hosted a free Thanksgiving dinner for everyone; an army of volunteers, both parishioners and non-parishioners, deliver food to shut-ins and transport those unable to drive to and from the family-style dinner that is served in the school gym. Parishioners, local businesses, and school students donate, prepare, and serve the meal, including desserts.

Lancaster
IGLESIA CATÓLICA SAN JUAN BAUTISTA

*N*amed for the patron saint of Puerto Rico, the homeland to the vast majority of Hispanics in Lancaster at its conception, Iglesia Católica San Juan Bautista now serves a great diversity of Hispanic ethnic groups in Lancaster County. Formal Hispanic ministry began with Bishop Daley, who invited the Vocationist Fathers in 1972 to Lancaster. From 1972 to 1982, the Vocationist priests directed the San Juan Bautista Center, using the lower church of Saint Anthony of Padua Parish for Mass, other liturgies, Bible study and community activities. Historic Saint Mary also responded to the needs of Hispanics. In 1961 Nuestra Señora de la Providencia Center was established, and the priests of Saint Mary provided a Sunday afternoon Mass and sacraments in Spanish, as well as other spiritual support to their Hispanic members.

Ministry to Hispanics in Lancaster was transformed tremendously during the pastorate of Vocationist Father Tomas Adinolfi by the purchase of their own church in 1982 (at their current location). Since 1982 the community of San Juan Bautista has steadily grown in numbers and ethnic composition. Marking this growth was its establishment by then-Bishop Keeler as a quasi-parish in 1988 with Father Bernardo Pistone as pastor and its full-fledged parish status by Bishop Dattilo in 2003 with Father Allan Wolfe as the first pastor of this first Hispanic parish in the diocese.

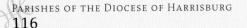

Assumption of the Blessed Virgin Mary, Lebanon

Assumption of the Blessed Virgin Mary , the mother church of Lebanon County, traces its roots to the 1700s, when Irish and German immigrants settled in the area. The first generation of missionaries in colonial America ministered to them at a mission site north of Lebanon. The first church in Lebanon was built in 1814, and Father Charles Kearns became the first pastor in 1823. A second church, built in the 1870s, was consecrated by Bishop Jeremiah Shanahan in 1880. This church was adorned with exquisite artifacts which were on display at the American Centennial Exhibition in Philadelphia.

As the Catholic population in Lebanon continued to grow, the other Lebanon parishes were formed from this mother parish: Saints Cyril and Methodius, Saint Gertrude, Saint Gregory, and Nuestra Senora de Gaudalupe. Our Lady of Fatima Mission, Jonestown, was established as a mission in 1953 to accommodate the Catholics of northern Lebanon County. A new chapel along busy Route 22 continues to serve locals and travelers alike.

The present third church was erected in 1974, incorporating many of the historic artifacts of the previous building.

A parish school was opened in 1859 and the present Lebanon Catholic School is the successor to this unbroken line of Catholic education in Lebanon County. The parish has also given such distinguished sons to the Church as William Cardinal Keeler, Bishop Kevin Rhoades, and Monsignor Damian McGovern.

OLD ST. MARY'S CHURCH

[28]

Our Lady of Fatima, Jonestown

Lebanon
SAINT BENEDICT THE ABBOT

On July 1, 1995, Saint Benedict the Abbot parish was established on the west end of Lebanon. It is composed of the former SS. Cyril and Methodius Slovak parish and Our Lady of Guadeloupe Hispanic parish. SS. Cyril and Methodius church, which was blessed in 1906, the oldest Catholic church in Lebanon city, was chosen as the worship site.

SS. Cyril and Methodius had been established after the Civil War, when the burgeoning steel industry in Lebanon County attracted many immigrants from Central and Eastern Europe.

The period after World War II began to attract many Hispanic-speaking peoples to the area. As a result, in the early 1970s, the Hispanic parish of Our Lady of Guadeloupe was established; a former Methodist church on Eighth Street was purchased for use as a worship site.

The jointure of these two congregations in 1995 brought into existence one of the diocese's successful multicultural parishes.

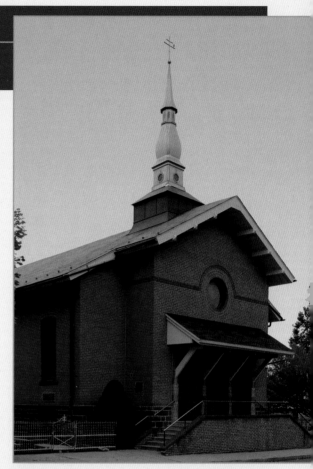

Lebanon
SAINT CECILIA

To combine resources within Lebanon's Catholic community, two parishes—Saint Gregory the Great and Saint Gertrude—merged in 1995. The newly formed parish, named Saint Cecilia, uses the former Saint Gertrude's church structure, dedicated in1907, as a worship space. A religious education building is attached to the church. Sisters of Saint Francis, who arrived at Saint Gertrude's in 1916, continue to serve the parish.

To raise funds, the 10-year-old parish hosts an annual fastnacht festival that attracts thousands from the greater Lebanon area. Parishioners make the fastnachts—German for donuts—24 hours a day, beginning the Sunday before Ash Wednesday until the Shrove Tuesday festival. This tradition recalls the long custom of using up all household cooking fat before the Lenten season begins. In this way, each year for three days, the parish—now numbering 1,600 families—honors the German, Austrian, and Eastern European immigrants who arrived in the early 1900s, worked in local steel mills, and planted the seeds of Catholicism in Lebanon.

The town of Lewisburg was laid out by Lewis Derr in 1785. There is a possibility that Derr was a Catholic for, in the original town plan, we find streets named Saint Anthony, Saint Mary, Saint John, Saint Louis, Saint Catherine and Saint George. On this same plan, lots at the corner of Saint John and Second Streets have written the words "Roman Chapple." I. H. Mauser in his 1886 centennial history of Lewisburg states that a chapel stood on this lot, "the first church along the West Branch of the Susquehanna."

Sacred Heart of Jesus, Lewisburg

On December 20, 1788, the entire town of Lewisburg was sold to Carroll Ellenckhuysen, a Catholic merchant from Holland. In 1790 a priest, Father John Heilborn, became the agent and owner for the sale of lots. There has always been a faithful group of Catholics in Lewisburg. Bishop Leech dedicated the present church on November 11, 1935, the day of Bishop McDevitt's death.

Since then, the church has been expanded; a viable campus ministry has been conducted at Buckell University, and Saint George mission in Mifflinburg was established in 1999.

Statue of Saint George

1937

Saint George, Mifflinburg

Lewistown
SACRED HEART OF JESUS

1964

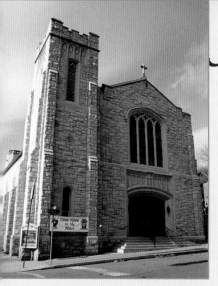

As early as the 1750s Catholics were settled in the area surrounding what is now Sacred Heart of Jesus in Lewistown. However, it was not until 1830 that a wooden chapel, named All Saints, was constructed. With the growth in the Catholic population in the post-Civil War years, the mission was raised to parish status in 1871. A brick church, given the name Sacred Heart of Jesus, was constructed, and Father John Pape served as the first resident pastor. Through the years Sacred Heart has remained the only Catholic parish in Mifflin County. The current church, the first church in the area to be built of native sandstone, was constructed in 1921.

The church community continued to grow. In 1948 a school opened, and in 1956 priests from Sacred Heart began celebrating Mass in Mifflintown. On April 5, 1959, Bishop Leech solemnly blessed this first Catholic church in Juniata County, placing it under the patronage of Saint Jude Thaddeus. The church continues to be served from the Lewistown parish.

In 1964, after extensive renovation, Sacred Heart church was rededicated. In the second half of the century the parish saw the establishment of many ministries reflecting the changes of Vatican II. Renovations to the church were made again in 1988 and in the opening years of the new century.

In 2005 the congregation marked the milestone of its 175th anniversary with a year-long celebration that included an anniversary Mass celebrated by Bishop Rhoades and a youth pilgrimage to Rome led by Father John Bateman, pastor.

Mifflintown
SAINT JUDE THADDEUS

Saint Jude Thaddeus Parish began through a small and devout group who lived in Juniata County in the 1950s. These Catholics united to face the challenges of practicing their faith in a rural county where there was strong religious prejudice. In 1956 priests from Sacred Heart Church in Lewistown began celebrating Mass in the Odd Fellow's Hall in Mifflintown. Land was purchased and a church was soon under construction. On April 5, 1959, Bishop Leech blessed the first (and still the only) Catholic Church in Juniata County under the patronage of Saint Jude Thaddeus.

The church remained a mission of Sacred Heart in Lewistown until October 21, 1965, when it was declared a parish and was placed under the care of the Glenmary Fathers. When the Glenmary Fathers relinquished charge of the parish, the Oblates of Saint Francis DeSales took up the challenge. Upon the death of Father Thomas Rush in 1988, Saint Jude, once again, became dependant upon Sacred Heart in Lewistown to provide a priest for their faith community. Much of the parish responsibility was given to Deacon John Rocco, who served the parish until his death in 2002.

Entering the 21st Century, the parish now has over 165 families, a significant Hispanic population, and a weekly bi-lingual Mass. There are plans for the further expansion of the facilities, including a new church to seat 400, social hall area, and classrooms for religious education.

Lititz
SAINT JAMES

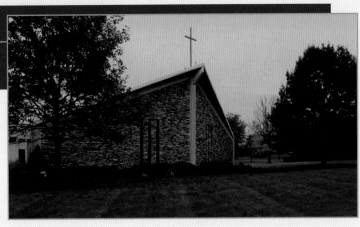

The development of Saint James Parish began in 1914 when the Redemptorist Congregation established Saint Clement Mission in Ephrata. Bishop John Shanahan gave the 12 townships of northern Lancaster County into the pastoral care of the Redemptorists. Redemptorist Father William White searched the countryside seeking Catholics in the Lititz area, who had to travel to Lancaster for Sunday Mass.

The Lititz mission rented a small storefront room for Sunday Mass until November 1919, when Saint James Evangelical Lutheran Church at Front and Water Streets was offered for sale and purchased in the name of the Redemptorist Fathers. The first High Mass was celebrated at that location on August 1, 1920.

Saint James mission grew, and in 1977 Bishop Joseph Daley granted it parish status. The first Mass at the new Saint James Church, Woodcrest Avenue, Lititz, was celebrated on July 2, 1978. A parish center and education facilities were added to serve the growing community, which now consists of approximately 1,100 families.

The Social Justice Network of Saint James Church shares in the feeding and caring for the needy in and around Lititz, as well as in missions in South Africa, and ministers most notably through its work with Habitat for Humanity, A Woman's Concern, Pro-Life, Beads of Peace, and Bread for the World.

Littlestown
SAINT ALOYSIUS

1962

Saint Aloysius Parish, Littlestown, traces its roots to the earliest colonial days when Jesuit missionaries first visited the Conewago Valley. Mass was celebrated in Mass houses until 1791, when a hotel in the town, then called Petersburg, was purchased and remodeled for use as a church, named in honor of Saint Aloysius Gonzago, the Patron of Christian Youth. In those early years Saint Aloysius was attached as a mission to Sacred Heart, Conewago.

In 1842 Saint Aloysius became a parish and a new church was completed; in 1867 a school was established. The present church was built in 1892 under the direction of the first resident pastor, Father Thomas Crotty. In 1962 the church was renovated to restore and modernize the sanctuary. In the late 1960s the school closed, and by 1971 the school building was transformed into a multi-purpose center for religious education and the varied activities of the active congregation.

In 2002 the church underwent another major restoration. Through the years the congregation has seen an admirable number of vocations to the religious life and the priesthood. Today Saint Aloysius includes long-established families and newcomers alike, all contributing to the religious vitality of the congregation.

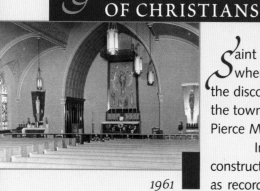

1961

Saint Patrick (later the Cathedral) was the only other parish in Dauphin County when Our Lady Help of Christians was established in Lykens in 1853. After the discovery of coal in the Valley in 1825, mining became the leading industry in the town. The development of the mines brought a great influx of people. Father Pierce Maher traveled from Saint Patrick to serve the Catholics among them.

In 1852 Father Sylvester Eagle became the first pastor and began the construction of the stone church. Saint John Neumann probably blessed this church, as records show that he baptized six children there on September 11, 1853. All Catholics in the Lykens Valley attended this church.

On May 17, 1896, Bishop Thomas McGovern dedicated the new (present) church. At that time the parish numbered 120 families. In 1906 the Sisters of Mercy opened a parochial school. The educational system of the parish developed to include a four-year high school, quite an undertaking for such a small congregation.

First graduation class, 1909

On August 22, 1875, Bishop Jeremiah Shanahan laid the cornerstone for Sacred Heart of Jesus in Williamstown. It was attended by the priest from Lykens until Father Charles Kenny was appointed its first pastor in 1887.

In 1905 the Sisters of Mercy opened a parish school in Williamstown. One can see the value placed on education by these industrious people, as a high school also was opened in Sacred Heart Parish. The two high schools were subsequently combined in the Williamstown building until it closed in 1967.

The decrease in demand for anthracite coal after World War II caused an exodus from the Valley. A reduction in the number of available clergy brought a merger of the parishes in July 1995. Sacred Heart Church in Williamstown continues to serve as a worship site.

Our Lady Help of Christians, Lykens

Sacred Heart of Jesus, Williamstown

Our Lady of Good Counsel, Marysville

O ur Lady of Good Counsel in Marysville and Saint Bernadette in Duncannon serve Catholics in an area extending 25 miles along the Susquehanna River and reaching 10 miles inland, encompassing 10 towns.

Marysville's Catholics date to 1900, when expert Italian stone masons immigrated to build the Rockville railroad bridge. Through the years Masses were celebrated in private homes, a meeting hall, and the former post office building. Finally, in 1956 Our Lady of Good Counsel dedicated its newly built church and became a parish.

In 1939 Father Francis Dinkel, pastor in Enola, began celebrating monthly Masses in Duncannon. By 1950 weekly Masses were being celebrated in a rented storeroom, and in 1954 the faithful built a church, dedicated to Saint Bernadette of Lourdes. Construction of a social hall, kitchen, and meeting room followed, and in 1960 a baptistery was added to the church.

Today, both congregations are recognized for the involvement of their faithful: Marysville parishioners hold two annual spaghetti dinner fundraisers, and volunteers oversee all outreach ministries; in Duncannon members are active, especially, the Council of Catholic Women, known for coconut and peanutbutter Easter candy fundraisers, and the parishioners who teach CCD. The congregations share a youth group.

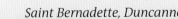

Laying of the Cornerstone, Marysville, 1957

Current pastor Father John Trigilio, Jr., PhD, ThD, is president of Confraternity of Catholic Clergy, host of the weekly TV series "Web of Faith" on EWTN, and author of *Catholicism for Dummies* (2003), *The Everything Bible* (2004), *Women in the Bible for Dummies* (2005), and *Pope John Paul II for Dummies* (2006)

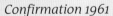

Confirmation 1961

Saint Bernadette, Duncannon

Manheim
SAINT RICHARD

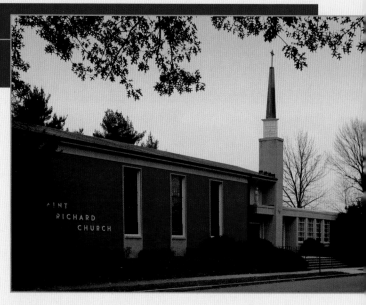

Saint Richard, Manheim, traces its formal beginning to 1949, when Father Lawrence Gustin from Saint Peter, Elizabethtown, conducted a religious education class in a private Manheim residence. Interest in a Catholic presence in the community grew, and in November 1953 Mass was celebrated in Union Hall with 125 in attendance. For the next four years the Catholic community continued to worship there while they planned and built their church and social hall. Land was donated by Harry M. Witmyer of Manheim.

Ground was broken in 1956, and in November 1957 Saint Richard Church was dedicated by Bishop George L. Leech. The congregation continued as a mission of Saint Peter until 1967, when Father Dale Sneeringer was appointed administrator. Beginning in 1971 the care of the congregation was entrusted to Oblates of Saint Francis DeSales, and finally, in June 1978, Saint Richard was granted parish status, with Father Joseph Tustin, O.S.F.S., as the first pastor.

In 1997 the congregation celebrated the 40th anniversary of the construction of the church. Through the years the parish has enjoyed continued growth and in the new century includes over 325 families.

McSherrystown
ANNUNCIATION OF THE BLESSED VIRGIN MARY

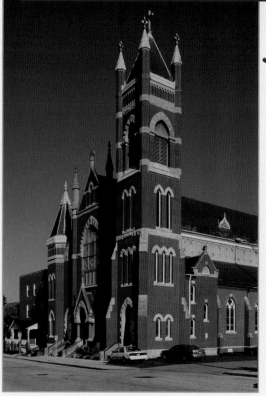

McSherrystown, which has always been predominantly Catholic in population, was laid out as a village in 1765. The graceful spire of historic Conewago chapel can be seen from the town, and that is where the populace attended Sunday Mass. After the Civil War, a bustling cigar industry brought many Catholics to the area, and a chapel was erected in McSherrystown. Father Pius Hemler was appointed the first pastor in 1900, and construction of the church and rectory followed. On a trip to Bavaria in 1923, Reverend Dr. L. Augustus Reudter acquired the large carved crucifix that presently hangs above the altar.

The Sisters of Saint Joseph opened a parochial school there in 1854. In 1908 a new school was built to provide grade and high school education. This school was destroyed by fire in 1938, following which Delone Catholic High School was built through the generosity of Charles J. Delone, Esquire. The families of this staunchly Catholic community have given over 15 priests and 40 religious women to the service of the Church.

Mechanicsburg
SAINT JOSEPH

$\int$aint Joseph owes its beginnings to Mary Moriarty Brindle, who from age 15 through adulthood labored to establish a Catholic presence in Mechanicsburg. With just two years of Catholic education, Mary began to host meetings in her home and write letters to the diocese in an effort to establish a church. Visits to Mechanicsburg by priests were sporadic through the late 1800s, so Mary diligently maintained her weekly meetings and continued her appeals to the diocese.

Impressed with Mary's persistence, Bishop John Shanahan used his own personal funds to build a chapel in 1900. Mary urged parishioners of the fledgling Catholic population to stand at the windows during Mass so the chapel might appear crowded to passersby. Her letters to the diocese are preserved in the diocesan Archives.

The mission attained parish status in 1950, and the Catholic population has continued to grow steadily in the ensuing 50-plus years. Today, Saint Joseph serves more than 2,000 families with two resident priests. A new parish life and education center, dedicated in August 2005, houses a school served by the Sisters of Saints Cyril and Methodius.

Former Saint Joseph Church

Mechanicsburg
SAINT ELIZABETH ANN SETON

$\mathcal{T}$he parish of Saint Elizabeth Ann Seton was formally established on April 21, 1977. Father Daniel Menniti was named the first pastor. In May 1978, ground was broken for the construction of a modified colonial design church, which would reflect the colonial period in which Saint Elizabeth Ann Seton had lived.

The new church, dedicated on June 17, 1979, displays an innovative and vibrant parish that launched an array of educational, charitable, and social activities.

Today, the religious education programs, charitable outreach, care of the sick and elderly, and unique social events, such as the annual Apple Festival, all exhibit the willingness of parishioners to contribute their time and talents to the well-being of the parish and community.

Under the current leadership of Father Richard Waldron since 1982, the parish continues to thrive. The parish is currently in Phase II of a building construction and renovation project to upgrade the existing facility and expand the educational and social areas.

The Catholic Christian community of Saint Elizabeth Ann Seton Parish places special emphasis on guiding and teaching God's children in the ways of Christ, a plan that Saint Elizabeth set in motion.

Summer Bible School 2005

Mechanicsburg
SAINT KATHARINE DREXEL

Saint Katharine Drexel was established in 1988 by then-Bishop Keeler to provide a parish home for the Catholic population of Cumberland County's fast-growing Silver Spring Township; Father James O'Brien became its first pastor. Mass was celebrated initially in the Silver Spring Fire Company and, as the congregation continued to grow, at Saint Timothy Lutheran Church. With the announcement that Mother Katharine Drexel, who had traveled through the township numerous times en route to the Carlisle Indian Industrial School, was to be beatified, the name for the fledgling parish presented itself. It became the first in the world named in her honor.

Ground was broken in 1990, the church was dedicated the following September, and with the canonization of the good saint on October 1, 2000, the name was changed from Blessed to Saint Katharine Drexel. A parish center was added in 2004.

Appropriately, the new parish adopted the two guiding themes espoused by Saint Katharine, devotion to the Eucharist and care of the less fortunate. The parish carries on her work in various programs and outreaches, including paying tuition for three high school students and distributing books to needy students of all ages. Now numbering 926 families, the parish is recognized for its commitment to "Building a Community of Faith."

Middletown
SEVEN SORROWS OF THE BLESSED VIRGIN MARY

Lacking a priest in Middletown in the late 1700s, Catholics walked or drove over the rough, narrow paths cut through the wilderness to Elizabethtown for Sunday Mass. They organized a separate mission in the 1850s, and by 1855, Father John McCosker—affectionately known as "Good Father John"—had been appointed to it. The faithful still trekked to worship in Elizabethtown, but parishioners also hosted monthly

Masses until their homes could no longer accommodate the growing congregation. Liturgies then moved to a brick schoolhouse. In 1857, Father McCosker secured land for a church to be named Seven Sorrows of the Blessed Virgin Mary, and the first Mass in the new structure was celebrated in 1859.

The parish continues to thrive and today numbers more than 1,700 families. The parish has a nursing ministry that offers free blood pressure screenings, distributes educational materials about stroke prevention and breast cancer, and sponsors health fairs. Other outreach includes visits to shut-ins and the hospitalized and an annual summer festival, among others. The parish has developed a reputation for being especially friendly and open.

Originally a mission of Our Lady, Help of Christians, Lykens, the parish of Queen of Peace, Millersburg, had its beginning in the early 1900s when Mass for the small number of Catholics scattered throughout the area was celebrated in private homes, usually on a weekday.

Nineteen people attended the mission's first Sunday Mass on July 29, 1952, held in the Ulsh building in Millersburg; that same year, the mission was elevated to parish status. In 1953 a private residence on Moore Street was purchased for use as a chapel, which was placed under the patronage of Our Blessed Mother with the title "Queen of Peace."

By 1976 with a congregation of 80 families, the parish proceeded with plans for a new church and expanded parish activities. The small congregation added a school and launched religious education and community outreach programs.

The parish continued to grow and today numbers 237 families, who carry on their faith tradition in this rural community.

Milton
SAINT JOSEPH

Pearly Bells of Saint Joseph, 150th anniversary

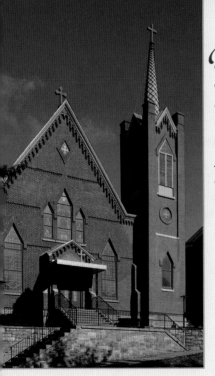

Saint Joseph had its beginning prior to the Revolutionary War and thus ranks among the oldest Catholic communities in the country. Its colonial members endured persecution, exclusion, and oppression but managed to persist. The first recorded history of a church structure (log cabin) is a deed dated 1805 (while Lewis and Clarke journeyed on their westward expedition) in which John and Margaret Keffer transferred to a Jesuit, Father Francis Neale, a two-acre tract for one dollar. The parish cemetery, with graves dating to the late 1700s, is located on this tract. It was not until 1845 that Saint Joseph's first church structure was dedicated.

The Milton congregation is one of the few in the diocese that have belonged successively to the Sees of Baltimore, Philadelphia, and now Harrisburg.

Today the parish counts 500 families and is active in aiding the needs of the community through its local agencies. The parish community maintains a strong ecumenical faith relationship with the churches through the local food bank and the activities of the Milton Area Ministerium. In the year 2005 Saint Joseph celebrated its 200th year of Catholicism in the Susquehanna Valley.

Church rededication,
September 26, 1999

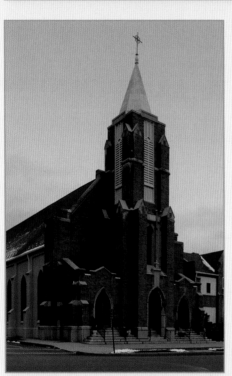

Known locally as "The Church of Our Lady," the present parish was formed in July 1995 by the consolidation of the parishes of Our Lady, Mount Carmel; Saint Joseph, Mount Carmel; Saint Joseph, Locust Gap; Saint Joseph, Locustdale; and Saint Ignatius, Centralia. The history of the parish is the story of the coming of the immigrants to America, in these parishes, mainly from Ireland and Poland. In 1964 these parishes (with the exception of Locustdale and Centralia) took the bold step of consolidating their parochial schools (along with the other parishes in Mount Carmel) into the first interparochial school in the country. This forward step made it possible to enrich the whole educational program. These parishes, all begun in the 19th century, served their individual congregations well until declining populations and a lack of clergy forced them to consolidate their gains by merging into one parish.

The Church of Our Lady was selected as the worship site for the new parish. Religious artifacts from all the former parishes were masterfully integrated into the church to reflect the traditions of all parishioners.

Mount Carmel
DIVINE REDEEMER

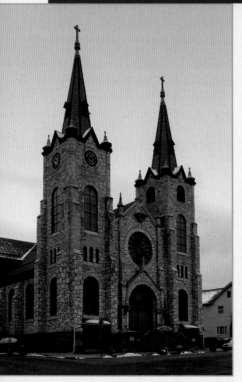

Divine Redeemer Parish was established in July 1995 as a result of the merger of the former parishes Holy Cross, Saint John the Baptist, Our Mother of Consolation, and Saint Peter, all in Mount Carmel, and Saint Paul Chapel, Atlas. Although only a decade old, this new parish traces its roots to 1892, the founding year for both Holy Cross and Saint John the Baptist. The church building of Our Mother of Consolation is the worship site of the new parish.

The newly formed congregation celebrated its founding with a Mass of Dedication on July 2, 1995. During the prayer of dedication, representatives of the former parishes carried the altar stones from their churches in procession. In the following three years the new parish installed a new altar and extensively refurbished and renovated the church. The newly renovated edifice incorporates articles from all the merged parishes. Divine Redeemer celebrated the completion of the project with a Dedication Mass and parish celebration in February 1998.

Like their immigrant ancestors, the present congregation has seized upon the opportunity to build a faith community for themselves and all generations to follow.

Mount Joy

MARY, MOTHER OF THE CHURCH

The merger of Presentation of the Blessed Virgin Mary Parish in Marietta and Assumption of the Blessed Virgin Mary Parish in Mount Joy became complete and official on July 1, 1995. This date reflects the founding of Mary, Mother of the Church Parish. The mission at Mount Joy was founded in the 1870s from Saint Anthony Parish, Lancaster. In 1881 Saint Peter Parish, Elizabethtown, assumed the care of this mission. It was raised to parish status in 1979 when a new church was built and dedicated.

The town of Marietta was an important transportation center in the eighteenth century. The Catholic community functioned as a mission until a church was built in 1869. In 1892 the parish had its first resident pastor, Father John O'Reilly. The Sisters of Charity opened a parochial school in 1873. At times, the mission at Safe Harbor and a chapel at Billmeyer were attended from Marietta.

At the time of the merger of these two communities into Mary, Mother of the Church Parish, the church at Mount Joy was chosen as the worship site. In 2003 a new education building and rectory were added to the parish complex.

Myerstown

MARY, GATE OF HEAVEN

Mary, Gate of Heaven, was founded in 1926 when Father Leopold Stump, pastor of Saint Gertrude, Lebanon, joined with local Italian and German families to purchase property at Railroad and Center Streets, Myerstown, on which a grain storage warehouse and several other buildings were situated. They converted the

Church dedication, 1926

warehouse into a church, which they gave the name Mary, Gate of Heaven, English for Maria, Porta Coeli, the mother church in Abruzzi, Italy, of the mission's Italian founding families. Shortly thereafter, the warehouse-turned-church, a mission of Saint Gertrude, Lebanon, was dedicated. There were about 150 founding members in this Italian and German ethnic faith community, and Father Stump, a German immigrant, labored to learn Italian in order to minister to all his congregation.

The mission attained parish status in 1968, ending its 42-year-long relationship with Saint Gertrude, and Father Frederick Farace, then an assistant pastor at Saint Gertrude, served as the first pastor. In 1970 the new parish dedicated their present church on McKinley Avenue, Jackson Township. The 80-year-old Catholic community currently hosts an array of social and community outreach efforts and fundraisers, including semi-annual spaghetti dinners and annual Summerfest and Mardi Gras celebrations, among others.

New Bloomfield
SAINT BERNARD PARISH

S aint Bernard Parish, New Bloomfield, Pennsylvania, traces its beginning to 1798 when Father Stanislaus Cerfourmont purchased land in Juniata Township. Initially, Masses were celebrated in a Mass house and, later, at mission churches in Enola and New Cumberland. By 1937 Mass was being celebrated at Carson Long Military Institute for the increased number of Catholics in the area.

In 1946 land was purchased on McClure Street, New Bloomfield, for construction of a church. Reverend Monsignor Joseph Schmidt was the founding pastor and great benefactor of Saint Bernard church, named for the great saint and doctor and in memory of Father Schmidt's own father, Bernard Schmidt. A

rectory, built adjacent to the church, was dedicated in 1970. In 1985 the church was expanded to seat 185.

By 2002 Saint Bernard Parish had grown to 335 families. The need to expand resulted in the purchase of land west of New Bloomfield along Route 274. In 2002, Bishop Dattilo officiated at a solemn groundbreaking for a new church and returned in 2003 for its dedication. Weekend Masses are celebrated in the new church, and weekday daily Masses continue to be celebrated at what is now the Mass Chapel on McClure Street.

New Cumberland
SAINT THERESA OF THE INFANT JESUS

W hen Father Roy Keffer was appointed pastor on the West Shore in 1926, he was given charge of a huge mission territory extending some 75 miles along the Susquehanna River. Included in this area of 750 square miles were 29 towns. The courageous steps taken to meet the religious needs of Catholics in the area were further complicated by the Great Depression and the religious antagonisms generated by the 1929 presidential campaign.

After building the parish church in Enola, Father Keffer opened a new mission in New Cumberland on April 29, 1928. Saint Theresa's parish experienced a steady growth, and after years of crowding and inconvenience, a combination church and school was dedicated in 1949. Most of the present parishes on the West Shore were eventually broken off from Saint Theresa's. A new commodious church building was dedicated in 1968. In the ensuing years the parish plant has been supplemented with a new rectory and school addition.

New Freedom
SAINT JOHN THE BAPTIST

First Easter in new church, 1989

Old Church

The first seeds of Catholicism in New Freedom were planted by German settlers and Redemptorist missionaries. The faithful worshiped in a log cabin built in 1841 under the direction of now-Saint John Neumann. Early announcement books show Mass was celebrated in both German and English. Named Saint John the Baptist, the church became a mission of Saint Mary's in York. Traveling priests serving country missions ministered to Saint John's until the first resident priest arrived in 1871. In 1899, the mission received parish status.

With the church population presently approaching 2,000 families, the parish continues its century-long growth; a new church was dedicated in 1989, and a new school building, in 2005. The annual Christmas Bazaar is one of many activities funding the parish's expansion and its outreach ministries, including the Southern York Clothing Bank. Saint John's also joins with several other churches to operate the Southern York County Food Pantry. A parish picnic, launched in 1922, still brings parishioners together for fun and fellowship.

New Holland
OUR LADY OF LOURDES

Our Lady of Lourdes Parish, New Holland, was established as a mission by the Redemptorist Fathers from Ephrata. As early as 1919 Father William White, C.SS.R., celebrated Mass twice monthly in a rented room in New Holland.

In 1920 the growing congregation moved to the Legion Hall in New Holland, where, for the next twenty years, Mass was celebrated on all Sundays and Holy Days.

In July 1940 ground was broken for a church on land donated by the Lewis Strob family. The first Mass in the new church was celebrated on Christmas Day 1940. On April 20, 1941, the church was dedicated in honor of Our Lady of Lourdes.

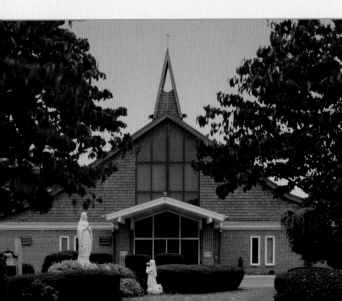

By the early 1970s the thriving Catholic population had outgrown the church. In 1972 the current church was built, and five years later, on January 5, 1977, the mission became a parish with Father Edward Bober, C.SS.R, as the first pastor.

The Redemptorist Order served the parish until June 1999 when, upon the withdrawal of the Order, the parish reverted to the Diocese of Harrisburg. The parish has continued to grow through the years and at present has nearly 700 families.

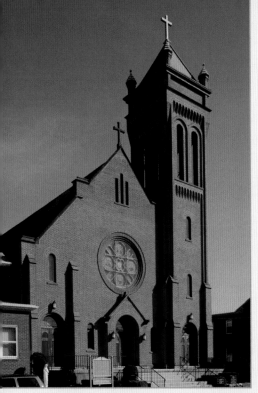

*E*arly records of Catholics in the New Oxford area date back to the first English settlers. Worshippers traveled faithfully to Conewago Chapel, until a frame structure, erected in 1852, offered the community their own place of worship. Jesuit priests served the church, named Immaculate Conception of the Blessed Virgin Mary. A mission to Conewago, it attained parish status in 1891. Over the next decade, the church grew, adding a rectory and a two-room school. A convent housed the Sisters of Christian Charity, who arrived in 1900.

1980

A new brick church, dedicated in 1901, replaced the wooden building, and the Sisters of Mercy oversaw the school beginning in 1913. To beautify church grounds, parish members constructed a distinctive grotto in the parish cemetery in the 1940s. Imbedded in the grotto are stones from holy sites and battlefields around the world. To celebrate the parish centennial, Father Daniel O'Brien supervised the replacement of the main front doors, estimating that more than six million people had passed through the old doors to worship there.

Palmyra

HOLY SPIRIT

*I*n 1913 Walter T. Bradley, owner of the limestone quarries outside Palmyra, noted 400 Catholics working at the quarries and at the Hershey Chocolate Factory. For decades, Catholics in the area attended Mass in nearby Hershey. In 1955 Bishop Leech purchased land for a worship site and two years later dedicated a new church, naming it Holy Spirit, and a social hall. The church remained a mission

attended by Saint Joan of Arc until 1965, when Father Francis Lahout, became the first resident pastor.

Today, Holy Spirit Parish holds several events to fund charitable causes, church maintenance, and more than thirty parish ministries. Every spring the Men's Society hosts the Lenten Fish Fry, serving nearly 5,000 meals. The Women's Society sells crafts and baked goods during the annual Christmas Bazaar and hosts a Summer Flea Market and Auction. The Summer Festival, held for more than 20 years, attracts hundreds of people from the surrounding communities, as parishioners transform parish grounds into a carnival featuring homemade foods and live entertainment.

In 2002, Holy Spirit began a capital campaign for a new church building, projected for 2007.

Quarryville
SAINT CATHERINE OF SIENA

The construction of an iron furnace in 1809 brought an influx of Irish immigrants to southern Lancaster County, and Father Bernard McCabe celebrated Mass in a grove of oak and hickory trees that is now the Quarryville cemetery. In 1844 he built a small chapel and called it Saint Catherine of Siena. The fledgling congregation attained mission status in the late 1800s, first to Saint Mary's, and then to Saint Anthony's, both in Lancaster.

A new church, built in 1896, reflected a Romanesque style with steeple and bell tower. Road conditions from November through March, however, forced worshippers to meet in private homes

during the winter months. The first resident pastor, Father Herman Fischer, arrived in 1930.

Outgrowing the century-old church, parishioners dedicated a new one with religious education and meeting rooms in 1999 and celebrated the blessing of a new parish hall in July 2005.

Roaring Creek
OUR LADY OF MERCY

Priests from Danville and Bloomsburg traveled once monthly to serve eight Catholic families living in the Roaring Creek Valley about 1900. The first recorded Mass took place in a tenant building, although worshippers also celebrated Mass in private homes. After the purchase of a schoolhouse in 1905, services increased to twice monthly; Holy Ghost Fathers from Mount Carmel and priests from Marion Heights and Danville traveled by horse and buggy over mountains to reach the small mission. The first resident pastor, Father Harry Strickland, built a church in 1915, and Our Lady of Mercy attained parish status in 1923.

The parish, comprised mainly of settlers from Slovakia, Poland, and Lithuania, struggled through the Depression years. Father Steven Zajac, pastor in 1930, held Mass in the rectory to save fuel. He also instituted a Sunday School program to educate parish youth, a program first overseen by the Sisters of the Immaculate Heart of Mary from Centralia and then from Mount Carmel. Today, volunteer catechists from the parish's more than 600 members continue religious education.

Parish Christmas carolers

Selinsgrove
SAINT PIUS X

Swiss Catholic and Revolutionary War hero Major Anthony Selin planted the first seeds of Catholicism in Selinsgrove in 1791, when he invited priests from Philadelphia to the area to baptize his two children.

Selinsgrove Center Christmas party, 1992

Later, a failed attempt to construct a brick chapel began in 1828, when Irish settlers building the nearby Pennsylvania Canal purchased land but never completed its construction. After a post-World War II power-plant construction attracted many Catholics to the area, Bishop Leech established Selinsgrove as a mission, attaching it to Saint Michael's in Sunbury. Without a proper worship space, priests celebrated Mass at the American Legion Hall.

Saint Pius X was the first Catholic congregation in Snyder County. In the 1950s the mission was placed under the care of Saint Thomas Moore, Northumberland, and land was purchased for a permanent worship site. The present church was completed in 1959, and five years later, in 1964, the mission attained parish status, with Father Anthony Burakowski serving as the first resident pastor. The parish ministers to the Selinsgrove Center and nearby Susquehanna University. In the new millennium the parish has purchased land, and plans are underway for construction of a new church for this growing congregation.

Shamokin
MOTHER CABRINI

Mother Cabrini Parish, Shamokin, was founded in July 1995, formed by the merger of five parishes: Saint Edward the Confessor, Assumption of the Blessed Virgin Mary, Saint Stanislaus, and Saint Michael the Archangel, all in Shamokin, and Saint Anthony of Padua, Ranshaw. The Saint Edward church building became the worship site for the new parish. Father Dennis Grumsey, OFM Conv., was named pastor of the new congregation. The church was renovated to incorporate elements from all five of the merged congregations and in 1998 was re-blessed by Bishop Dattilo.

One of the incorporated items, a Eucharistic mosaic composed of pieces of marble and glass and pure gold leaf, reflects the now-merged former parishes, which, as noted by Father Grumsey, "like pieces of a mosaic have been joined to form an exquisite new picture." The parish newsletter fittingly bears the name *The Mosaic*.

Mother Cabrini celebrated its tenth anniversary in summer 2005 with festivities reflecting both the individual histories that each of the original parishes brought to the merger and the oneness of the new congregation.

Shippensburg
OUR LADY OF THE VISITATION

*O*ur Lady of the Visitation Parish traces its beginning to land acquisition in1840 and, two years later, construction of a church, named Saint Mary's of the Visitation. However, in the 1860s the size of the congregation, comprised largely of transient railroad workers, dwindled, and the church and property were sold. For the next seventy-five years Shippensburg Catholics traveled to Chambersburg for Mass.

Beginning in 1939, with a faith community of over 200, Mass was celebrated in a former one-room Shippensburg school. Finally in 1950, Our Lady of the Visitation parish was established, with Father Edward Gerrity as the first pastor. Our Lady of Refuge, Doylesburg, was attached as a mission. Property adjacent to what is now Shippensburg University was purchased and the buildings remodeled by parishioners for use as a worship site and rectory.

The parish flourished, and in 1967 the present church and rectory were dedicated. In 1999 the new social hall and education building were completed and dedicated. Catholic students from Shippensburg University became involved in all parish activities of the church, which serves also as the university Newman Center.

Growth of parish and programs continued through the century. The parish welcomed the new millennium with a celebration of its 50th anniversary and in this new century promises continued growth and vitality.

Spring Grove
SACRED HEART OF JESUS

*F*ather William Homan from Saint Patrick's, York, celebrated the first recorded Mass in Spring Grove at the home of Mr. and Mrs. William J. Allen on August 1, 1901. Masses continued to be celebrated in private homes until several prominent Catholic families raised $15,000 for a church space purchased from the Reformed Congregation in 1903. Sacred Heart of Jesus was dedicated in May 1904, with Father William Boyle serving as its first resident pastor. It reverted to a mission in 1909, first to Saint Mary's, then to Saint Patrick's for 50 years, then to Saint Rose of Lima, and finally to Saint Francis Preparatory School.

Renovations to update the aging church building began in 1975, and Sacred Heart again attained parish status on Thanksgiving Day 1976. Completed in 1982, a parish center provides space for a yearly Christmas Bazaar and a summer yard sale. In addition, a weekly 200 Club raises funds to support church upkeep and the Harvest of Hope Food Pantry, to which parishioners donate food, funds, and their time ministering to those in need.

Steelton
PRINCE OF PEACE PARISH

*D*emographic changes in Steelton in recent years necessitated restructuring within the Catholic community. Under a directive from Bishop Dattilo, five parishes— Saint James, Saint Ann, Saint Peter, Saint John the Evangelist, and the Assumption of the Blessed Virgin Mary—were merged to form Prince of Peace Parish on July 1, 1995.

Working to build a foundation for the new parish, which has Assumption of the Blessed Virgin Mary church as its worship site, the first pastor, Father Samuel Houser, sifted through the contents of each church property to select and utilize items to honor each parish and make religious articles and furnishings available for other churches.

Parishioners' fundraising activities include an annual parish picnic, spaghetti/ravioli dinners, bingo and lottery. Outreach ministries for this 10-year-old parish include the Legion of Mary, the Parish Council of Catholic Women, Prince of Peace Seniors Group, Funeral Luncheon Committee, and the Kolo Club "Marian." Prince of Peace School offers kindergarten through eighth grade; the CCD program provides children and youth with religious instruction, and Deacon Michael Grella directs the RCIA.

Sunbury
SAINT MONICA

*S*aint Monica Parish, Sunbury, was founded in July 1995, by the merger of Saint Michael Parish, Sunbury, and Saint Thomas More Parish, Northumberland. Both of these communities are strategically located at the confluence of the north and west branches of the Susquehanna River in Northumberland County. The area is steeped in Indian lore and was probably a stopping place for early Jesuit missionaries traveling the Susquehanna from Canada and Maryland in the eighteenth century. Sunbury was listed as a mission of Father Louis DeBarth from Lancaster in 1795. This early Catholic group lost its identity for fifty years. Father Leo Foin was appointed first resident pastor in March 1902. In 1950 a church, auditorium and school building were erected.

Northumberland also has a rich early history. Property was purchased as early as November 7, 1774. Presentday history of Catholicity in the community begins in 1937. It was not until 1955 that Father Matthias Siedlecki was appointed first resident pastor.

Original church

Saint Patrick in Trevorton dates back to 1850 when Father Charles Kenny arrived on horseback and celebrated Mass in private homes. Two years later, Father Michael Sheridan, pastor at Danville, came on regular circuit visits to celebrate Mass and offer sacraments. He is credited with being the first priest to plan a church building in the area and for naming the church after Ireland's patron saint. Construction was begun in 1857, and the church, built of mountain rock, was dedicated in 1860. Legend says the pastor, Father George Gostenchnigg, carried the bell for the new church on his shoulders from Sunbury. Sadly, as a result of suffering heat exhaustion in a journey from Trevorton to Milton, he died from pneumonia just days before the dedication

The parish, which celebrated its 150th anniversary in 2000, has 286 families, who participate in an array of activities, including a bereavement ministry that oversees the funeral luncheon, visits and telephones the deceased's family, and continues support through a one-year letterwriting effort to lend aid during the grieving process

Waynesboro

SAINT ANDREW

Waynesboro area's first Mass was celebrated in 1816 and the second, in 1819, both in private homes. In 1819 Missionary Father Nicholas Zocchi built the first Catholic church in Waynesboro on the site of the present Saint Andrew's cemetery at a cost of 400 dollars. The church served 3 families and 18 others. Between 1819 and 1850, Masses were infrequent and, during a two-year period, were suspended. After the church building became unusable in 1845, six members of the congregation constructed a new church on Saint Andrew's present site. For several years priests from Emmitsburg traveled to Waynesboro about every three months to minister to the faithful there. In 1854 the Saint Andrew congregation was attached to Chambersburg as a mission, and Masses began to be celebrated every fifth Sunday. The mission attained parish status in 1893.

The thriving parish added a rectory in 1894, a new church structure in 1908, and a school in 1925. Today 691 families participate in numerous outreach activities, including an annual picnic and an Oktoberfest celebration with games for children and an auction, dance, and country-club dinner for adults.

December 2002

ishop (now Saint) John Neumann authorized the purchase of property for a new church and cemetery for the growing German Catholics and for overflow members of Saint Patrick's Church in York in 1852. Called Immaculate Conception of the Blessed Virgin Mary, the church structure was completed within a year, and parishioners heard the first German Mass before it was dedicated by Bishop Neumann in 1853 as a German national parish. By 1884, the vibrant parish needed a new, larger church structure, and the cornerstone for it was laid on May 25. Growing rapidly, the parish opened a second, larger school, staffed by the Good Sisters of the Third Order of Saint Francis, in 1869.

Now, over a century later, the parish, still bi-lingual, except now with Spanish congregants, celebrates one Sunday Mass in Spanish. Saint Mary's 1,070 families participate in a variety of outreach efforts, including the daily operation of a thrift shop, located next door to the rectory and staffed by volunteers.

York
SAINT JOSEPH

Church carnival, 2002

After a 1908 census conducted by Father George Breckel, pastor of Immaculate Conception, showed more than 300 Catholics in East York, Bishop John Shanahan authorized construction of a chapel. The next year the mission church, called Saint Joseph, was built. With 180 faithful filling the new chapel to capacity, Father Breckel celebrated the first Mass on Christmas Day 1909. Four years later, the church achieved parish status, and within two years, parishioners added a rectory, parish school, and hall. In 1954 the original church was demolished to make way for a larger church and school

In 1979, at the invitation of Bishop Daley, the Capuchin Franciscan Friars of the Province of Saint Augustine, Pittsburgh, assumed the responsibility for the pastoral care of the parish.

In May 1996, under the leadership of Father John Daya, OFM, Cap., a new church was dedicated on acreage adjoining the parish school on Kingston Road.

Today more than 2,700 families participate in a myriad of activities, including a lending library, an outreach to the sick and homebound, and a peace and justice outreach, among others. Saint Joseph continues its vibrant growth, still demonstrating care and concern for each other and the wider community.

York
SAINT PATRICK

Saint Patrick church, 1809

Although no written records of Saint Patrick's exist prior to 1776, the faithful gathered in a privately owned Mass-House as early as 1741. In those colonial years when anti-Catholic sentiment made public worship impossible, missionaries from Lancaster, Conewago, Baltimore, and Emmitsburg visited the area. The prospects of independence softened those sentiments, and in 1776 Joseph Schmidt purchased the present site of Saint Patrick church, then the site of a stone chapel. A brick church was built in 1810, and visiting priests continued to minister to the congregation until Father Lorence Huber became the first resident pastor in 1819. In 1852 German members separated from Saint Patrick to form Saint Mary's. Almost a half century later, in 1898, the present church was dedicated.

A parochial school opened in 1851, run by The Sisters of Charity until 1934, and then by Sisters, Servants of the Immaculate Heart of Mary, who oversee it today.

Today the parish's 1,075 families participate in an array of outreach ministries and activities, including peace and justice and crisis pregnancy outreaches, Legion of Mary, and Marriage Encounter, among others.

York
SAINT ROSE OF LIMA

aint Rose of Lima Church, named for the first saint of the New World, was founded in 1907 as a mission of Saint Patrick's to minister to York's growing Catholic population. Initially, parishioners worshipped in a brick structure purchased from Saint Matthew's Lutheran congregation. Saint Patrick's priests served the new church until Reverend Thomas Dougherty arrived as its first resident pastor. Three years later, parishioners purchased land and built the present Romanesque rectory, said to be the finest in the diocese.

The cornerstone was laid in 1915 for a new structure providing space for a church, an auditorium, and a school. Sisters of Saint Joseph from Chestnut Hill came in 1919 to oversee the parish school, which opened in the same year. Today, 2,100 families participate in a variety of outreach ministries, including a youth group that has clocked many service hours to the parish and its surrounding communities.

1994

York Haven
HOLY INFANT PARISH

oly Infant Parish traces its beginning to 1923, when priests from Immaculate Conception Parish in York began to minister to the Catholic people in Saginaw. A small chapel was built under the patronage of Saint Joseph the Worker. It served about 60 Catholics for 24 years before the Union Quarry closed, forcing members to move elsewhere for work. Its second phase began in 1944, when Bishop Leech granted permission to move the mission several miles north to York Haven, where people worked at the local paper and power companies. In 1948 ground was broken in York Haven for a new church, which was dedicated to the Holy Infant.

A mission of Immaculate Conception Parish in York, Holy Infant thrived with groups such as the Holy Name Society and the Council of Women serving its community. Parishioners worked hard to eliminate building debt and increase membership in an effort to attain parish status. Finally, in May 1972, Holy Infant was erected as a parish. Now parishioners gather at the church's Grotto for special Marian devotions and have established a "Love of Neighbor" fund to aid needy parish families.

Acri, Reverend John A.

Amalanthan, Reverend Jayaseelan

Amoako-Attah, Reverend Anthony, O.P.

Anthappa, Reverend Anthony

Arrazola, Reverend Rodrigo A.

Aumen, Reverend Paul, C.P.P.S.

Bateman, Jr., Reverend John B.

Bennett, Reverend Michael X.

Berger, Reverend Robert F.

Bierster, Reverend Monsignor Leo N.

Blackwell, Jr., Reverend Edward A.

Brenner, Reverend Monsignor Thomas R.

Bryan, Reverend Paul V., C.Ss.R.

Burger, Very Reverend Philip G., V.F.

Campion, Reverend John R.

Capitani, Reverend Sylvan P., D.Min.

Carolin, Reverend Joseph C.

Cawley, Reverend William M.

Clark, Reverend Paul M.

Coakley, Reverend Lawrence R.

Conrad, Reverend Brian P.

Cramer, II, Reverend Donald W.

Creaven, Reverend John, C.Ss.R.

Culkin, Reverend Michael J.

Dalessandro, Reverend Dennis G.

Danneker, Reverend David L., Ph.D.

Devine, Reverend Patrick A.

Dibiccaro, Reverend Dominic M.

Drucker, Reverend James N.

Farace, Reverend Frederick A., S.T.L.

Fauser, Reverend Steven W.

Fennessy, Reverend Joseph H.

Fisher, Reverend Paul R.

Fontanella, Reverend Andrew J.

Forrey, Jr., Reverend William C.

Fregapane, Reverend Monsignor Mercurio A.

Froehlich, Reverend James, O.F.M. CAP

Gaffney, Reverend Edward M., O.P.

Gallagher, Reverend Adrian, O.F.M. CONV

Geiger, Reverend William G., C.Ss.R.

Gillelan, Very Reverend Robert M., V.F.

Glasgow, Reverend Robert

Goodman III, Reverend Leo M.

Gotwalt, Very Reverend Joseph F., V.F.

Grab, Reverend Michael J.

Greaney, Reverend John F.

Greany, Reverend Brendan, C.Ss.R.

Gribbin, Reverend Monsignor Robert C.

Gross, Reverend Lawrence C.

Grumsey, Reverend Dennis, O.F.M. CONV

Grzybowski, Reverend Robert O.F.M. CONV

Guzman, Reverend Walter F.

Hahn, Reverend Peter I.

Haney, Very Reverend Ronald T.

Haviland, Reverend William T.

Heintzelman, Reverend Gerard T.

Helwig, Reverend Paul C.

Hemler, Reverend Thomas J.

Hereshko, Reverend David W.

Hilbert, Reverend Joseph C.

Hillier, Reverend David A.

Hohenwarter, Jr., Reverend Norman C.

Hoke, Reverend John D., Lt. CHC, USMC

Hoke, Reverend Thomas R.

Houser, Reverend Samuel E.

Hwang, Reverend Euihyeon

Karwacki, Very Reverend Francis J., V.F.

Keating, Jr., Reverend Edward J.

Keller, Reverend David S.

Kelly, Reverend John W., C.Ss.R.

Kemper, Reverend John C., S.S.

King, Very Reverend William J., J.C.D.

Kofchock, Reverend Joseph T.

Kujovsky, Reverend Monsignor Thomas J.

Kumontis, Reverend Monsignor Francis M.

Laicha, Reverend Michael M.

Langan, Reverend Thomas F.

Lavelle, Reverend Edward R.

Lavoie, Reverend Raymond J.

Lawrence, Very Reverend Kenneth F., V.F.

Lawrence, Reverend Monsignor Robert E., V.F.

Leitem, Reverend Leon, O.F.M. CAP

Letteer, Reverend Michael C.

Lum, Reverend Donald Lasap Khawng

Luong, Reverend Tri M.

Lyons, Very Reverend James M.

Lytle, Reverend Gerald A.

Mahoney, Reverend Daniel J.

Malesic, Very Reverend Edward C., J.C.L.
Mammarella, Reverend Dominick A.
Mannion, Reverend Thomas I.
Marickovic, Reverend Thomas C.
Marinak, Reverend Andrew P.
Marut, Reverend Paul, O.F.M. CONV
McAndrew, Reverend David T.
McCreary, Reverend Robert E., O.F.M. CAP
McFadden, Very Reverend J. Michael
McGarrity, Reverend Patrick, C.Ss.R.
McGinley, Reverend Bernard P.
McLernon, Reverend Thomas M.
McNeil, Reverend Lawrence J.
Meluskey, Reverend Andre J.
Menei, Reverend Francis T.
Menniti, Reverend Daniel J., S.T.D., Ph.D., J.D.
Messaro, Reverend Michael A., M.SS.CC.
Messner, Reverend Michael E.
Miller, Reverend C. Anthony
Mitzel, Very Reverend Daniel C.
Moran III, Reverend Martin O.
Moratelli, Reverend Ronald J.
Moss, Reverend Darius G. C.
Msoka, Reverend Gabriel A., A.J.
Nguyen, Reverend Hoa Van
Nichols, Reverend Joseph E.
Nugent, Reverend Robert, S.D.S.
Nkwasibwe, Reverend Frederick L., A.J.
O'Blaney, Reverend James, C.Ss.R.
O'Brien, Reverend Daniel P.
O'Brien, Very Reverend James R., V.F.
Ogden, Reverend Louis P.
Olszewski, Reverend Clarence A.
Oniwe, Reverend Bernard Mary Ayo, O.P.
Oranyeli, Reverend Christopher A., O.P.
Orloski, Reverend Raymond J.
Overbaugh, Reverend Monsignor Hugh A.
Overbaugh, Reverend Monsignor Lawrence R.
Oye, Reverend Paul Bola, O.P.
Palomino, Reverend Ignacio
Peck, Reverend John J., O.S.B.
Persing, Reverend Charles L.
Petruha, Reverend Louis, O.F.M. CAP
Pistone, Very Reverend Bernardo
Plociennik, Reverend Robert, O.F.M. CONV
Podlesny, Reverend James R., O.S.B.
Powell, Reverend Daniel F. X.
Quinlan III, Very Reverend Edward J.
Quinn, Reverend Bernard
Rable, Reverend Cyril J.
Reid II, Reverend Michael P.
Rhoades, Most Reverend Kevin C., D.D.
Richardson, Reverend Monsignor William M.
Rindos, Reverend Paul T.

Rivera-Lopez, Reverend Ramon Luis
Rodriguez, Reverend Luis R.
Rost, Reverend Monsignor George W.
Rothan, Reverend Michael W.
Rozman, Reverend Thomas J.
Scala, Reverend Thomas A.
Scanlin, Reverend Joseph T.
Sceski, Reverend Alfred P.
Schmalhofer, Reverend John D.
Sempko, Reverend Walter A.
Sharman, Reverend Robert F.
Shear, Reverend Michael P.
Sheetz, Reverend Stephen A.
Sherdel, Reverend Lawrence
Shuda, Reverend Paul R.
Slough, Reverend Charles R.
Small, Reverend James, C.Ss.R.
Smith, Reverend Kenneth G.
Smith, Reverend Monsignor Thomas H.
Smith, Reverend Monsignor Vincent J.
Snyder, Reverend Chester P.
Stahmer, Reverend Andrew J.
Stahura, Reverend Joseph L.
Steffen, Reverend Carl J.
Sterner, Reverend James M.
Strome, Reverend Robert L.
Sullivan, Reverend D. Edward
Sullivan, Reverend Neil S.
Sullivan, Reverend William J.
Szada, Jr., Reverend John A.
Tamburro, Reverend Francis J.
Tancredi, Reverend Carl T., D. Min.
Thompson, Reverend Kevin, O.F.M. CAP
Thoms, Reverend Jeffrey F.
Topper, Reverend Charles J., Ed.D.
Topper, Reverend Monsignor Vincent J.
Trigilio, Jr., Reverend John, Ph.D., Th.D.
Troche, Reverend Sigfried, M.SS.CC.
Waldron, Reverend Richard P.
Waltersheid, Reverend William J.
Wangwe, Reverend Fred, A.J.
Weary, Reverend William M.
Weiss, Reverend Mark E.
Weitzel, Reverend Stephen D.
Wolfe, Reverend Allan F.
Yohe, Jr., Reverend Robert A.
Youtz, Reverend Monsignor Richard A., V.F.
Ziolkowski, Reverend Adam, O.F.M. CONV

DECEASED CLERGY
OF THE DIOCESE OF HARRISBURG

BISHOPS	BORN-DIED
Daley, Bishop Joseph	1915-1983
Dattilo, Bishop Nicholas	1931-2004
Leech, Bishop George	1890-1985
McDevitt, Bishop Philip	1858-1935
McGovern, Bishop Thomas	1832-1898
Schott, Auxiliary Bishop Lawrence	1907-1963
Shanahan, Bishop Jeremiah	1834-1886
Shanahan, Bishop John	1846-1916

PRIESTS	BORN-DIED
Adair, Rev. Msgr. Paul	1907-1982
Adams, Rev. Msgr. Donald	1928-1996
Albanese, Rev. Francis	1881-1952
Allen, Rev. Msgr. Charles	1894-1970
Allwein, Rev. Cyril James	1910-1957
Armour, Rev. James	n/d/a-n/d/a
Aurentz, Rev. John	1919-1996
Azbe, Rev. Francis	n/d/a-1932
Bade, Rev. J. Henry	n/d/a-1890
Balfe, Rev. Joseph	1811-1881
Baluta, Rev. Leonard	1884-1925
Barr, Rev. James	1852-1908
Barrett, Rev. Edward	1930-2001
Barrett, Rev. Martin	1917-1969
Barrett, Rev. Michael	1919-1996
Barry, Rev. Richard	n/d/a-1872
Bartol, Rev. Msgr. Thomas	1893-1969
Bastible, Rev. Francis	1844-1873
Bechter, Rev. John	n/d/a-1842
Beierschmitt, Rev. Msgr. Leo	1921-2002
Benton, Rev. Msgr. Gilbert	1857-1910
Blascovich, Rev. Joseph	1949-1999
Bleistein, Rev. Aloysius	1874-1935
Boetzkes, Rev. John	n/d/a-1891
Bolen, Rev. Msgr. John	1900-1966
Boll, Rev. Joseph	1838-1893

PRIESTS	BORN-DIED
Boyle, Rev. William A.	1894-1960
Boyle, Rev. William F.	1863-1937
Bozic, Rev. Joseph	n/d/a-1900
Braddock, Rev. Edger	n/d/a-n/d/a
Bradley, Rev. Msgr. Joseph	1917-1996
Brady, Rev. Msgr. Carl	1899-1981
Brandt, Rev. Arthur	1882-1960
Bratina, Rev. Anthony	1901-1931
Braubitz, Rev. Joseph	1924-1988
Breckel, Rev. Francis	1860-1901
Breckel, Rev. Msgr. George	1870-1959
Bridy, Rev. Msgr. William	1922-1989
Brown, Rev. George	1879-1963
Browne, Rev. Joseph	1904-1963
Brozys, Rev. Vincent	1890-1960
Brueggemann, Rev. Peter	1871-1937
Buckley, Rev. Miles	n/d/a-1899
Burakowski, Rev. Anthony	1913-2002
Burger, Rev. Clement	1871-1907
Burhard, Rev. Edward	1872-1939
Burke, Rev. Msgr. William J.	1894-1975
Burke, Rev. William J.	n/d/a-1899
Burns, Rev. Robert	1944-2001
Butler, Rev. Francis	1901-1965
Byrne, Rev. James	1937-1988
Byrnes, Rev. John	1906-1937
Campbell, Rev. Bernard	n/d/a-n/d/a
Carey, Rev. Daniel	1876-1933
Casey, Rev. V. Leonard	1922-1997
Cavanaugh, Rev. William	1900-1983
Celia, Rev. Joseph	1940-2005
Ceponis, Rev. Joseph	1912-1997
Cerney, Rev. A.	n/d/a-n/d/a
Chizzolo, Rev. Vigilio	1868-1925
Christ, Rev. Msgr. Adam	1856-1930
Christ, Rev. Msgr. Henry	1859-1939
Ciarlantini, Rev. Lino	1906-1974
Clarke, Rev. Msgr. James	1874-1952
Codori, Rev. John	n/d/a-1947
Connaghan, Rev. John	1870-1941
Conrad, Rev. Msgr. Francis	1903-1981
Costigan, Rev. Patrick	n/d/a-1915
Coyle, Rev. James	1914-1958
Coyne, Rev. Joseph	1943-2001
Crane, Rev. Peter	1874-1946
Creeden, Rev. Louis	1920-1979
Crotty, Rev. Thomas	1858-1934
Crowley, Rev. Daniel	1904-1964
Curran, Rev. Michael	n/d/a-1858

D'Alessandro, Rev. Patrick	1923-1996
Dailey, Rev. William	1876-1932
Danneker, Rev. John	1872-1951
DeBarth, Rev. Louis	1764-1844
DeChico, Philip	1948-2006
Delarm, Rev. Curtis	1963-2005
Deller, Rev. Edward	1927-1995
Dinkel, Rev. Msgr. Francis	1907-1984
Dobinis, Rev. Msgr. Stanley	1886-1963
Dombrowski, Rev. Msgr. Charles	1900-1979
Dorff, C.SS.R., Rev. John	n/d/a-2002
Dougherty, Rev. Louis	1919-1978
Dougherty, Rev. Raymond	1917-1992
Dougherty, Rev. Thomas	1875-1945
Dryer, Rev.	n/d/a-1860
Dwen, Rev. Patrick	1795-1838
Eagle, Rev. Sylvester	1828-1866
Eberle, Rev. John	n/d/a-1956
Echterling, Rev. Joseph	1881-1914
Effertz, Rev. Henry	n/d/a-1914
Ehehalt, Rev. Christian	1881-1938
Enright, Rev. Patrick	1887-1971
Eovacious, Rev. Thomas	1909-1951
Feeser, Rev. Albert	1863-1939
Feeser, Rev. Francis	1888-1960
Field, Rev. Edward	n/d/a-1884
Filippelli, Rev. Francis	1928-1968
Fischer, Rev. Hermann	1892-1937
Fleming, Rev. Thomas	n/d/a-1900
Foin, Rev. Jules	1854-1924
Foin, Rev. Leo	n/d/a-1930
Forgeng, Rev. Louis	1914-1972
Frisch, Rev. John	1800-1872
Fuhr, Rev. Msgr. Rudolph	1905-1994
Gallagher, Rev. Raymond	1911-1966
Gallen, Rev. Joseph	n/d/a-1885
Galligan, Rev. Charles	1863-1915
Gallitzin, Rev. Demetrius	1770-1840
Ganss, Rev. Henry	1855-1912
Gergen, Rev. Philip	1899-1961
Gerrity, Rev. Edward	1916-1981
Gieringer, Rev. Msgr. Paul	1896-1975
Gies, Rev. Herman	1884-1945
Gilligan, Rev. John	n/d/a-1873
Gladek, Rev. Luke	1880-1936
Gostenchnigg, Rev. George	1819-1860
Gotwalt, Rev. Msgr. Joseph	1904-1988
Gralinski, Rev. Thomas	1915-2005
Gratza, Rev. John	n/d/a-n/d/a

Grotemeyer, Rev. Johann	1840-1888
Gruss, Rev. Ferdinand	1909-1962
Gunville, Rev. John	1910-1973
Gustin, Rev. Msgr. Lawrence	1903-1976
Hager, Rev. Msgr. Joseph	1903-1992
Halaburda, Rev. Walter	1932-2000
Halftermeyer, Rev. Eugene	n/d/a-1909
Hartnett, Rev. Robert	1892-1966
Hassett, Rev. Msgr. Maurice	1869-1953
Hauck, Rev. Cletus	1907-1969
Hayden, Rev. Ambrose	1901-1967
Hayes, Rev. Thomas	1844-1918
Hazuda, Rev. Andrew	1909-1946
Heim, Rev. Gerard	1936-1991
Heltshe, Rev. Msgr. Francis	1903-1967
Hemler, Rev. Pius	n/d/a-1906
Herzog, Rev. Msgr. Henry	1875-1939
Hickey, Rev. James	1840-1884
Hoenninger, Rev. Albert	1884-1964
Hogan, Rev. George	n/d/a-1822
Holland, Rev. John	n/d/a-1823
Hollern, Rev. John J.	1866-1912
Homola, Rev. Michael	1923-2003
Hooman, Rev. William	1850-1906
Horrigan, Rev. Msgr. William	1886-1971
Horstman, Rev. I.	n/d/a-n/d/a
Howard, Rev. William	1878-1939
Howarth, Rev. Henry	1872-1955
Hribick, Rev. Stephen	1920-1978
Hric, Rev. George	1888-1946
Huber, Rev. Msgr. James	1853-1940
Hudak, Rev. Msgr. Francis	1930-2005
Huegel, Rev. Msgr. Peter	1877-1958
Huygen, Rev. William	1881-1942
Igoe, Rev. James	1851-1888
Johnson, Rev. Thomas	1884-1954
Jones, Rev. Woodrow	1913-1984
Jordan, Rev. Stephen	1923-1994
Joyce, Rev. Raymond	1893-1927
Kaelin, Rev. Joseph	n/d/a-1904
Kaminsky, Rev. Francis	1903-1969
Kane, Rev. Anthony	1910-1986
Kane, Rev. Thomas	1907-1973
Kappes, Rev. Augustine	1874-1930
Kattein, Rev. Emil	n/d/a-n/d/a
Kaul, Rev. Msgr. Anthony	1846-1935
Kealy, Rev. John	1899-1961
Kealy, Rev. Msgr. Joseph	1917-1997

PRIESTS	BORN-DIED
Kedjiora, O.F.M.Conv., Rev. Gerald	n/d/a-2002
Keenan, Rev. Msgr. Bernard	1779-1877
Keffer, Rev. Msgr. Roy	1896-1971
Keller, Rev. Msgr. Harold	1897-1967
Kennedy, Rev. Andrew	1873-1933
Kennedy, Rev. Timothy	n/d/a-1904
Kenny, Rev. Charles	n/d/a-1896
Kirchner, Rev. Leo	1895-1942
Kirchner, Rev. Msgr. Francis	1911-1964
Klimas, Rev. John	1894-1958
Klonowski, Rev. Florian	n/d/a-1893
Klonowski, Rev. Jerome	n/d/a-1893
Kobularik, Rev. Robert	1948-1999
Koch, Rev. Charles	1853-1925
Koch, Rev. Msgr. John	1840-1917
Kohl, Rev. Germanus	n/d/a-1914
Koppernagel, Rev. Clement	1829-1891
Kosko, Rev. Michael	1886-1955
Krichten, Rev. Leo	1894-1964
Kuhlmann, Rev. Aloysius	n/d/a-1881
Kulla, Rev. James	n/d/a-n/d/a
Kumerant, Rev. Louis	n/d/a-1922
Kunkel, Rev. Henry	1858-1890
Lahout, Rev. Francis	1928-2003
Laurinitis, Rev. Stanislaus	1916-1989
Lavelle, Rev. Msgr. George	1903-1974
Lawler, Rev. Thomas	1925-1987
Lawley, Rev. Msgr. John	1886-1948
Leitch, Rev. Msgr. Thomas	1922-1983
Lentocha, Rev. Msgr. George	1923-1997
Leuffert, Rev. John	n/d/a-n/d/a
Liebich, Rev. Philip	1896-1968
Loague, Rev. Hugh	n/d/a-1916
Loague, Rev. William	n/d/a-1892
Loszewski, Rev. Chester	1911-1964
Ludes, Rev. Henry	1884-1918
Lyons, Rev. Msgr. William	1918-1993
Machnikowski, Rev. John	n/d/a-n/d/a
Magorien, Rev. Hugh	n/d/a-1864
Maguire, Rev. Msgr. John	1895-1963
Maher, Rev. Daniel	n/d/a-1899
Maher, Rev. Msgr. Robert	1911-1990
Maher, Rev. Pierce	1812-1873
Mahony, Rev. John	1874-1946
Marcincavage, Rev. Msgr. Alphonse	1911-1985
Marshall, Rev. Francis	n/d/a-1861
Martersteck, Rev. Francis	n/d/a-n/d/a
Martin, Rev. William	1864-1932
Martini, Rev. Kenneth	1922-1988

Mattern, Rev. Msgr. Bernard	1911-1992
Mayan, Rev. Anthony	1904-1973
McAnulty, Rev. Msgr. John	1914-1971
McArdle, Rev. Patrick	n/d/a-1917
McBride, Rev. Michael	1849-1897
McCann, Rev. Arthur	1861-1917
McCarthy, Rev. Francis	n/d/a-1901
McCarthy, Rev. John	n/d/a -1908
McClary, Rev. Edward	1878-1910
McCloskey, Rev. John	1870-1900
McCosker, Rev. John	n/d/a-1862
McCullagh, Rev. Peter	n/d/a-1910
McCullough, Rev. Msgr. Francis	1909-1990
McDermott, Rev. Charles	1917-1983
McDermott, Rev. Daniel	1844-1927
McDermott, Rev. James	n/d/a-1913
McDonnell, Rev. Joseph	1883-1960
McDonnell, Rev. William	1943-1990
McElwee, Rev. Mark	1898-1947
McEntee, Rev. Thomas	1888-1946
McGee, Rev. Msgr. Patrick	1888-1976
McGinnis, Rev. Arthur	1835-1873
McGough, Rev. Msgr. Thomas	1901-1997
McGovern, Rev. John	1869-1941
McGovern, Rev. Msgr. Damian	1922-2000
McGrath, Rev. James	1871-1945
McGuire, Rev. Msgr. Hubert	1916-2003
McIlhenny, Rev. William	n/d/a-1915
McIlvaine, Rev. John	n/d/a-1918
McKenna, Rev. Louis	n/d/a-1907
McLaughlin, Rev. Hugh	1936-2005
McLaughlin, Rev. Philip	n/d/a-n/d/a
McLaughlin, Rev. Richard	1888-1958
McManus, Rev. Francis	1870-1946
McMonigle, Rev. Charles	1830-1891
Melchoir, Rev. John	1872-1947
Menko, Rev. Michael	1899-1958
Mersch, Rev. Aegedius	n/d/a-n/d/a
Metz, Rev. John	1916-1983
Meurer, Rev. Mathias	n/d/a-n/d/a
Meuwese, Rev. Msgr. Aloysius	1859-1931
Mignot, Rev. Francis	1920-1978
Miller, Rev. Paul	1929-2004
Milner, Rev. Samuel	n/d/a-1926
Moder, Rev. Albin	n/d/a-n/d/a
Monahan, Rev. James	1875-1935
Mongelluzzi, Rev. Msgr. Francis	1914-1971
Mulcahy, Rev. Msgr. George	1908-1971

PRIESTS	BORN-DIED
Murphy, Rev. Joseph	1866-1941
Murray, Rev. Edward	n/d/a-1880
Murray, Rev. Msgr. Charles	1909-1970
Muthaplakel, Rev. James	n/d/a-2003
Nagot, Rev. Francis	1734-1816
Neufeld, Rev. Francis	1834-1891
Nichols, Rev. John	1867-1942
Noel, Rev. James	1954-1980
Noel, Rev. Msgr. Francis	1859-1939
Noonan, Rev. Patrick	n/d/a-1873
O'Brien, Rev. Andrew	n/d/a-n/d/a
O'Brien, Rev. John	n/d/a-1879
O'Callaghan, Rev. William	n/d/a-1939
O'Connell, Rev. Matthew	n/d/a-1872
O'Donnell, Rev. John	1875-1967
O'Flynn, Rev. Edward	1876-1948
O'Flynn, Rev. Michael	1891-1947
O'Hanrahan, Rev. Timothy	1895-1935
O'Neill, Rev. Mark	1844-1895
O'Reilly, Rev. Daniel	n/d/a-n/d/a
O'Rielly, Rev. James	1831-1913
O'Rielly, Rev. John	1850-1892
O'Reilly, Rev. Michael	1856-1908
Onofrey, Rev. Msgr. John	1896-1973
Pape, Rev. John	n/d/a-1901
Park, Rev. Msgr. Charles	1892-1972
Paukovits, Rev. John	1917-1982
Pavilanis, Rev. Stanislaus	1888-1926
Petrasek, Rev. Msgr. Charles	1905-1980
Petrovits, Rev. Msgr. Joseph	1886-1963
Peza, Rev. Michael	n/d/a-n/d/a
Phelan, Rev. Patrick	1877-1957
Pieper, Rev. Msgr. William	1834-1912
Pietrowicz, Rev. Charles	n/d/a-1909
Pohl, Rev. Frank	1885-1955
Poist, Rev. Pius	1900-1939
Power, Rev. Michael	1848-1895
Procopio, Rev. Charles	1927-1997
Rafferty, Rev. Terence	n/d/a-1899
Reardon, Rev. Msgr. Dennis	1888-1964
Reilly, Rev. D.	n/d/a-1892
Reilly, Rev. Msgr. Owen	1896-1883
Reilly, Rev. Thomas	n/d/a-1883
Relt, Rev. Henry	1849-1895
Resetrics, Rev. Joseph	1884-1969
Reudter, Rev. L. Augustus	1863-1934
Rice, Rev. George	1883-1926
Rolko, Rev. Stephen	1930-1993
Russel, Rev. James	1828-1893

PRIESTS	BORN-DIED
Sama, Rev. Benjamin	n/d/a-1920
Sass, Rev. James	n/d/a-n/d/a
Sawdy, Rev. Wallace	1922-2006
Scanlon, Rev. Matthew	n/d/a-1938
Scheld, Rev. Charles	n/d/a-1885
Schlebbe, Rev. Fred	n/d/a-n/d/a
Schleuter, Rev. Clement	n/d/a-1906
Schmelz, Rev. Frederick	n/d/a-1898
Schmidt, Rev. Francis	1846-1899
Schmidt, Rev. Msgr. Joseph	1894-1985
Schwarze, Rev. Anthony	1806-1892
Schweich, Rev. Msgr. Joseph	1896-1961
Seimetz, Rev. John	n/d/a-n/d/a
Seubert, Rev. Francis	1859-1900
Seubert, Rev. George	1875-1927
Shanahan, Rev. Edward	1898-1972
Shanahan, Rev. John	1848-1927
Shaull, Rev. Msgr. Walter	1918-1992
Sheridan, Rev. Michael	n/d/a-n/d/a
Shields, Rev. John	1881-1940
Shorb, Rev. Basil	1810-1871
Siedlecki, Rev. Msgr. Matthias	1915-1990
Simpson, Rev. Thomas	1919-1990
Smarsh, Rev. Joseph	1905-1967
Smith, Rev. John	1931-1999
Smith, Rev. Joseph E.	n/d/a-1923
Smith, Rev. Joseph P.	1911-1969
Smyth, Rev. John	1885-1943
Stankiewicz, Rev. Boleslaus	1916-1971
Stanton, Rev. Msgr. John	1895-1961
Steffy, Rev. Martin	1876-1926
Stenzel, Rev. Emil	n/d/a-1886
Stief, Rev. Peter	1885-1958
Stock, Rev. Mark	1884-1951
Stofko, Rev. Msgr. Karl	1915-1988
Strickland, Rev. Henry	1884-1944
Strzelec, Rev. Thaddeus	1917-2005
Stumpf, Rev. Leopold	1883-1959
Suknaic, Rev. John	1921-2004
Sullivan, Rev. Daniel	n/d/a-1908
Sullivan, Rev. Patrick	n/d/a-1934
Tangney, Rev. Jeremiah	1894-1918
Taylor, Rev. Msgr. Francis	1929-1997
Thompson, Rev. Msgr. John	1872-1927
Tighe, Rev. Msgr. Charles	1902-1966
Topper, Rev. Anthony	1892-1968
Tormey, Rev. John Francis	1928-1990
Treyer, Rev. Francis	n/d/a-1859
Vaughn, Rev. Frederick	1909-1992

PRIESTS	BORN-DIED
Wagman, Rev. Msgr. Cletus	1913-2001
Wagner, Rev. Frederick	1876-1924
Weaver, Rev. Charles	1905-1960
Weaver, Rev. Msgr. Paul	1890-1962
Weaver, Rev. William	1896-1950
Weber, Rev. John	1888-1948
Welsh, Rev. Francis	1867-1940
Whalen, Rev. Joseph	1882-1941
Whalen, Rev. Will	1882-1949
Wiest, Rev. Stephen	1857-1910
Wittman, Rev. Arthur	1878-1952
Wojno, Rev. Vincent	1886-1949
Wright, C.SS.R., Rev. John	n/d/a-2001
Yeager, Rev. Louis	1895-1983
Zajac, Rev. Msgr. Stephen Charles	1898-1963
Zan, Rev. Augustine	1911-1999
Zangari, Rev. Salvatore	1918-2004
Zarkoski, O.F.M., Conv., Rev. Martin	1908-1992
Zator, Rev. Fabian	1906-1978
Zednowicz, Rev. Joseph	1917-1989
Zuvich, Rev. Anthony	1876-1919

DEACONS	BORN-DIED
Alden, Harold	1922-1991
Bankos, Stephen	1929-1997
Banks, Halmon	1920-1993
Beaston, Lee	1931-1989
Broussard, J.	1923-1992
Bucher, Henry	1915-1990
Camplese, Anthony	1920-1978
Colonell, Arthur	1921-1996
Conway, Edward	1919-1992
E'Del, Ralph	1919-1984
Formica, Alphonse	1936-1991
Grier, John	1921-1981
Kashi, George	1945-2001
Kole, Gerald	1945-2002
Kruger, Charles	1926-1997
Leszczynski, Edward	1931-1999
Lydon, Michael	1920-1999
MacAdam, Morris	1923-1996
Robertson, Robert	1929-2001
Rocco, John	1924-2002
Runkle, Ralph	1917-2005
Sahd, Joseph	1924-1998
Skiffington, Eugene	1934-1989
Smith, William	1931-1994
Vecera, James	1933-1987

To Lindsey & Matthew,
May the two of you always in
carry the joy of reading in both
your hearts. We love you
very, very much. Love mom + Dad

Dec 25, 1998
matthew 4 mos.

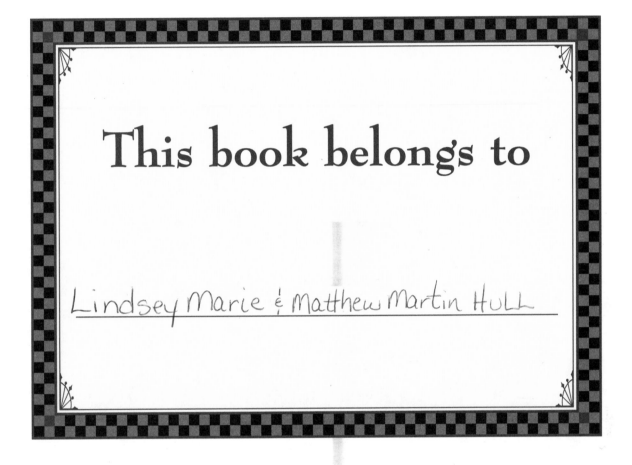

This book belongs to

Lindsey Marie & Matthew Martin Hull

MOTHER GOOSE

Special Limited Edition

Rearranged and edited in this form by
EULALIE OSGOOD GROVER

Illustrated by
FREDERICK RICHARDSON

Cover art design by
SHANNON OSBORNE THOMPSON

Dalmatian Press

AN INTRODUCTION

by YOLANDA D. FEDERICI
Director of Children's Books
Chicago Public Library

Mother Goose and the rhymes attributed to her are acknowledged favorites with children. Young children, even the littlest ones, show preferences in their choice of the sounds, words and books they want to hear read aloud. Before their hands can hold books, babies show an interest in the rhythmic lilt of Mother Goose rhymes. A three-month-old baby, for example, will listen with a wondering intentness to "Little Bo-peep has lost her sheep." And "Bye, Baby Bunting," or "Hush-a-Bye, Baby," have a soothing rhythm that will lull a child to sleep. The many finger games and plays that identify parts of the body, like "This little pig went to market," will bring many moments of delight. When the child has some control of his arms and hands, he will take part in, "Pat a cake, pat a cake," and many of the other action rhymes. Later, the picture book itself will attract the children, and they will point to the colorful illustrations that accompany their favorite rhymes and demand that those be read.

As children grow, they learn the riddles and the ABC and counting rhymes. Then they want the longer ballads read aloud. There is actually something for everyone in Mother Goose. Even scholarly adults are intrigued by her possible origin, by the hidden meaning in the simple verses, and even which particular historical characters are being lampooned in them. Parents share with their children their own pleasant memories of hours of fun as children with such rhymes as "Hickery, Dickery, Dock," "Bah, Bah, black sheep," and all the other old friends in Mother Goose. Few books have the quality of appeal that lasts from one generation to another.

The longevity of this old lady and her offerings is probably due to the folk quality that is inherent in her origin as much as the lively nonsense, good commonsense, and variety in the verses. Some of the rhymes can be traced to popular ballads, folk songs and games, political satire, ancient proverbs, cries of street vendors, real or legendary events. These were known long before they were designated as Mother Goose rhymes. In fact, until the eighteenth century Mother Goose did not have a name in print in English literature.

Her name may have come from Charlemagne's mother who was known as Queen Goosefoot. *Mère l'Oye,* or Mother Goose, was well known in

France for centuries as the supposed originator of any fabulous tale, particularly those for children.

Additions from old sources keep on increasing the number of pieces attributed to Mother Goose. These are taken from old proverbs, riddles, charms, and tongue-twisters. When adequate research is not done, familiar poems for children, whose authorship is declared anonymous, are frequently included. For example, "Twinkle, Twinkle Little Star" was written by Jane Taylor. Sara J. Hale wrote "Mary Had a Little Lamb," and Eliza Lee Follen wrote "The Three Little Kittens."

In every generation, distinguished authors and artists have felt the lure of doing their own Mother Goose collection. There is something about this folk character and her rhymes that stimulates imaginative people who remember her charm for young children, and who want to add their own interpretation. Mother Goose has worn many different costumes but those that seem to suit her best are the ones currently worn as everyday clothing during the eighteenth century when she first acquired her name in print.

Her perennial attraction for children is the variety of interesting characters that troop through the pages of her books, and not all of the characters are good. "Little Boy Blue," for example, is asleep on the job. "Little Polly Flinders" is a careless little girl. And Simple Simon did his best to get something for nothing from the pieman. But Mother Goose is full of happy, busy children who are independent and ingenious. Another attraction is the natural contact that the child-characters have with the great grown-up world. The rhymes tell about festivals, vocations, courtship, marriage, and death. There are many adult characters in adult situations, like "Jack Sprat could eat no fat," "There was a crooked man," "Old woman, old woman, shall we go a-shearing?" "A Farmer went trotting upon his gray mare," and many others.

Friendly animals are everywhere, with cats and mice as special favorites, as in "I like little pussy, her coat is so warm," and "Hickery, Dickery, Dock/ The mouse ran up the clock." Other rhymes are humorous and full of fantasy, such as "High diddle diddle/The cat and the fiddle" and "Three wise men of Gotham/Went to sea in a bowl." For older children, there is a more mature humor as in "The man in the wilderness/Asked me/How many strawberries/Grew in the sea." Action-filled and quickly resolved plots also charm the young and the older children: "The Queen of hearts/She made some tarts," "Sing a song of sixpence," "Old King Cole," and so on. Then there are the riddles which seem at first glance incomprehensible yet always fascinate the young.

Here is the wealth of Mother Goose presented for the delight of children and adults of all ages. She is a very old lady who remains youthful and vigorous; and remarkably she is able to charm every new generation.

A FOREWORD

Children, as well as their interested parents, will eagerly welcome this beautiful edition of the one great nursery classic, just as a worthy edition of Shakespeare is welcomed by discriminating adult readers.

But some may ask what there is in these simple melodies, attributed to Mother Goose, which gives them so secure and beloved a place in the home, the school and the public library. Is it the humor, the action, the rhythm, or the mystery of the theme which appeals so strongly to critical little minds in each generation of childhood, and even to adult minds so fortunate as to have retained some of the refreshing naiveté of early years?

It is useless to try to explain the charm of these nonsense melodies. The children themselves do not know why they love them. No mother can tell us the magic of the spell which seems to be cast over her restless baby as she croons to it a Mother Goose lullaby. No primary teacher quite understands why the mere repetition or singing of a Mother Goose jingle will transform her listless, inattentive class into one all eagerness and attention. But mother and teacher agree that the best of these verses have an even more potent influence than that of innocently diverting and entertaining the child. The healthy moral, so subtly suggested in many of the rhymes, is unconsciously absorbed by the child's receptive mind, helping him to make his own distinction between right and wrong, bravery and cowardice, generosity and selfishness.

From a literary standpoint, also, these rhymes have proved of real value in creating a taste for the truly musical in poetry and song. They train the ear and stir the imagination of the child as no other verses do. Many famous poets and writers trace their first inspiration, and love for things literary, back to the nursery songs and fairy tales of their childhood.

Teachers well know that children who have reveled in these rhymes and stories, at the time of their strongest appeal, step naturally and appreciatively into the great fields of good literature which are beyond.

Knowing these things to be true, we do not hesitate to place this venerable classic on the shelf beside our Shakespeare, and to send our children there for delight and inspiration. They will understand Shakespeare the better for having known and loved Mother Goose.

But what about the personality of this classic writer? Was she really Mistress Elizabeth Goose who is said to have lived in Boston about two hundred years ago, and who crooned her nonsense jingles to a large and happy family of grandchildren? We are told that their father, Thomas Fleet, who was a printer by trade, thought to turn an honesty penny with his mother-in-law's popular verses, so he published them in a small volume under the title of "Songs for the Nursery: or, Mother Goose's Melodies." A goose with a very long neck and a wide-open mouth flew across the title page, at least so the story goes. But we have to believe that it is only a story, for no copy of the book can be found, and nothing but tradition identifies Elizabeth Goose, the Boston grandmother, with the famous rhymester.

We might feel sorry to be obliged to discredit this picturesque story of Mother Goose, if her real history were not even more mysterious. We know very little about the beloved patron of childhood, but what we do know is as follows:

Mother Goose is most certainly of respectable French origin, for in 1697 a distinguished French writer, Charles Perrault, published in Paris a little book of familiar stories called "Contes de ma Mère l'Oye," or "Tales of My Mother Goose." Her identity, however, he leaves a mystery, except that in the frontispiece of his book is pictured an old woman by her fireside telling stories to an eager little family group.

This volume contained the only prose tales that have ever been credited to Mother Goose, and they are still among the most popular

stories in nursery or school room. The titles are as follows: "Little Red Riding Hood;" "The Sisters Who Dropped From Their Mouths Diamonds and Toads;" "Bluebeard;" "The Sleeping Beauty;" "Puss in Boots;" "Cinderella;" "Riquet With the Tuft;" and "Tom Thumb."

It is through her verses, however, that Mother Goose has won her well-deserved fame. The first collection under her name was published in London about 1765 by John Newbery. It may be, if Oliver Goldsmith were living, he could tell us more about the origin of these verses than we are now ever likely to know. It is more than probable that he himself edited the little volume for John Newbery, and that he wrote the clever preface, "By a very Great Writer of very Little Books," as well as the quaint moral which supplements each rhyme.

About twenty-five years later this book was reprinted in our country by Isaiah Thomas of Worcester, Massachusetts. Several copies of this edition are preserved, one of which has been photographed and reproduced in facsimile by W. H. Whitmore of Boston. Other publishers also reprinted the English edition, one being done for John Newbery's grandson, Francis Power, in 1791.

In 1810 another collection of melodies appeared under the title of "Gammer Gurton's Garland." It was quite evidently a rival of Mother Goose, though it contained nearly all of her verses, besides many far less interesting ones gathered from other sources.

Gammer Gurton's popularity, however, was short, and Mother Goose was revived about 1825 by a Boston firm, Munroe and Francis. Since that time her fame has never waned. In spite of the present multiplicity of beautiful books for children, they are constantly exhausting large editions of the one universally beloved book of melodies. Some of these volumes have been collected and edited by men of the highest literary judgment and ability, such as Goldsmith (with hardly a doubt), Ritson, Halliwell, Andrew Lang, Charles Eliot Norton, Charles Welsh and Edward Everett Hale. Certainly there is not another collection of juvenile literature which can boast such a list of scholarly editors. The deepest gratitude is due them for their careful and discriminating effort to preserve for the children of future generations this rich heritage of nursery melodies.

Many less discriminating editors, however, have ruthlessly mutilated and adapted many of the rhymes to suit their fancy, thinking, possibly, that as Mother Goose is only a title, the verses attributed to her belong to the general public to use as it sees fit. On the contrary, Mother Goose's melodies belong to the children, and no addition or change should be made except by those who are in such close sympathy with the child-heart that they may act with the child's authority.

This present edition of "Mother Goose" preserves the best of the verses which became so popular in England and America as to first demand their publication. It is the only truly classic edition that has been published in modern times. The two authorities which have been followed are the edition published for John Newbery's grandson in London in 1791, and probably edited by Oliver Goldsmith, and the edition published in Boston in 1833 by Munroe and Francis, called "The Only True Mother Goose Melodies." It is from this copy that the following quaint introduction by "Ma'am Goose" is quoted.

Not all the favorites among the nursery rhymes are here, only those that first helped to make the fame of the fictitious but no less worthy patron of childhood. May her fame and her melodies be lovingly preserved to give joy and inspiration to many future generations of little children.

EULALIE OSGOOD GROVER

Hear What Ma'am Goose Says!

My dear little Blossoms, there are now in this world, and always will be, a great many grannies besides myself, both in petticoats and pantaloons, some a deal younger, to be sure, but all monstrous wise and of my own family name. These old women, who never had chick or child of their own, but who always know how to bring up other people's children, will tell you with long faces that my enchanting, quieting, soothing volume, my all-sufficient anodyne for cross, peevish, won't-be-comforted little bairns, ought be laid aside for more learned books, such as *they* could select and publish. Fudge! I tell you that all their batterings can't deface my beauties, nor their wise pratings equal my wiser prattlings; and all imitators of my refreshing songs might as well write another Billy Shakespeare as another Mother Goose—we two great poets were born together, and shall go out of the world together.

No, no, my melodies will never die,
While nurses sing, or babies cry.

THE VOLLAND CREED

*It is the Volland ideal that books for children should contain
nothing to cause fright, suggest fear, glorify mischief,
extenuate malice or condone cruelty. That is why they are called*
"books good for children"

From "The Only True Mother Goose Melodies
Published by Munroe & Francis, Boston, 1833

OLD MOTHER GOOSE

Old Mother Goose, when
　She wanted to wander,
Would ride through the air
　On a very fine gander.

Mother Goose had a house,
　'Twas built in a wood,
An owl at the door
　For a porter stood.

She had a son Jack,
　A plain-looking lad,
He was not very good,
　Nor yet very bad.

She sent him to market,
　A live goose he bought:
"Here! mother," says he,
　"It will not go for nought."

Jack's goose and her gander
　Grew very fond;
They'd both eat together,
　Or swim in one pond.

Jack found one morning,
　As I have been told,
His goose had laid him
　An egg of pure gold.

Jack rode to his mother,
　The news for to tell.
She called him a good boy,
　And said it was well.

And Old Mother Goose
　The goose saddled soon,
And mounting its back,
　Flew up to the moon.

Old Mother Goose, when
She wanted to wander,
Would ride through the air
On a very fine gander.

Cock-a-doodle-doo,
My dame has lost her shoe:
My master's lost his fiddlestick,
And knows not what to do.

Peter, Peter, pumpkin eater,
Had a wife and couldn't keep her;
He put her in a pumpkin shell,
And then he kept her very well.

Peter, Peter, pumpkin eater,
Had another, and didn't love her;
Peter learned to read and spell,
And then he loved her very well.

I had a little hobby-horse,
And it was dapple gray;
Its head was made of pea-straw,
Its tail was made of hay.
I sold it to an old woman
For a copper groat;
And I'll not sing my song again
Without another coat.

Monday's bairn is fair of face,
Tuesday's bairn is full of grace,
Wednesday's bairn is full of woe,
Thursday's bairn has far to go,
Friday's bairn is loving and giving,
Saturday's bairn works hard for its
    living;
But the bairn that is born on the
    Sabbath day
Is bonny and blithe and good and
    gay.

Three young rats with black felt
    hats,
Three young ducks with white
    straw flats,
Three young dogs with curling
    tails,
Three young cats with demi-veils,
Went out to walk with three
    young pigs
In satin vests and sorrel wigs;
But suddenly it chanced to rain
And so they all went home again.

"Billy, Billy, come and play,
While the sun shines bright as day."

"Yes, my Polly, so I will,
For I love to please you still."

"Billy, Billy, have you seen
Sam and Betsy on the green?"

"Yes, my Poll, I saw them pass,
Skipping o'er the new-mown grass."

"Billy, Billy, come along,
And I will sing a pretty song."

Hie to the market, Jenny come trot,
Spilt all her buttermilk, every drop,
Every drop and every dram,
Jenny came home with an
    empty can.

Shoe the colt,
Shoe the colt,
Shoe the wild mare;
Here a nail,
There a nail,
Colt must go bare.

If all the world were apple pie,
    And all the sea were ink,
And all the trees were bread and
    cheese,
    What should we have to drink?

Lady-bird, Lady-bird,
Fly away home,
Your house is on fire,
Your children will burn.

One misty, moisty morning,
  When cloudy was the weather,
I chanced to meet an old man clothed all in leather.
He began to compliment, and I began to grin,
  How do you do, and how do you do?
  And how do you do again?

I like little pussy, her coat is so warm,
And if I don't hurt her she'll do me no harm;
So I'll not pull her tail, nor drive her away,
But pussy and I very gently will play.

Little Bo-peep has lost her sheep,
And can't tell where to find them;
Leave them alone, and they'll come home,
And bring their tails behind them.

Mary had a little lamb
    With fleece as white as snow.
And everywhere that Mary went
    The lamb was sure to go.

It followed her to school one day—
    That was against the rule.
It made the children laugh and
      play
    To see a lamb at school.

And so the teacher turned it out,
    But still it lingered near,
And waited patiently about
    Till Mary did appear.

"Why does the lamb love Mary so?"
    The eager children cry.
"Why, Mary loves the lamb, you
      know!"
    The teacher did reply.

Birds of a feather flock together,
And so will pigs and swine;
Rats and mice have their choice,
And so will I have mine.

Go to bed first,
A golden purse;
Go to bed second,
A golden pheasant;
Go to bed third,
A golden bird.

My mother said, I never should
Play with the gypsies in the wood.
If I did, then she would say:
Naughty girl to disobey.
Your hair shan't curl and your
    shoes shan't shine,
You gypsy girl you shan't be mine.
And my father said that if I did,
He'd rap my head with the teapot
    lid.

My mother said that I never should
Play with the gypsies in the wood.
The wood was dark, the grass was
    green;
By came Sally with a tambourine.
I went to sea—no ship to get
    across;
I paid ten shillings for a blind
    white horse.
I upped on his back and was off
    in a crack,
Sally tell my mother I shall never
    come back.

There's a neat little clock,—
In the schoolroom it stands,—
And it points to the time
With its two little hands.

And may we, like the clock,
Keep a face clean and bright,
With hands ever ready
To do what is right.

Little Nanny Etticoat
In a white petticoat,
  And a red nose;
The longer she stands
  The shorter she grows.

Jack, be nimble; Jack, be quick;
Jack, jump over the candlestick.

Who killed Cock Robin?
"I," said the sparrow,
"With my little bow and arrow,
I killed Cock Robin."

Who saw him die?
"I," said the fly,
"With my little eye,
I saw him die."

Who caught his blood?
"I," said the fish,
"With my little dish,
I caught his blood."

Who'll make his shroud?
"I," said the beetle,
"With my thread and needle.
I'll make his shroud."

Who'll carry the torch?
"I," said the linnet,
"I'll come in a minute,
I'll carry the torch."

Who'll be the clerk?
"I," said the lark,
"If it's not in the dark,
I'll be the clerk."

Who'll dig his grave?
"I," said the owl,
"With my spade and trowel
I'll dig his grave."

Who'll be the parson?
"I," said the rook,
"With my little book,
I'll be the parson."

Who'll be chief mourner?
"I," said the dove,
"I mourn for my love,
I'll be chief mourner."

Who'll sing a psalm?
"I," said the thrush,
"As I sit in a bush.
I'll sing a psalm."

Who'll carry the coffin?
"I," said the kite,
"If it's not in the night,
I'll carry the coffin."

Who'll toll the bell?
"I," said the bull,
"Because I can pull,
I'll toll the bell."

All the birds of the air
Fell sighing and sobbing,
When they heard the bell toll
For poor Cock Robin.

Rain, rain, go away,
Come again another day;
Little Johnny wants to play.

Pretty John Watts,
We are troubled with rats,
Will you drive them out of the house?
We have mice, too, in plenty,
That feast in the pantry,
But let them stay
And nibble away,
What harm in a little brown mouse?

I'll tell you a story
  About Mary Morey,
And now my story's begun.
I'll tell you another
  About her brother,
And now my story's done.

Hush-a-bye, Baby, upon the tree top,
When the wind blows the cradle will rock;
When the bough breaks the cradle will fall,
Down tumbles cradle and Baby and all.

Ride away, ride away,
　　Johnny shall ride,
And he shall have pussy~cat
　　Tied to one side;
And he shall have little dog
　　Tied to the other,
And Johnny shall ride
　　To see his grandmother.

Little Jenny Wren fell sick,
Upon a time;
In came Robin Redbreast
And brought her cake and wine.

"Eat well of my cake, Jenny,
Drink well of my wine."
"Thank you, Robin, kindly,
You shall be mine."

Jenny she got well,
And stood upon her feet,
And told Robin plainly
She loved him not a bit.

Robin being angry,
Hopped upon a twig,
Saying, "Out upon you! Fie upon
        you!
Bold-faced jig!"

⁓⊙⋈⊙⁓

Dance, little baby, dance up high!
Never mind, baby, mother is by.
Crow and caper, caper and crow,
There, little Baby, there you go!

Up to the ceiling, down to the
        ground,
Backwards and forwards, round
        and round;
Dance, little baby and mother will
        sing,
With the merry coral, ding, ding,
        ding!

There was an old woman of
        Gloucester,
Whose parrot two guineas it cost
        her,
But its tongue never ceasing,
Was vastly displeasing
To the talkative woman of
        Gloucester.

⁓⊙⋈⊙⁓

I am a pretty wench,
And I come a great way
        hence,
And sweethearts I can get
        none:
But every dirty sow
Can get sweethearts enough,
And I pretty wench can get
        none.

⁓⊙⋈⊙⁓

What are little boys made of,
        made of?
What are little boys made of?
Snaps and snails and puppy dogs
        tails;
And that's what little boys are
        made of, made of.

What are little girls made of,
        made of?
What are little girls made of?
Sugar and spice and all that's nice;
And that's what little girls are
        made of, made of.

Dickery, dickery, dock,
The mouse ran up the clock;
The clock struck one,
The mouse ran down,
Dickery, dickery, dock.

A, B, C, D, E, F, G,
H, I, J, K, L, M, N, O, P,
Q, R, S, and T, U, V,
W, X, and Y and Z.
Now I've said my A, B, C,
Tell me what you think of me.

The little robin grieves
    When the snow is on the ground,
For the trees have no leaves,
    And no berries can be found.

The air is cold, the worms are hid;
    For robin here what can be done?
Let's strow around some crumbs of bread,
    And then he'll live till snow is gone.

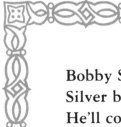

Bobby Shaftoe's gone to sea,
Silver buckles on his knee;
He'll come back and marry me,
        Pretty Bobby Shaftoe.

Bobby Shaftoe's fat and fair,
Combing down his yellow hair,
He's my love forevermore,
        Pretty Bobby Shaftoe.

See-saw, sacradown,
Which is the way to London town?
One foot up, the other foot down,
That is the way to London town.

A cat came fiddling out of a barn,
With a pair of bagpipes under her
        arm;
She could sing nothing but fiddle-
        de-dee,
The mouse has married the
        bumble-bee;
Pipe, cat—dance, mouse—
We'll have a wedding at our good
        house.

Little Betty Blue
Lost her holiday shoe.
What will poor Betty do?
Why, give her another
To match the other,
And then she will walk in two.

Robin Hood, Robin Hood,
Is in the mickle wood!
Little John, Little John,
He to the town is gone.

Robin Hood, Robin Hood,
Telling his beads,
All in the greenwood
Among the green weeds.

Little John, Little John,
If he comes no more,
Robin Hood, Robin Hood,
We shall fret full sore!

There was a lady loved a swine,
Honey, quoth she,
Pig-hog wilt thou be mine?
Hoogh, quoth he.

I'll build thee a silver sty,
Honey, quoth she,
And in it thou shalt lie.
Hoogh, quoth he.

Pinned with a silver pin,
Honey, quoth she,
That thou may go out and in.
Hoogh, quoth he.

Wilt thou have me now,
Honey? quoth she.
Speak or my heart will break.
Hoogh, quoth he.

Little Tommy Tittlemouse
Lived in a little house;
He caught fishes
In other men's ditches.

About the bush, Willie, about the bee-hive,
About the bush, Willie, I'll meet thee alive.

Bah, bah, black sheep,
    Have you any wool?
Yes, marry, have I,
    Three bags full;
One for my master,
    One for my dame,
But none for the little boy
    Who cries in the lane.

Hickety, pickety, my black hen,
She lays eggs for gentlemen:
Gentlemen come every day
To see what my black hen doth lay.

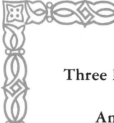

Three little kittens lost their
    mittens,
  And they began to cry,
  Oh! mother dear, we very
    much fear
  That we have lost our mittens.
Lost your mittens! You naughty
    kittens!
  Then you shall have no pie.
    Mee-ow, mee-ow, mee-ow.
  No, you shall have no pie.
    Mee-ow, mee-ow, mee-ow.

The three little kittens found their
    mittens,
  And they began to cry,
  Oh! mother dear, see here, see
    here,
  See, we have found our
    mittens.
Put on your mittens, you silly
    kittens,
  And you may have some pie.
    Purr-r, purr-r, purr-r,
  Oh! let us have the pie,
    Purr-r, purr-r, purr-r.

The three little kittens put on
    their mittens,
  And soon ate up the pie;
  Oh! mother dear, we greatly
    fear
  That we have soiled our
    mittens.

Soiled your mittens! you naughty
    kittens!
  Then they began to sigh,
    Mee-ow, mee-ow, mee-ow.
  Then they began to sigh,
    Mee-ow, mee-ow, mee-ow.

The three little kittens washed
    their mittens,
  And hung them out to dry;
  Oh! mother dear, do you not
    hear,
  That we have washed our
    mittens.
Washed your mittens! Oh! you're
    good kittens.
  But I smell a rat close by.
    Hush! hush! mee-ow.
    mee-ow.
  We smell a rat close by,
    Mee-ow, mee-ow, mee-ow.

Tweedle-dum and Tweedle-dee
Resolved to have a battle,
For Tweedle-dum said Tweedle-
    dee
Had spoiled his nice new rattle.
Just then flew by a monstrous
    crow,
As big as a tar barrel,
Which frightened both the
    heroes so,
They quite forgot their quarrel.

Willie boy, Willie boy,
    Where are you going?
O, let us go with you
    This sunshiny day.

I'm going to the meadow
    To see them a-mowing,
I'm going to help the girls
    Turn the new hay.

Three children sliding on the ice
    Upon a summer's day,
As it fell out, they all fell in,
    The rest they ran away.

Oh, had these children been at school,
    Or sliding on dry ground,
Ten thousand pounds to one penny
    They had not then been drowned.

Ye parents who have children dear,
    And ye, too, who have none,
If you would keep them safe abroad,
    Pray keep them safe at home.

Wee Willie Winkie runs through the town,
Upstairs and downstairs, in his nightgown;
Tapping at the window, crying at the lock:
"Are the babes in their beds, for it's now ten o'clock?"

There was an old woman who lived in a shoe,
She had so many children she didn't know what to do.
She gave them some broth without any bread,
She whipped them all soundly and put them to bed.

Peter Piper picked a peck of
    pickled peppers;
A peck of pickled peppers Peter
    Piper picked.
If Peter Piper picked a peck of
    pickled peppers,
Where's the peck of pickled
    peppers
Peter Piper picked?

When I was a little girl,
About seven years old,
I hadn't got a petticoat,
To cover me from the cold.

So I went into Darlington,
That pretty little town,
And there I bought a petticoat,
A cloak, and a gown.

I went into the woods
And built me a kirk,
And all the birds of the air,
They helped me to work.

The hawk with his long claws
Pulled down the stone,
The dove with her rough bill
Brought me them home.

The parrot was the clergyman,
The peacock was the clerk,
The bullfinch played the organ,
We made merry work.

Here we go round the mulberry
    bush,
The mulberry bush, the mulberry
    bush,
Here we go round the mulberry
    bush.
On a cold and frosty morning.

This is the way we wash our
    hands,
Wash our hands, wash our hands,
This is the way we wash our
    hands,
On a cold and frosty morning.

This is the way we wash our
    clothes.
Wash our clothes, wash our
    clothes,
This is the way we wash our
    clothes,
On a cold and frosty morning.

This is the way we go to school,
Go to school, go to school,
This is the way we go to school,
On a cold and frosty morning.

This is the way we come out of
    school,
Come out of school, come out of
    school,
This is the way we come out of
    school,
On a cold and frosty morning.

There was a man and he had naught,
  And robbers came to rob him;
He crept up to the chimney top,
  And then they thought they had him.
But he got down on the other side,
  And then they could not find him;
He ran fourteen miles in fifteen days,
  And never looked behind him.

There was an old man,
And he had a calf,
And that's half;
He took him out of the stall,
And put him on the wall,
And that's all.

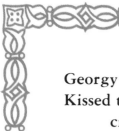

Georgy Porgy, pudding and pie,
Kissed the girls and made them
cry.
When the boys came out to play,
Georgy Porgy ran away.

"Where are you going to, my pretty
maid?"
"I'm going a-milking, sir," she said.
"May I go with you, my pretty
maid?"
"You're kindly welcome, sir," she
said.
"What is your father, my pretty
maid?"
"My father's a farmer, sir," she
said.
"What is your fortune, my pretty
maid?"
"My face is my fortune, sir," she
said.
"Then I can't marry you, my pretty
maid!"
"Nobody asked you, sir!" she said.

My Maid Mary she minds the
dairy,
While I go a-hoeing and mowing
each morn;
Gaily run the reel and the little
spinning wheel.
While I am singing and mowing
my corn.

Dear, dear! what can the matter be?
Two old women got up in an
apple tree;
One came down, and the other
stayed till Saturday.

If all the seas were one sea,
What a great sea that would be!
And if all the trees were one tree,
What a great tree that would be!
And if all the axes were one axe,
What a great axe that would be!
And if all the men were one man,
What a great man he would be!
And if the great man took the
great axe,
And cut down the great tree,
And let it fall into the great sea,
What a splish splash that would be!

Thirty white horses upon a red
hill,
Now they tramp, now they champ,
Now they stand still.

A wise old owl sat in an oak,
The more he heard the less he
spoke;
The less he spoke the more he
heard.
Why aren't we all like that wise
old bird?

Bow, wow, wow!
Whose dog art thou?
Little Tom Tinker's dog,
Bow, wow, wow!

Pussy-Cat sits by the fire;
    How can she be fair?
In walks the little dog;
    Says: "Pussy, are you there?
How do you do, Mistress Pussy?
    Mistress Pussy, how d'ye do?"
"I thank you kindly, little dog,
    I fare as well as you!"

Here am I, little jumping Joan,
When nobody's with me
I'm always alone.

Jog on, jog on, the footpath way,
    And merrily jump the style,
        boys;
A merry heart goes all the day,
    Your sad one tires in a mile,
        boys.

There was an old woman had
    three sons,
Jerry and James and John,
Jerry was hanged, James was
    drowned,
John was lost and never was
    found;
And there was an end of her three
    sons,
Jerry and James and John!

Every lady in this land
Has twenty nails, upon each hand
Five, and twenty on hands and
    feet:
All this is true, without deceit.

Over the water, and over the sea,
And over the water to Charley,
I'll have none of your nasty beef,
Nor I'll have none of your barley;
But I'll have some of your very
    best flour
To make a white cake for my
    Charley.

Johnny shall have a new bonnet,
    And Johnny shall go to the
        fair,
And Johhny shall have a blue
    ribbon
    To tie up his bonny brown
        hair.
And why may not I love Johnny?
    And why may not Johnny love
        me?
And why may not I love Johnny,
    As well as another body?
And here's a leg for a stocking,
    And here's a leg for a shoe,
And here's a kiss for his daddy,
    And two for his mammy, I
        trow.
And why may not I love Johnny?
    And why may not Johnny love
        me?
And why may not I love Johnny,
    As well as another body?

There were once two cats of
    Kilkenny.
Each thought there was one cat
    too many;
So they fought and they fit,
And they scratched and they bit,
Till, excepting their nails,
And the tips of their tails,
Instead of two cats, there weren't
    any.

There was an old woman lived under the hill,
And if she's not gone she lives there still.
Baked apples she sold, and cranberry pies,
And she's the old woman that never told lies.

Simple Simon met a pieman
  Going to the fair;
Says Simple Simon to the pieman:
  "Pray let me taste your ware."

Says the pieman to Simple Simon:
  "Show me first your penny;"
Says Simple Simon to the pieman:
  "Indeed I have not any."

Sing a song of sixpence, a bag full of rye,
Four and twenty blackbirds baked in a pie;
When the pie was opened the birds began to sing,
And wasn't this a dainty dish to set before the king?
The king was in the parlor counting out his money;
The queen was in the kitchen eating bread and honey;
The maid was in the garden hanging out the clothes,
There came a little blackbird and nipped off her nose.

To market, to market, to buy a fat pig,
Home again, home again, jiggety, jig.

Ride a cock horse
To Banbury Cross
To see what Tommy can buy:
A penny white loaf,
A penny white cake,
And a two-penny apple pie.

Little Tee Wee,
He went to sea
In an open boat;
And while afloat
The little boat bended,
And my story's ended.

Intery, mintery, cutery-corn,
Apple seed and apple thorn;
Wire, brier, limber-lock,
Five geese in a flock,
Sit and sing by a spring,
O-u-t, and in again.

Who made the pie?
I did.
Who stole the pie?
He did.
Who found the pie?
She did.
Who ate the pie?
You did.
Who cried for pie?
We all did.

Elizabeth, Elspeth, Betsy and Bess,
They all went together to seek a
    bird's nest;
They found a bird's nest with five
    eggs in it,
They all took one and left four
    in it.

Little girl, little girl, where have
    you been?
Gathering roses to give to the
    queen.
Little girl, little girl, what gave
    she you?
She gave me a diamond as big as
    my shoe.

Jerry Hall, he was so small,
A rat could eat him, hat and all.

There was a man of double deed,
Sowed his garden full of seed.
When the seed began to grow,
'Twas like a garden full of snow;

When the snow began to melt,
'Twas like a ship without a belt;
When the ship began to sail,
'Twas like a bird without a tail;

When the bird began to fly,
'Twas like an eagle in the sky;
When the sky began to roar,
'Twas like a lion at the door;

When the door began to crack,
'Twas like a stick across my back;
When my back began to smart,
'Twas like a penknife in my heart;
When my heart began to bleed,
'Twas death and death and
    death indeed.

Little Miss Muffet
Sat on a tuffet,
Eating some curds and whey;
There came a great spider,
And sat down beside her,
And frightened Miss Muffet away.

Three wise men of Gotham
Went to sea in a bowl,
And if the bowl had been stronger
My song had been longer.

There were two birds sat upon a stone,
    Fal de ral–al de ral–laddy.
One flew away and then there was one,
    Fal de ral–al de ral–laddy.
The other flew after and then there was none,
    Fal de ral–al de ral–laddy.
So the poor stone was left all alone,
    Fal de ral–al de ral–laddy.
One of these little birds back again flew,
    Fal de ral–al de ral–laddy.
The other came after and then there were two,
    Fal de ral–al de ral–laddy.
Says one to the other: "Pray, how do you do?"
    Fal de ral–al de ral–laddy.
"Very well, thank you, and pray how are you?"
    Fal de ral–al de ral–laddy.

This is the house that Jack built.
This is the malt
That lay in the house that Jack
    built.
This is the rat,
That ate the malt
That lay in the house that Jack
    built.
This is the cat,
That killed the rat,
That ate the malt
That lay in the house that Jack
    built.
This is the dog,
That worried the cat,
That killed the rat,
That ate the malt
That lay in the house that Jack
    built.

This is the cow with the crumpled
    horn,
That tossed the dog,
That worried the cat,
That killed the rat,
That ate the malt
That lay in the house that Jack
    built.
This is the maiden all forlorn,
That milked the cow with the
    crumpled horn,
That tossed the dog,
That worried the cat,
That killed the rat,
That ate the malt
That lay in the house that Jack
    built.
This is the man all tattered and
    torn,
That kissed the maiden all forlorn,
That milked the cow with the
    crumpled horn,
That tossed the dog,
That worried the cat,
That killed the rat,
That ate the malt
That lay in the house that Jack
    built.

This is the priest all shaven and
  shorn,
That married the man all tattered
  and torn,
That kissed the maiden all forlorn,
That milked the cow with the
  crumpled horn,
That tossed the dog,
That worried the cat,
That killed the rat,
That ate the malt
That lay in the house that Jack
  built.
This is the cock that crowed in
  the morn,
That waked the priest all shaven
  and shorn,
That married the man all tattered
  and torn,
That kissed the maiden all forlorn,
That milked the cow with the
  crumpled horn,
That tossed the dog,
That worried the cat,
That killed the rat,
That ate the malt
That lay in the house that Jack
  built.

This is the farmer sowing the corn,
That kept the cock that crowed in
  the morn.
That waked the priest all shaven
  and shorn,
That married the man all tattered
  and torn,
That kissed the maiden all forlorn,
That milked the cow with the
  crumpled horn,
That tossed the dog,
That worried the cat,
That killed the rat,
That ate the malt
That lay in the house that Jack
  built.

Bye, Baby bunting,
Father's gone a-hunting,
Mother's gone a-milking,
Sister's gone a-silking,
And Brother's gone to buy a skin
To wrap the Baby bunting in.

Little Polly Flinders
Sat among the cinders
    Warming her pretty little toes;
Her mother came and caught her,
Whipped her little daughter
    For spoiling her nice new clothes.

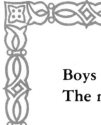

Boys and girls come out to play,
The moon doth shine as bright as
    day,
Leave your supper and leave your
    sleep,
And meet your playfellows in the
    street;
Come with a whoop and come with
    a call,
And come with a good will, or not
    at all.
Up the ladder and down the wall,
A halfpenny roll will serve us all.
You find milk and I'll find flour,
And we'll have a pudding in half
    an hour.

There was a little man,
  And he had a little gun,
And his bullets were made of lead,
    lead, lead;
  He went to the brook,
  And saw a little duck,
And shot it through the head, head,
    head.

  He carried it home
  To his good wife Joan,
And bade her a fire to make, make,
    make;
  To roast the little duck
  He had shot in the brook,
And he'd go fetch the drake, drake,
    drake.

A was an Apple pie;
  B bit it;
    C cut it;
      D dealt it;
        E ate it;
          F fought for it;

G got it;
  H had it;
    I inspected it
    J joined it;
      K kept it;
        L longed for it;
          M mourned for it;

N nodded at it;
  O opened it;
    P peeped in it;
      Q quartered it;
      R ran for it;
        S stole it;

T took it;
  V viewed it;
    W wanted it;
      X, Y, Z, and ampers-and,
        All wished for a piece in
        hand.

Here we go up, up, up,
  And here we go down, down,
    downy,
Here we go backward and forward,
  And here we go round, round,
    roundy.

Tom, Tom, the piper's son,
Stole a pig, and away he run;
   The pig was eat,
   And Tom was beat,
And Tom ran crying down the street.

Jack and Jill went up the hill
    To fetch a pail of water;
Jack fell down and broke his crown,
    And Jill came tumbling after.

London Bridge is broken down,
Dance over my Lady Lee;
London Bridge is broken down,
With a gay lady.

How shall we build it up again?
Dance over my Lady Lee;
How shall we build it up again?
With a gay lady.

Build it up with silver and gold,
Dance over my Lady Lee;
Build it up with silver and gold,
With a gay lady.

Silver and gold will be stole away,
Dance over my Lady Lee;
Silver and gold will be stole away,
With a gay lady.

Build it up with iron and steel,
Dance over my Lady Lee;
Build it up with iron and steel,
With a gay lady.

Iron and steel will bend and bow,
Dance over my Lady Lee;
Iron and steel will bend and bow,
With a gay lady.

Build it up with wood and clay,
Dance over my Lady Lee;
Build it up with wood and clay,
With a gay lady.

Wood and clay will wash away,
Dance over my Lady Lee;
Wood and clay will wash away,
With a gay lady.

Build it up with stone so strong,
Dance over my Lady Lee;
Huzza! 'twill last for ages long,
With a gay lady.

As I was walking in a field of
        wheat,
I picked up something good to
        eat;
Neither fish, flesh, fowl, nor
        bone,
I kept it till it ran alone.

Wine and cakes for gentlemen,
    Hay and corn for horses,
A cup of ale for good old wives,
    And kisses for young lasses.

See, see! What shall I see?
A horse's head where his tail
        should be.

Little fishes in a brook,
Father caught them on a hook,
Mother fried them in a pan,
Johnnie eats them like a man.

Pussy cat, pussy cat, where have you been?
I've been to London to see the Queen.
Pussy cat, pussy cat, what did you there?
I frightened a little mouse under the chair.

Pat a cake, pat a cake, Baker's man;
So I do, master, as fast as I can.
Pat it and prick it and mark it with T,
And then it will serve for Tommy and me.

Little Boy Blue, come blow your horn,
The sheep's in the meadow, the cow's in the corn.
What! Is this the way you mind your sheep,
Under the haycock fast asleep?

There was an old woman tossed in a blanket
    Seventeen times as high as the moon;
But where she was going no mortal could tell,
    For under her arm she carried a broom.

"Old woman, old woman, old woman," said I,
"Whither, ah whither, ah whither so high?"
"To sweep the cobwebs from the sky,
    And I'll be with you by and by."

My dear, do you know
How, a long time ago,
    Two poor little children,
Whose names I don't know,

Were stolen away
On a fine summer's day,
    And left in a wood,
As I've heard people say?

And when it was night,
So sad was their plight,
    The sun it went down,
And the moon gave no light!

They sobbed and they sighed,
And they bitterly cried,
    And the poor little things
They laid down and died.

And when they were dead,
The robins so red
    Brought strawberry leaves
And over them spread.

And all the day long
They sang them this song:
"Poor babes in the wood!
Poor babes in the wood!
    And don't you remember
The babes in the wood?"

A hill full, a hole full,
Yet you cannot catch a bowl full.

Rock-a-bye baby,
Thy cradle is green;
Father's a nobleman,
Mother's a queen,
And Betty's a lady
And wears a gold ring,
And Johnny's a drummer
And drums for the king.

If I'd as much money as I could
    spend,
I never would cry old chairs to
    mend,
Old chairs to mend, old chairs to
    mend;
I never would cry, old chairs to
    mend.
If I'd as much money as I could
    tell,
I never would cry old clothes to
    sell,
Old clothes to sell, old clothes to
    sell;
I never would cry, old clothes to
    sell.

Pussy-cat Mole jumped over a coal,
And in her best petticoat burnt a
    great hole.
Poor pussy's weeping, she'll have
    no more milk
Until her best petticoat's mended
    with silk.

Cold and raw the north winds blow
Bleak in the morning early,
All the hills are covered with snow,
And winter's now come fairly.

The man in the moon came down too soon
To inquire the way to Norridge;
The man in the south, he burnt his mouth
With eating cold plum porridge.

Four-and-twenty tailors
    Went to kill a snail;
The best man among them
    Durst not touch her tail;
She put out her horns
    Like a little Kyloe cow.
Run, tailors, run, or
    She'll kill you all just now.

Lucy Locket lost her pocket,
Kitty Fisher found it;
There was not a penny in it,
But a ribbon round it.

Old Sir Simon the king,
And young Sir Simon the squire,
And old Mrs. Hickabout
Kicked Mrs. Kickabout
Round about our coal fire.

Round and round the rugged rock
The ragged rascal ran.
How many R's are there in that?
Now tell me if you can.

Bessy Bell and Mary Gray,
They were two bonny lasses;
They built their house upon the lea,
And covered it with rushes.

Bessy kept the garden gate,
And Mary kept the pantry;
Bessy always had to wait,
While Mary lived in plenty.

Swan, swan, over the sea;
Swim, swan, swim!
Swan, swan, back again;
Well swum, swan!

There is a well
As round as an apple, as deep as a
cup,
And all the king's horses can't fill
it up.

As little Jenny Wren
Was sitting by her shed.
She waggled with her tail,
And nodded with her head.

She waggled with her tail,
And nodded with her head,
As little Jenny Wren
Was sitting by the shed.

There was a little boy and a
little girl
Lived in an alley;
Says the little boy to the little
girl,
"Shall I, oh, shall I?"

Says the little girl to the little
boy,
"What shall we do?"
Says the little boy to the little
girl,
"I will kiss you."

The boughs do shake and the bells
do ring,
So merrily comes our harvest in,
Our harvest in, our harvest in,
So merrily comes our harvest in.

We've ploughed, we've sowed,
We've reaped, we-ve mowed,
We've got our harvest in.

Little Tom Tucker
Sings for his supper.
What shall he eat?
White bread and butter.
How will he cut it
Without e'er a knife?
How will he marry
Without e'er a wife?

"To bed, to bed," says Sleepy-Head;
    "Let's stay awhile," says Slow;
"Put on the pot," says Greedy-Sot,
    "We'll sup before we go."

Diddle, diddle, dumpling, my son John,
Went to bed with his breeches on,
One stocking off, and one stocking on,
Diddle, diddle, dumpling, my son John.

High diddle diddle,
The cat and the fiddle,
The cow jumped over the moon;
The little dog laughed
To see such craft,
And the dish ran away with the spoon.

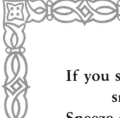

If you sneeze on Monday, you
    sneeze for danger;
Sneeze on a Tuesday, kiss a
    stranger;
Sneeze on a Wednesday, sneeze for
    a letter;
Sneeze on a Thursday, something
    better.
Sneeze on a Friday, sneeze for
    sorrow;
Sneeze on a Saturday, joy
    tomorrow.

Margaret wrote a letter,
Sealed it with her finger,
Threw it in the dam
For the dusty miller.
Dusty was his coat,
Dusty was the silver,
Dusty was the kiss
I'd from the dusty miller
If I had my pockets
Full of gold and silver,
I would give it all
To my dusty miller.

Clap, clap handies,
Mammie's wee, wee ain;
Clap, clap handies,
Daddie's comin' hame;
Hame till his bonny wee bit laddie:
Clap, clap handies,
My wee, wee ain.

Dance to your daddie,
    My bonnie laddie,
Dance to your daddie, my bonnie
    lamb!
    You shall get a fishie,
    On a little dishie,
You shall get a fishie when the
    boat comes home.

Dance to your daddie,
    My bonnie laddie,
Dance to your daddie, and to your
    mammie sing!
    You shall get a coatie,
    And a pair of breekies,
You shall get a coatie when the
    boat comes in.

Cocks crow in the morn
    To tell us to rise,
And he who lies late
    Will never be wis
For early to bed
    And early to rise
Is the way to be healthy,
    Wealthy and wise.

Oh where, oh where has my little
    dog gone?
Oh where, oh where can he be?
With his ears cut short and his
    tail cut long,
Oh where, oh where is he?

The two gray kits,
And the gray kits' mother,
All went over
The bridge together.

The bridge broke down,
They all fell in;
"May the rats go with you,"
Says Tom Bolin.

Robin and Richard
    Were two sleepyheads;
They spent the day
    Just lazing in bed.
Then up starts Robin
    And looks at the sky:
"Oh, brother Richard,
    The sun's very high.
You go before
    With the bottle and bag,
And I will come after
    On little Jack nag."

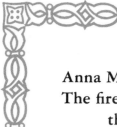

Anna Maria she sat on the fire;
The fire was too hot, she sat on
  the pot;
The pot was too round, she sat on
  the gound;
The ground was too flat, she sat
  on the cat;
The cat ran away with Maria on
  her back.

Cobbler, cobbler mend my shoe
Get it done by half past two;
Stitch it up, and stitch it down,
Then I'll give you half a crown.

Thirty days hath September,
April, June, and November;
February has twenty-eight alone,
All the rest have thirty—one,
Excepting leap-year, that's the
  time
When February's days are twenty-
  nine.

The cock's on the housetop
  blowing his horn;
The bull's in the barn a-threshing
  of corn;
The maids in the meadows are
  making of hay;
The ducks in the river are
  swimming away.

Ladies and gentlemen come to
  supper—
Hot boiled beans and very good
  butter.

Christmas is coming, the geese are
  getting fat,
Please to put a penny in an old
  man's hat;
If you haven't got a penny a
  ha'penny will do,
If you haven't got a ha'penny,
  God bless you.

John Bull, John Bull,
Your belly's so full,
You can't jump over
A three-legged stool.

As I walked by myself,
And talked to myself,
Myself said unto me:
"Look to thyself,
Take care of thyself,
For nobody cares for thee."

I answered myself,
And said to myself
In the self—same repartee:
"Look to thyself,
Or not look to thyself,
The self—same thing will be."

Is John Smith within?—Yes, that he is.
Can he set a shoe?   Ay, marry, two.
Here a nail and there a nail,
Tick–tack–too.

I had a little hen, the prettiest ever seen,
She washed me the dishes and kept the house clean.
She went to the mill to fetch me some flour,
And always got home in less than an hour.
She baked me my bread, she brewed me my ale,
She sat by the fire and told many a fine tale.

When I was a little boy I lived by myself,
And all the bread and cheese I got I put upon a shelf;
The rats and the mice, they made such a strife,
I was forced to go to London to buy me a wife.
The streets were so broad and the lanes were so narrow,
I was forced to bring my wife home in a wheelbarrow;
The wheelbarrow broke and my wife had a fall,
And down came the wheelbarrow, wife and all.

'Twas once upon a time, when Jenny Wren was young,
So daintily she danced and so prettily she sung,
Robin Redbreast lost his heart, for he was a gallant bird,
So he doffed his hat to Jenny Wren, requesting to be heard.

"O, dearest Jenny Wren, if you will but be mine,
You shall feed on cherry pie and drink new currant wine,
I'll dress you like a goldfinch or any peacock gay,
So, dearest Jen, if you'll be mine let us appoint the day."

Jenny blushed behind her fan and thus declared her mind:
"Since, dearest Bob, I love you well, I take your offer kind;
Cherry pie is very nice and so is currant wine,
But I must wear my plain brown gown and never go too fine."

How many days has my baby to play?
Saturday, Sunday, Monday,
Tuesday, Wednesday, Thursday, Friday,
Saturday, Sunday, Monday.

Humpty Dumpty sat on a wall,
Humpty Dumpty had a great fall;
All the king's horses and all the king's men
Couldn't put Humpty Dumpty together again.

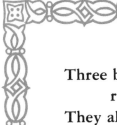

Three blind mice! See how they
run!
They all ran after the farmer's
wife,
Who cut off their tails with a
carving knife.
Did you ever see such a thing in
your life
As three blind mice?

Sleep, baby, sleep,
Our cottage value is deep:
The little lamb is on the green,
With woolly fleece so soft and
clean —
Sleep, baby, sleep.

Sleep, baby, sleep,
Down where the woodbines creep;
Be always like the lamb so mild,
A kind, and sweet, and gentle
child.
Sleep, baby, sleep.

One, he loves; two, he loves;
Three, he loves, they say;
Four, he loves with all his heart;
Five, he casts away.
Six, he loves; seven, she loves;
Eight, they both love.
Nine, he comes; ten, tarries;
Eleven, he courts; twelve, he
marries.

Here sits the Lord Mayor,
    Here sits his two men,
Here sits the cock,
    Here sits the hen,
Here sits the little chickens,
    Here they run in,
Chin chopper, chin chopper,
    Chin chopper, chin!

As I was going to sell my eggs
I met a man with bandy legs,
Bandy legs and crooked toes;
I tripped up his heels,
And he fell on his nose.

March winds and April showers
Bring forth May flowers.

I see the moon,
And the moon sees me;
God bless the moon,
And God bless me.

Nose, nose,
    Jolly red nose,
And what gave thee
    That jolly red nose?
Nutmeg and ginger,
    Cinnamon and cloves,
That's what gave me
    This jolly red nose.

Little King Boggen he built a fine hall,
Pie-crust and pastry-crust, that was the wall;
The windows were made of black puddings and white,
And slated with pancakes,—you ne'er saw the like!

As I went to Bonner
I met a pig
Without a wig,
Upon my word and honor.

Pussy-cat ate the dumplings, the
  dumplings,
Pussy-cat ate the dumplings.
Mamma stood by, and cried, "Oh,
  fie!
Why did you eat the dumplings?"

There was a little woman, as I've
  been told,
Who was not very young, nor yet
  very old;
Now this little woman her living
  got
By selling codlins, hot, hot, hot!

Dickery, dickery, dare,
The pig flew up in the air;
The man in brown soon brought
  him down,
Dickery, dickery, dare.

You shall have an apple,
You shall have a plum,
You shall have a rattle,
When papa comes home.

Donkey, donkey, old and gray,
Open your mouth and gently bray;
Lift your ears and blow your horn,
To wake the world this sleepy
  morn.

Hannah Bantry,
In the pantry,
Gnawing at a mutton bone;
How she gnawed it,
How she clawed it,
When she found herself alone.

If you are to be a gentleman,
And I suppose you'll be,
You'll neither laugh nor smile,
For a tickling of the knee.

Ring-a-ring-a-roses,
A pocket full of posies;
Hush! hush! hush! hush!
We're all tumbled down.

One, Two—buckle my shoe;
Three, Four—open the door;
Five, Six—pick up sticks;
Seven, Eight—lay them straight;
Nine, Ten—a good fat hen;
Eleven, Twelve—I hope you're
  well;
Thirteen, Fourteen—draw the
  curtain;
Fifteen, Sixteen—the maid's in the
  kitchen;
Seventeen, Eighteen—she's in
  waiting;
Nineteen, Twenty—my stomach's
  empty.

Little Jack Horner
Sat in a corner
Eating a Christmas pie;
He put in his thumb,
And pulled out a plum,
And said: "Oh, what a good boy am I!"

Miss Jane had a bag and a mouse was in it;
She opened the bag, he was out in a minute.
The cat saw him jump and run under the table,
And the dog said: "Catch him, Puss, soon as you're able."

The Queen of Hearts,
She made some tarts
All on a summer's day;
The Knave of Hearts,
He stole those tarts,
And took them clean away.

The King of Hearts
Called for the tarts,
And beat the Knave full sore;
The Knave of Hearts
Brought back the tarts,
And vowed he'd steal no more.

Goosey, goosey, gander, where dost thou wander?
Upstairs and downstairs and in my lady's chamber;
There I met an old man that wouldn't say his prayers,
I took him by his hind legs and threw him downstairs.

"I went up one pair of stairs."
"Just like me."

"I went up two pairs of stairs."
"Just like me."

"I went into a room."
"Just like me."

"I looked out of a window."
"Just like me."

"And there I saw a monkey."
"Just like me."

Mary had a pretty bird,
Feathers bright and yellow,
Slender legs—upon my word
He was a pretty fellow!

The sweetest note he always sung,
Which much delighted Mary.
She often, where the cage was
        hung,
Sat hearing her canary.

As I went through the garden gap,
Who should I meet but Dick
        Redcap!
A stick in his hand, a stone in
        his throat,
If you'll tell me this riddle,
I'll give you a groat.

St. Dunstan, as the story goes,
Once pulled the devil by his nose,
With red hot tongs, which made
        him roar,
That could be heard ten miles or
        more.

Terence McDiddler,
        The three-stringed fiddler,
Can charm, if you please,
        The fish from the seas.

A duck and a drake,
And a halfpenny cake,
With a penny to pay the old baker.
A hop and a scotch
Is another notch,
Slitherum, slatherum, take her.

Punch and Judy
Fought for a pie;
Punch gave Judy
A knock in the eye.
Says Punch to Judy,
Will you have any more?
Says Judy to Punch,
My eye is too sore.

Cry, baby, cry,
Put your finger in your eye,
And tell your mother it wasn't I.

See saw, Margery Daw,
  Jacky shall have a new master:
Jacky must have but a penny a day
Because he can work no faster.

Daffy-down-dilly is now come to town
With a petticoat green and a bright yellow gown.

"Cock, cock, cock, cock,
 I've laid an egg,
   Am I to gang ba-are-foot?"

"Hen, hen, hen, hen,
 I've been up and down
 To every shop in town,
 And cannot find a shoe
 To fit your foot,
 If I'd crow my hea-art out."

The lion and the unicorn
    Were fighting for the crown.
The lion beat the unicorn
    All about the town.
Some gave them white bread,
    And some gave them brown;
Some gave them plum-cake,
    And sent them out of town.

A frog he would a-wooing go,
　Heigh ho! says Rowley,
Whether his mother would let
　　him or no.
　With a rowley, powley,
　　gammon and spinach,
　Heigh ho! says Anthony
　Rowley.

So off he set with his opera hat,
　Heigh ho! says Rowley,
And on the road he met with
　a rat.
　With a rowley, powley,
　　gammon and spinach,
　Heigh ho! says Anthony
　Rowley.

Pray, Mister Rat, will you go
　　with me?
　Heigh ho! says Rowley,
Kind Mistress Mousey for to
　　see?
　With a rowley, powley,
　　gammon and spinach,
　Heigh ho! says Anthony
　Rowley.

They came to the door of
　Mousey's hall,
　Heigh ho! says Rowley,
They gave a loud knock, and
　　they gave a loud call.
　With a rowley, powley,
　　gammon and spinach,
　Heigh ho! says Anthony
　Rowley.

Pray, Mistress Mouse, are you
　　within?
　Heigh ho! says Rowley,
Oh yes, kind sirs, I'm sitting
　　to spin.
　With a rowley, powley,
　　gammon and spinach,
　Heigh ho! says Anthony
　Rowley.

Pray, Mistress Mouse, will you
　　give us some beer?
　Heigh ho! says Rowley,
For Froggy and I are fond of
　　good cheer.
　With a rowley, powley,
　　gammon and spinach,
　Heigh ho! says Anthony
　Rowley.

As I was going to Derby
   Upon a market day,
I met the finest ram, sir,
   That ever was fed on hay.

This ram was fat behind, sir,
   This ram was fat before,
This ram was three yards high,
   sir,
   Indeed he was no more.

The wool upon his back, sir,
   Reached up unto the sky,
The eagles built their nests
   there,
   For I heard the young ones
   cry.

The wool upon his tail, sir,
   Was three yards and an ell,
Of it they made a rope, sir,
   To pull the parish bell.

The space between the horns,
   sir,
   Was as far as man could
   reach,
And there they built a pulpit,
   But no one in it preached.

This ram had four legs to walk
   upon,
   This ram had four legs to
   stand,
And every leg he had, sir,
   Stood on an acre of land.

Now the man that fed the ram,
   sir,
   He fed him twice a day,
And each time that he fed him,
   sir,
   He ate a rick of hay.

The man that killed the ram, sir,
   Was up to his knees in
   blood,
And the boy that held the pail,
   sir,
   Was carried away in the
   flood.

Indeed, sir, it's the truth, sir,
   For I never was taught to
   lie,
And if you go to Derby, sir,
   You may eat a bit of the
   pie.

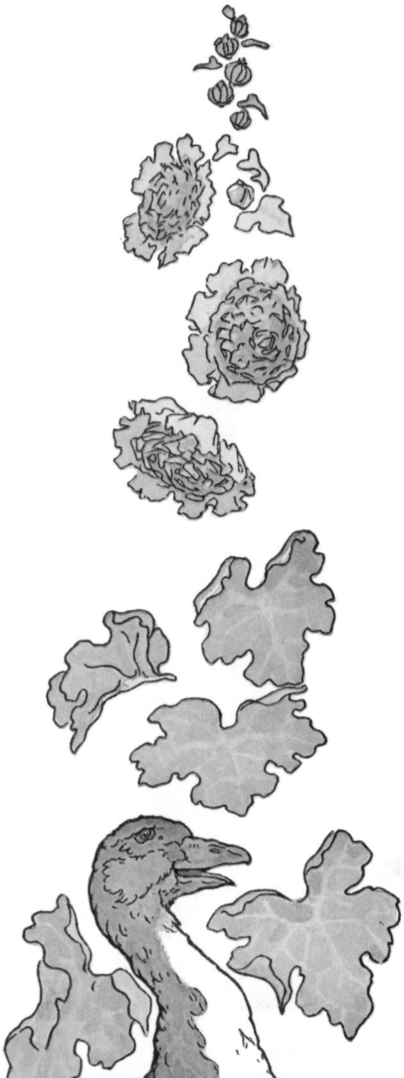

Old King Cole
Was a merry old soul,
And a merry old soul was he;
He called for his pipe,
And he called for his bowl,
And he called for his fiddlers three.

Mistress Mary, quite contrary,
How does your garden grow?
With silver bells and cockle shells
And pretty maids all in a row.

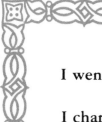

I went to the toad that lies under
 the wall,
I charmed him out, and he came at
 my call;
I scratched out the eyes of the owl
 before,
I tore the bat's wing; what would
 you have more?

See a pin and pick it up,
All the day you'll have good luck.
See a pin and let it lay,
Bad luck you'll have all the day.

Hot-cross buns!
Hot-cross buns!
One a penny, two a penny,
Hot-cross buns!

If ye have no daughters,
Give them to your sons.
One a penny, two a penny,
Hot-cross buns!

Oh, I am so happy!
 A little girl said,
As she sprang like a lark
 From her low trundle bed.
It is morning, bright morning,
 Good morning, papa!
Oh, give me one kiss
 For good morning, mamma!

Diddlty, diddlty, dumpty,
The cat ran up the plum tree;
Give her a plum and down she'll
 come,
Diddlty, diddlty, dumpty.

As Tommy Snooks and Bessie
 Brooks
Were walking out one Sunday;
Says Tommy Snooks to Bessie
 Brooks,
"To-morrow—will be Monday."

Ride a cock horse to Shrewsbury
 Cross,
To buy little Johnny a galloping
 horse.
It trots behind and it ambles
 before
And Johnny shall ride till he can
 ride no more.

Now I lay me down to sleep,
I pray the Lord my soul to keep;
And if I die before I wake,
I pray the Lord my soul to take.

If wishes were horses,
 Beggers might ride;
If turnips were watches,
 I would wear one by my side.

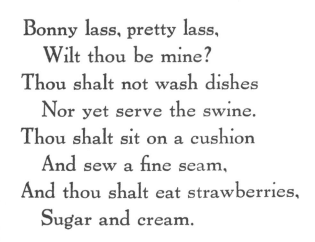

Bonny lass, pretty lass,
  Wilt thou be mine?
Thou shalt not wash dishes
  Nor yet serve the swine.
Thou shalt sit on a cushion
  And sew a fine seam,
And thou shalt eat strawberries,
  Sugar and cream.

Handy-spandy, Jacky dandy,
Loves plum cake and sugar candy.
He bought some at a grocer's shop,
And pleased away went hop, hop, hop.

Ding–dong–bell, the cat's in the well.
   Who put her in?   Little Johnny Green.
   Who pulled her out?   Great Johnny Stout.
      What a naughty boy was that
      To drown poor pussy cat
   Who never did him any harm,
   And killed the mice in his father's barn.

This pig went to market,
That pig stayed at home;
This pig had roast meat,
That pig had none;
This pig went to the barn door,
And cried "week, week," for more.

Come when you're called,
Do what you're bid,
Shut the door after you,
Never be chid.

A was an archer,
    who shot at a frog;
B was a butcher,
    and had a great dog.
C was a captain,
    all covered with lace;
D was a drunkard,
    and had a red face.
E was an esquire,
    with pride on his brow;
F was a farmer,
    and followed the plough.
G was a gamester,
    who had but ill-luck;
H was a hunter,
    and hunted a buck.
I was an innkeeper,
    who loved to carouse;
J was a joiner,
    and built up a house.
K was King William,
    once governed this land;
L was a lady,
    who had a white hand.
M was a miser,
    and hoarded up gold;
N was a nobleman,
    gallant and bold.

O was an oyster girl,
    and went about town;
P was a parson,
    and wore a black gown.
Q was a queen,
    who wore a silk slip;
R was a robber,
    and wanted a whip.
S was a sailor,
    and spent all he got;
T was a tinker,
    and mended a pot.
U was a usurer,
    a miserable elf;
V was a vintner,
    who drank all himself.
W was a watchman,
    and guarded the door;
X was expensive,
    and so became poor.
Y was a youth,
    that did not love school;
Z was a zany,
    a poor harmless fool.

Blind man, blind man,
    Sure you can't see?
Turn round three times,
    And try to catch me.
Turn east, turn west,
    Catch as you can,
Did you think you'd caught me?
    Blind, blind man!

There were two blackbirds sitting on a hill,
One named Jack and the other named Jill.
Fly away, Jack!   Fly away, Jill!
Come again, Jack!   Come again, Jill!

Cross patch, draw the latch,
  Sit by the fire and spin;
Take a cup and drink it up,
  Then call your neighbors in.

Old Mother Hubbard
Went to the cupboard
    To get her poor dog a bone;
But when she came there
The cupboard was bare,
    And so the poor dog had none.

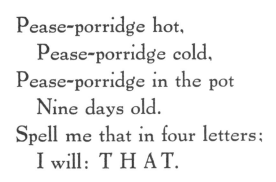

Pease-porridge hot,
   Pease-porridge cold,
Pease-porridge in the pot
   Nine days old.
Spell me that in four letters;
   I will: T H A T.

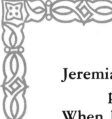

Jeremiah Obadiah, puff, puff,
    puff.
When he gives his messages he
    snuffs, snuffs, snuffs,
When he goes to school by day,
    he roars, roars, roars,
When he goes to bed at night
    he snores, snores, snores,
When he goes to Christmas treat
    he eats plum-duff,
Jeremiah Obadiah, puff, puff,
    puff.

Down by the river
    Where the green grass
    grows
Pretty Polly Perkins
    Bleaches her clothes.
She laughs and she sings,
    And she sings so sweet.
She calls, Come over,
    Across the street.
He kissed her, he kissed her,
    He took her to town;
He bought her a ring
    And a damascene gown.

Christmas comes but once a year,
And when it comes it brings
    good cheer,
A pocket full of money, and a
    cellar full of beer.

A swarm of bees in May
Is worth a load of hay;
A swarm of bees in June
Is worth a silver spoon;
A swarm of bees in July
Is not worth a fly.

Betty Botter bought some butter,
But she said, the butter's bitter;
If I put it in my batter
It will make my batter bitter,
But a bit of better butter,
That would make my batter
    better.
So she bought a bit of butter
Better than her bitter butter,
And she put it in her batter
And the batter was not bitter.
So t'was better Betty Botter
Bought a bit of better butter.

Mrs Mason bought a basin,
Mrs Tyson said, What a nice
    'un,
What did it cost? said
    Mrs Frost,
Half a crown, said Mrs Brown,
Did it indeed, said Mrs Reed,
It did for certain, said Mrs
    Burton.
Then Mrs Nix up to her tricks
Threw the basin on the bricks.

Polly, put the kettle on,
Polly, put the kettle on,
Polly, put the kettle on,
    We'll all have tea.
Sukey, take it off again,
Sukey, take it off again,
Sukey, take it off again,
    They're all gone away.

The sow came in with the saddle,
The little pig rocked the cradle,
The dish jumped up on the table
To see the pot swallow the ladle.
The spit that stood behind the door
Threw the pudding-stick on the floor.
"Odsplut!", said the gridiron,
  "Can't you agree?
I'm the head constable,
  Bring them to me!"

Little Robin Redbreast sat upon a tree,
Up went the Pussy-Cat, and down went he,
Down came Pussy-Cat, away Robin ran;
Says little Robin Redbreast: "Catch me if you can!"

Little Robin Redbreast jumped upon a spade,
Pussy-Cat jumped after him, and then he was afraid.
Little Robin chirped and sang, and what did Pussy say?
Pussy-Cat said: "Mew, mew, mew," and Robin flew away.

Away, birds, away!
Take a little and leave a little,
And do not come again;
For if you do,
I will shoot you through,
And there will be an end to you.

Hey, my kitten, my kitten.
    And hey, my kitten, my deary,
Such a sweet pet as this
    Was neither far nor neary.

For every evil under the sun,
There is a remedy, or there is none.
If there be one, try to find it;
If there be none, never mind it.

Hush-a-bye, baby, lie still with thy
    daddy,
Thy mammy has gone to the mill,
To get some meal to bake a cake,
So pray, my dear baby, lie still.

"Lend me thy mare to ride a mile."
"She is lamed, leaping over a stile."

"Alack! and I must keep the fair!
I'll give thee money for thy mare."

"Oh, Oh! say you so?
Money will make the mare to go!"

The King of France went up the
    hill,
With twenty thousand men;
The King of France came down
    the hill,
And ne'er went up again.

I had two pigeons bright and gay,
They flew from me the other day.
What was the reason they did go?
I cannot tell, for I do not know.

Mother and Father and Uncle Dick
Went to London on a stick;
The stick broke and made a smoke,
And stifled all the London folk.

Oh, my pretty cock, oh, my
    handsome cock,
I pray you, do not crow before
    day,
And your comb shall be made of
    the very beaten gold,
And your wings of the silver so
    gray.

A robin and a robin's son
Once went to town to buy a bun.
They couldn't decide on plum or
    plain,
And so they went back home again.

A farmer went trotting upon his gray mare,
    Bumpety, bumpety, bump,
With his daughter behind him, so rosy and fair,
    Lumpety, lumpety, lump.

A raven cried "Croak," and they all tumbled down,
    Bumpety, bumpety, bump;
The mare broke her knees and the farmer his crown,
    Lumpety, lumpety, lump.

The mischievous raven flew laughing away,
    Bumpety, bumpety, bump,
And vowed he would serve them the same next day,
    Lumpety, lumpety, lump.

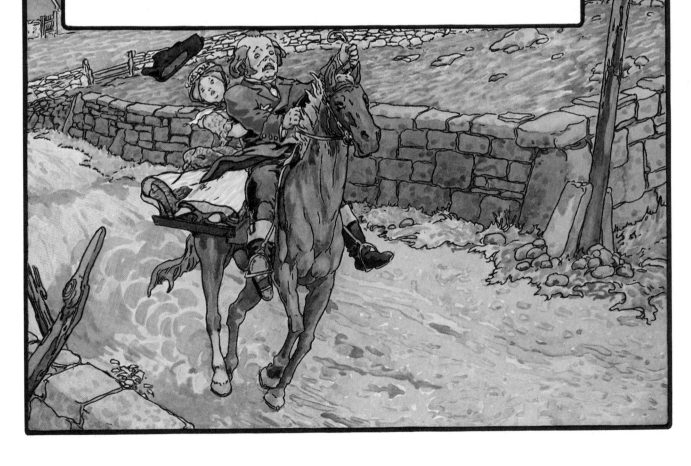

There was an old woman
    Sold puddings and pies;
She went to the mill,
    And dust flew in her eyes.
While through the streets,
To all she meets
    She ever cries:
"Hot Pies—Hot Pies."

"Old woman, old woman, shall we go a-shearing?"
"Speak a little louder, sir, I'm very thick o hearing."
"Old woman, old woman, shall I kiss you dearly?"
"Thank you, kind sir, I hear very clearly."

My little old man and I fell out;
I'll tell you what 'twas all about:
I had money and he had none,
And that's the way the noise begun.

I saw a ship a-sailing,
A-sailing on the sea;
And, oh! it was all laden
With pretty things for thee.

There were comfits in the cabin,
And apples in the hold;
The sails were all of silk,
And the masts were made of gold.

The four-and-twenty sailors
That stood between the decks,
Were four-and-twenty white mice
With chains about their necks.

The captain was a duck,
With a packet on his back;
And when the ship began to move,
The captain said, "Quack! quack!"

❧

Needles and pins, needles and
    pins,
When a man marries his trouble
    begins.

❧

Little boy, little boy, where
    were you born?
Up in the Highlands among the
    green corn.
Little boy, little boy, where did
    you sleep?
In the byre with the kye, in the
    cot with the sheep.

Tommy Trot, a man of law,
Sold his bed and lay upon
    straw;
Sold the straw and slept on
    grass,
To buy his wife a looking-glass.

❧

Magpie, magpie, flutter and flee,
Turn up your tail and good luck
    come to me.

❧

The greedy man is he who sits
And bites out of plates,
Or else takes up an almanac
And gobbles all the dates.

❧

A little cock-sparrow sat on a
    green tree,
And he chirruped, he chirruped,
    so merry was he;
A naughty boy came with his wee
    bow and arrow,
Determined to shoot this little
    cock-sparrow.
"This little cock-sparrow shall
    make me a stew,
And his giblets shall make me a
    little pie, too."
"Oh, no," says the sparrow "I
    won't make a stew."
So he flapped his wings and away
    he flew.

Jack Sprat could eat no fat.
His wife could eat no lean;
So 'twixt them both they cleared the cloth,
And licked the platter clean.

There was an old woman, and what do you think?
She lived upon nothing but victuals and drink;
Victuals and drink were the chief of her diet,
And yet this old woman could never be quiet.

What's the news of the day,
Good neighbor, I pray?
They say the balloon
Has gone up to the moon.

There was a crooked man,
    And he went a crooked mile,
He found a crooked sixpence
    Against a crooked stile;
He bought a crooked cat
    Which caught a crooked mouse,
And they all lived together
    In a little crooked house.

Bell horses, bell horses,
    What time of day?
One o'clock, two o'clock,
    Three and away.

One to make ready,
    And two to prepare;
Good luck to the rider,
    And away goes the mare.

One for the money,
    Two for show,
Three to make ready,
    And four to go.

Hector Protector was dressed
    all in green;
Hector Protector was sent to
    the Queen.
The Queen did not like him,
No more did the King;
So Hector Pretector was sent
    back again.

Of all the gay birds that e'er I
    did see,
The owl is the fairest by far to
    me,
For all day long she sits in a
    tree,
And when the night comes
    away flies she.

Sukey, you shall be my wife
And I will tell you why:
I have got a little pig,
And you have got a sty;
I have got a dun cow,
And you can make good cheese;
Sukey, will you marry me?
Say Yes, if you please.

Milkman, milkman, where have
    you been?
In Buttermilk Channel up to my
    chin;
I spilt my milk, and I spoilt my
    clothes,
And got a long icicle hung
    from my nose.

The girl in the lane,
That couldn't speak plain,
    Cried, gobble, gobble,
    gobble.
The man on the hill,
That couldn't stand still,
    Went hobble, hobble,
    hobble.

Smiling girls, rosy boys,
Come and buy my little toys,
Monkeys made of gingerbread,
And sugar horses painted red.

There was a piper had a cow,
    And he had naught to give her;
He pulled out his pipes and played her a tune,
    And bade the cow consider.

The cow considered very well,
    And gave the piper a penny,
And bade him play the other tune,
    "Corn rigs are bonny."

The man in the wilderness
  Asked me
How many strawberries
  Grew in the sea.
I answered him
  As I thought good,
As many red herrings
  As grew in the wood.

Hark! Hark!
The dogs do bark,
The beggars are coming to town;
Some in rags,
Some in tags,
And some in velvet gown.

As I was going to St. Ives
I met seven wives.
Every wife had seven sacks,
Every sack had seven cats,
Every cat had seven kits.
Kits, cats, sacks and wives,
How many were going to St. Ives?

Flour of England, fruit of Spain,
Met together in a shower of
    rain;
Put in a bag, tied round with a
    string;
If you tell me this riddle,
I'll give you a ring.

Up at Piccadilly oh!
    The coachman takes his
    stand,
And when he meets a pretty
    girl,
    He takes her by the hand;
        Whip away forever oh!
        Drive away so clever oh!
        All the way to Bristol oh!
    He drives her four-in-hand.

Here's to thee, old apple tree,
Whence thou may'st bud
And whence thou may'st blow,
And whence thou may'st bear
    apples enow;
Hats full and caps full,
Bushels full and sacks full,
And our pockets full too.

Old Roger is dead and laid in
    his grave,
    Laid in his grave, laid in his
    grave;

Old Roger is dead and laid in
    his grave,
    H'm ha! laid in his grave.

They planted an apple tree
    over his head,
    Over his head, over his
    head;
They planted an apple tree over
    his head,
    H'm ha! over his head.

The apples grew ripe and ready
    to fall,
    Ready to fall, ready to fall;
The apples grew ripe and ready
    to fall,
    H'm ha! ready to fall.

There came an old woman
    a-picking them all,
    A-picking them all,
    a-picking them all;
There came an old woman
    a-picking them all,
    H'm ha! picking them all.

Old Roger jumps up and gives
    her a knock,
    Gives her a knock, gives her
    a knock;
Which makes the old woman go
    hipperty-hop,
    H'm ha! hipperty-hop.

I had a little husband no bigger than my thumb,
I put him in a pint pot, and there I bid him drum;
I bought a little handkerchief to wipe his little nose,
And a pair of little garters to tie his little hose.

Great A, little a,
  Bouncing B;
The cat's in the cupboard,
  And she can't see.

Little Bobby Snooks was fond of
    his books,
And loved by his usher and master;
But naughty Jack Spry, he got a
    black eye,
And carries his nose in a plaster.

Friday night's dream, on Saturday
    told,
Is sure to come true, be it never so
    old.

This is the way the ladies ride,
    Prim, prim, prim.
This is the way the gentlemen ride,
    Trim, trim, trim.
Presently come the country folks.
    Hobbledy gee, hobbledy gee

I saw a fishpond all on fire
I saw a house bow to a squire
I saw a parson twelve feet high
I saw a cottage near the sky
I saw a balloon made of lead
I saw a coffin drop down dead
I saw two sparrows run a race
I saw two horses making lace
I saw a girl just like a cat
I saw a kitten wear a hat
I saw a man who saw these too
And said though strange
    they all were true.

Barber, barber, shave a pig.
How many hairs will make a wig?
Four and twenty; that's enough.
Give the barber a pinch of snuff.

Solomon Grundy,
Born on a Monday,
Christened on Tuesday,
Married on Wednesday,
Took ill on Thursday,
Worse on Friday,
Died on Saturday,
Buried on Sunday.
This is the end
Of Solomon Grundy.

Darby and Joan were dressed in
    black,
Sword and buckle behind their
    back;
Foot for foot, and knee for knee,
Turn about Darby's company.

She sells sea-shells on the sea
    shore;
The shells that she sells are
    sea-shells I'm sure.
So if she sells sea-shells on the
    sea shore,
I'm sure that the shells are
    sea-shore shells.

Bat, bat,
Come under my hat,
And I'll give you a slice of bacon:
And when I bake
I'll give you a cake,
If I am not mistaken.

As I was going up Primrose Hill,
    Primrose Hill was dirty;
There I met a pretty lass,
    And she dropped me a curtsey.

Little lass, pretty lass,
    Blessings light upon you;
If I had half-a-crown a day,
    I'd spend it all upon you.

There was a little boy went into a barn
    And lay down on some hay;
A calf came out and smelled about,
    And the little boy ran away.

When good King Arthur ruled his land
  He was a goodly king;
He stole three pecks of barley meal
  To make a bag-pudding.
A bag-pudding the king did make,
  And stuffed it well with plums,
And in it put great lumps of fat
  As big as my two thumbs.
The king and queen did eat thereof,
  And noblemen beside,
And what they could not eat that night
  The queen next morning fried.

"Jacky, come give me your fiddle,
  If ever you mean to thrive."
"Nay, I'll not give my fiddle
  To any man alive.

"If I should give my fiddle
  They'll think that I'm gone mad,
For many a joyful day
  My fiddle and I have had."

Doctor Foster went to
    Gloucester
In a shower of rain;
He stepped in a puddle,
Right up to his middle,
And never went there again.

❧❧❧

There was a mad man he had a
    mad wife,
And they lived in a mad town;
And they had children three at
    birth,
    And mad they were every
    one.
The father was mad, the mother
    was mad,
    And the children mad
    beside;
And they all got on a mad
    horse,
    And madly they did ride.
They rode by night and they
    rode by day,
    Yet never a one of them
    fell;
They rode so madly all the way,
    Till they came to the gates
    of hell.
Old Nick was glad to see them
    so mad,
    And gladly let them in:
But he soon grew sorry to see
    them so merry
And let them out again.

As I was going along, along,
A-singing a comical song, song,
    song,
The lane that I went was so long,
    long, long,
And the song that I sang was so
    long, long, long,
And so I went singing along.

❧❧❧

Cackle, cackle, Mother Goose,
Have you any feathers loose?
Truly have I, pretty fellow,
Half enough to fill a pillow.
Here are quills, take one or two,
And down to make a bed for
    you.

❧❧❧

In marble walls as white as
    milk,
Lined with a skin as soft as silk,
Within a fountain crystal-clear,
A golden apple doth appear.
No doors there are to this
    stronghold,
Yet thieves break in and steal
    the gold.

❧❧❧

Elsie Marley is grown so fine,
She won't get up to feed the
    swine,
But lies in bed till eight or nine.
Lazy Elsie Marley.

One, two, three, four, five,
I caught a hare alive;
Six, seven, eight, nine, ten,
I let him go again.

The north wind doth blow,
And we shall have snow,
And what will poor robin do then?
                    Poor thing!

He'll sit in the barn
And keep himself warm,
And hide his head under his wing.
                    Poor thing!

"You owe me five shillings,"
   Say the bells of St. Helen's.

"When will you pay me?"
   Say the bells of Old Bailey.

"When I grow rich,"
   Say the bells of Shoreditch.

"When will that be?"
   Say the bells of Stepney.

"I do not know,"
   Says the great Bell of Bow.

"Two sticks in an apple,"
   Ring the bells of Whitechapel.

"Halfpence and farthings,"
   Say the bells of St. Martin's.

"Kettles and pans,"
   Say the bells of St. Ann's.

"Brickbats and tiles,"
   Say the bells of St. Giles.

"Old shoes and slippers,"
   Say the bells of St. Peter's.

"Pokers and tongs,"
   Say the bells of St. John's.

It's once I courted as pretty a
     lass,
     As ever your eyes did see;
But now she's come to such a
     pass,
     She never will do for me.
She invited me to her house,
     Where oft I'd been before,
And she tumbled me into the
     hog-tub,
     And I'll never go there any
     more.

For want of a nail
     The shoe was lost,
For want of a shoe
     The horse was lost,
For want of a horse
     The rider was lost,
For want of a rider
     The battle was lost,
For want of a battle
     The kingdom was lost,
And all for the want
     Of a horse shoe nail.

Fee, fi, fo, fum,
I smell the blood of an
     Englishman:
Be he alive or be he dead,
I'll grind his bones to make my
     bread.

Six little mice sat down to spin;
Pussy passed by and she peeped
     in.
What are you doing, my little
     men?
Weaving coats for gentlemen.
Shall I come in and cut off
     your threads?
No, no, Mistress Pussy, you'd
     bite off our heads.
Oh, no, I'll not; I'll help you to
     spin.
That may be so, but you don't
     come in.

Baby and I
     Were baked in a pie,
The gravy was wonderful hot.
     We had nothing to pay
     To the baker that day
And so we crept out of the pot.

Dance, Thumbkin, dance;
　　(keep the thumb in motion)
Dance, ye merrymen, everyone.
　　(all the fingers in motion)
For Thumbkin, he can dance along.
　　(the thumb alone moving)
Thumbkin, he can dance alone.
　　(the thumb alone moving)
Dance, Foreman, dance,
　　(the first finger moving)
Dance, ye merrymen, everyone.
　　(all moving)
But Foreman, he can dance along,
　　(the first finger moving)
Foreman, he can dance alone.
　　(the first finger moving)
Dance, Longman, dance,
　　(the second finger moving)
Dance, ye merrymen, everyone.
　　(all moving)
For Longman, he can dance alone,
　　(the second finger moving)
Longman, he can dance alone.
　　(the second finger moving)
Dance, Ringman, dance,
　　(the third finger moving)
Dance, ye merrymen, dance.
　　(all moving)
But Ringman cannot dance alone,
　　(the third finger moving)

Ringman, he cannot dance alone.
　　(the third finger moving)
Dance, Littleman, dance,
　　(the fourth finger moving)
Dance, ye merrymen, dance.
　　(all moving)
But Littleman, he can dance alone,
　　(the fourth finger moving)
Littleman, he can dance alone.
　　(the fourth finger moving)

On Saturday night I lost my
　　wife,
And where do you think I
　　found her?
Up in the moon, singing a tune,
And all the stars around her.

Red stockings, blue stockings,
Shoes tied up with silver;
A red rosette upon my breast
And a gold ring on my finger.

There was a man in our town,
    And he was wondrous wise,
He jumped into a bramble-bush,
    And scratched out both his eyes;
And when he saw his eyes were out,
    With all his might and main
He jumped into another bush
    And scratched them in again.

INDEX BY FIRST LINE